Securing Prosperity

Securing Prosperity

THE AMERICAN LABOR MARKET:
HOW IT HAS CHANGED AND WHAT TO DO ABOUT IT

PAUL OSTERMAN

A Century Foundation Book

PRINCETON UNIVERSITY PRESS
Princeton and Oxford

The Century Foundation, formally the Twentieth Century Fund, sponsors and supervises timely analyses of economic policy, foreign affairs, and domestic political issues. Not-for-profit and nonpartisan, it was founded in 1919 and endowed by Edward A. Filene.

Copyright © 1999 by The Century Foundation
Published by Princeton University Press, 41 William Street,
Princeton, New Jersey 08540
In the United Kingdom: Princeton University Press, 3 Market Place, Woodstock,
Oxfordshire OX20 1SY

Second printing, and first paperback printing, 2001
Paperback ISBN 0-691-08688-5

The Library of Congress has cataloged the cloth edition of this book as follows
Osterman, Paul
Securing prosperity : the American labor market : How it has changed
and what to do about it / Paul Osterman.
p.   cm.
Includes bibliographical references and index.
ISBN 0-691-01011-0 (cloth : alk. paper)
1. Labor market—United States.   2. Trade-unions—United States.   3. Industrial relations—United States.   4. United States—Economic conditions—1981– .
5. United States—Economic policy—1981–1993.   6. United States—Economic policy—1993– .   I. Title.
HD5724.O765   1999
331.12′0973—dc21   99-17488

This book has been composed in Adobe Minion

The paper used in this publication meets the minimum requirements of
ANSI/NISO Z39.48-1992 (R1997) (*Permanence of Paper*)

www.pup.princeton.edu

Printed in the United States of America

3   5   7   9   10   8   6   4   2

To the people of EPISO, COPS,
Metro Alliance, and Valley Interfaith

Contents

Figures and Tables

FIGURES

TABLES

Foreword

As of this writing, America seems poised to end the century on a dizzy economic high. Unemployment and inflation are lower than many economists thought possible. The stock market continues its deafening boom, demonstrating remarkable resiliency by bouncing back from occasional sharp, but short-lived, declines. And the federal budget, plagued by large deficits "as far as the eye could see" at the outset of the 1990s, is now comfortably in the black and predicted to remain so for years. In a recent poll, over 70 percent of respondents said that 1999 is the best economic time of their lives.

On the other hand, a few spoilsports keep insisting that, upon closer inspection, the celebration of the present is masking disturbing and eventually corroding weaknesses beneath the economic glitter. Some of the points they make are unanswerable: Gaps between the rich and poor have continued to widen while the earnings of middle-income families have barely kept pace with inflation; as the expansion became one of the longest on record in 1998, household debt levels reached historic highs while the savings rate actually sank to zero; throughout the 1990s, stories in the daily business pages describing corporate "downsizings" ran side by side with stories about record corporate profits, often in the same industries. Prosperity also has failed to halt the growth in the number of Americans lacking health insurance and the reductions in guaranteed pension coverage.

Underlying these dissonant developments are complex transformations in the relationships between American employers and workers, which have resulted in gradual shifts in the balance of power from labor to management.

Such changes include the increased willingness of companies to lay off large numbers of workers even during profitable periods, the growing use of labor without perquisites on a "contingent" basis, new organizational strategies that diminish the need for middle managers, technological innovations that strengthen a company's capacity to replace workers, and the eroding threat of union organization. Even Federal Reserve Board Chairman Alan Greenspan has conceded that the risk of high inflation has diminished because workers have become more fearful about losing their jobs and therefore less willing to demand raises from their employers.

Because alterations in the labor market appear to explain a great deal about both the bright and the dark sides of the economy in the 1990s, the Century Foundation asked Massachusetts Institute of Technology Professor Paul Osterman to explore how American workplaces are evolving and the impact of those changes on workers. In this book, Osterman presents the most complete and nuanced portrait in years of the new American labor market. Based on extensive original research, including a survey of managers, Osterman's work shows conclusively that fundamental transformations have occurred while taking care not to overstate or mischaracterize the nature of those changes.

Osterman's argument about changes in the employer-employee relationship is reflected in his discussion of the different messages in the 1982 best-selling book on management, Thomas J. Peters and Robert H. Waterman, Jr.'s *In Search of Excellence,* and its modern counterpart, *Reengineering the Corporation* by Michael Hammer and James Champy. One central theme of *In Search of Excellence* was the importance of maintaining employment continuity, demonstrated by such passages as "many of the best companies view themselves as an extended family" and "when we look at excellent companies, we see full employment policies in times of recession." In contrast, the Hammer and Champy book focuses on how information technology can reduce costs through improvements in order processing, inventory management, supplier relations, and other functions. In many cases, the savings arise from eliminating the need for workers. Clearly times have changed.

Those who applaud the developments Osterman describes by and large also approve of the federal government's passivity throughout this period. Those who are concerned that the growing economic pie is failing to improve the living standards and financial security of many Americans are apt to believe that the government could help ensure that prosperity is more widely shared. Osterman belongs to the second camp and puts forward a range of sensible, concrete policy ideas that build on lessons learned from government successes here and abroad with respect to worker training, job information networks, pensions, and safety net programs.

The topics explored in this book are central to the agenda of the Century Foundation. Other related publications include *Created Unequal* by James K. Galbraith, *New Rules for a New Economy: Employment and Opportunity in Postindustrial America* by Stephen A. Herzenberg, John A. Alic, and Howard Wial, and *No One Left Behind: The Report of the Task Force on Retraining America's Workforce*. A number of other Century Foundation books and reports focusing on various aspects of changes in the economy and the labor market will be published in coming months.

We thank Paul Osterman for the diligence and care he devoted to the examination of this subject; the result is an important contribution to the study of the American workforce.

Richard C. Leone, President
The Century Foundation

Preface

—————

THIS IS A BOOK about what has happened in the American labor market over the past two decades and what we should do about it. It is motivated by a difficult set of intellectual puzzles about how firms and markets behave. It is also motivated by the fact that I share the unease of many people about the basic fairness of what is happening in today's economy. As such, the book tries to operate at two levels: a scholarly analysis of the past and a programmatic prescription for the future. A central premise of the book is that this is a transitional period from one form of labor market to another and the choices are more open than they have been for many years. This makes it an exciting time to think about the issues raised in the book, but it also means that there will inevitably be some uncertainty about just what is happening and what the possibilities are. It seems to me worth accepting this uncertainty as the price for having some impact, rather than waiting and writing a purely retrospective account of what happened and why.

Preparation of this book was supported by the Century Foundation (called, at the time I started, the Twentieth Century Fund), and I am grateful to Richard C. Leone, the president of the fund; Greg Anrig, my project officer; and Beverly Goldberg, who shepherded the book through publication. The entire experience of working with the fund was a pleasure.

Additional support for the survey of firms, which I draw upon in several chapters, was provided by the Sloan Foundation, for which I thank Hirsh Cohen, and the MIT Industrial Performance Center, for which I thank Richard Lester.

Midway through writing this book several colleagues and I received grants from the Ford Foundation and the Rockefeller Foundation to organize a series of conferences and seminars on topics related to the book. These discussions contributed to the book in important ways.

Publication of the book has given me the opportunity to meet Peter Dougherty of Princeton University Press. He is a truly outstanding editor, and I am grateful for his help.

Several first-class graduate students assisted me at various stages. I am grateful to Susan Eaton, who worked with me throughout the project, did much of the research on the company case studies used in the corporate responsibility discussion, and also struggled with back issues of the *Wall Street Journal* to understand how the causes of layoffs have shifted over time. Susan was responsible, thoughtful, and tremendously helpful. Brenda Lautsch worked with me as a colleague on the research that led to our report on Project QUEST, which is summarized in chapter 6. She did a terrific job, and it was great fun to work with her. I also received excellent assistance from Marianne Bittner and Eric Lindblad. Colleagues who read the manuscript and gave me valuable advice include Rosemary Batt, Harry Katz, Thomas Kochan, Richard Locke, Robert McKersie, and Michael Piore. Karen Boyajian did an outstanding job in preparing the final manuscript, and I am grateful for her hard work and the care she took.

Over the past several years I have benefited enormously from the opportunity to work with projects in the Southwest organized by various chapters of the Industrial Areas Foundation. To say that these have been an inspiration to me is an understatement. I am very appreciative to Sister Pearl Ceasar, Ernesto Cortes, Sister Judy Donovan, Sister Christine Stephens, and Elizabeth Valdez for letting me help.

Securing Prosperity

Introduction

WE LIVE IN AN ERA of economic paradox. The dynamism and power of the American economy are astounding. American industry remains the most productive in the world, and the economy spins off new products and industries at a pace that exceeds that of any other nation. Only imagination limits the possibilities inherent in information technology and the microelectronic revolution.

Yet despite the good economic news on many dimensions, there remains a widespread sense that the labor market is a riskier and more dangerous place than in the past. In some measure this feeling is based on what is in the air, as many firms continue to restructure and as rhetoric takes hold proclaiming that everyone is responsible for his or her own career and that one can expect little from one's employer. However, there is also hard reality: while many people are benefiting from the new economy, a larger number are not, and inequality has grown.

The good news/bad news character of the labor market can be seen both within and without the firm. Inside organizations employers are broadly implementing innovative ways of organizing work at an impressive rate. For many employees these new systems bring more interesting and more highly skilled employment, and the evidence shows that both blue- and white-collar workers prefer the new to the old way of structuring work. At the same time, the ties that bind the workforce to the firm have frayed, and the number of layoffs is rising. In addition, new work arrangements, captured by the phrase "contingent work," imply a much looser link between firm and employee. As we shall see, most contingent employees would prefer a more "regular" job. Finally, firms by and large do not seem to be sharing with their workforce the benefits they obtain from new organizational structures. Implementation of new work arrangements are associated with less employment security and no gains in compensation.

The external labor market has the same two-faced nature. It is undeniable that many people find the new labor market a congenial place. These people, roughly 20 percent of the working population, have experienced considerable wage gains. They have the good fortune to have high-level skills that are in strong demand. They believe that they indeed can manage their own careers, and high rates of job changing and weak attachments to employers pose no threat and may even be valued. The Silicon Valley is the epitome of this world, but it is not unique, and it would be foolish to deny the reality or extent of this attitude and experience.

At the same time, most do not share in this good fortune, and for them the external labor market is treacherous. Low-income labor markets have not disappeared, and the poverty rate has fallen very little. Even most employees higher in the labor queue have to view the new world with trepidation: as I shall show, when they lose their jobs, they suffer serious adverse consequences.

In short, the labor market is confusing. This book is an effort to step back and develop a broad understanding of the changes that have swept the labor market and, then, to think through an appropriate response. The book attempts to explain why even good news still makes so many people nervous and what we might do about it. In developing this argument I try to be realistic about the new economic realities that drive much of what we see. I also try to avoid looking back nostalgically or romantically to the glory days of the first thirty years of the postwar American economy. At the same time, it is important to understand that a political and intellectual struggle, sometimes overt and sometimes hidden, is taking place over the shape of the American labor market and the rules that will govern it for the foreseeable future. Economics and technology may frame this struggle, but choices remain open.

As I work to explain what has happened in the labor market and what we might do about it, two central themes will repeatedly demand our attention. First, in the new labor market, mobility, or job changing, has increased.

This is the result of a radical shift in how employers view their labor force and the degree of commitment they are willing to make. In the old labor market people changed jobs much less frequently, and there were few effective institutions to facilitate what movement existed. In the new labor market we will need to construct ways to enable people to navigate what has become a very treacherous set of transitions.

The second recurring theme is the shifting balance of power between employees and management. In the mid-1980s a fundamental transformation occurred. The 1960s were characterized by economic optimism and job security, a widening union/nonunion wage differential, and a national political environment that was interventionist and favorable to employees and provided a relatively (for America) strong safety net underneath the labor market. Many, although not all, of these characteristics continued into the 1970s. By the 1980s this had all turned around. Unions were in retreat, the government was reducing its role in policing the labor market, and economic insecurity was growing across a wide spectrum of employees. Management culture, and the attitude of employers toward employees, have also changed radically. All in all, the balance of power has shifted between firms and their workers. This has had far-reaching consequences, ranging from falling employment security to wage stagnation. I argue that we need to think hard about how to redress this imbalance.

How the Labor Market Has Changed

How has it come to be that the terms of trade in the labor market have tilted so much? To get a purchase on this question we need to step back from the normal division of academic labor and ask some broader questions. In the standard course of research we divide up "big" problems into what seem to be more manageable topics. For example, there is an enormous, and still growing, literature on wage stagnation and increased earnings inequality. Whether jobs are more insecure now than in the past is another topic hotly debated in both the popular and academic literature. Similarly, contingent work is a research theme of growing popularity.

There are obvious advantages to identifying discrete trends and studying them in depth. The risk is that we lose sight of the forest, the real story about the past two decades: the fact that the postwar institutional structure of the labor market has been destroyed and that we are living in a period in which a new institutional structure is being erected. The outcomes that trouble us about the labor market are symptoms of this larger development. What is at stake in the public and academic debate is what form the new rules will take.

The institutional structure of the labor market operates at two levels. Somewhat abstractly the term refers to "shared rules, which can be laws or collective understandings, held in place by custom, explicit agreement, or tacit agreement."[1] These shared understandings or norms can, as we shall see, have a powerful impact on behavior, and when the norms shift, behavior can change dramatically. At a more concrete level are the tangible institutions—unions, job-training programs, temporary help firms—whose activities influence labor market outcomes. The transformation of these concrete institutions is driven partly by economic "facts" and partly by changing norms and shared understandings about the labor market. Taken as a whole, the institutional structure provides a coherent set of practices and rules of thumb that shaped our expectations and guides the behavior of both firms and workers.

Looking back, we can discern what were the norms that undergirded the old structure. One example is that while blue-collar workers might be laid off, white-collar employees and managers were treated as fixed factors of production. Another was the long-standing view that layoffs take place in periods of economic decline but a firm that is doing well will share this good fortune with its employees. In labor relations, despite a 1938 Supreme Court opinion that permitted the permanent replacement of strikers,[2] "good" employers did not do this for forty years following the Court decision. When it came to wage setting, more attention was paid to maintaining constant relative wages across occupations and industries than to adjusting wages to the supply and demand conditions of the external labor market.

These rules and expectations were so widely accepted that much of the best-known academic research of the 1950s, 1960s, and even 1970s was devoted to documenting their existence, studying their consequences, and generating theories to explain their emergence and even their "optimality." Yet just listing these principles makes it clear how dramatically the labor market has shifted. Healthy employers lay off workers, including managers. Unions have declined, and strikers are often replaced. The wage structure has been blown apart.

It is obviously possible, and often fruitful, to study each of these developments in isolation. But it is also important to understand the whole picture. The rules of the postwar labor market—its institutional structure—fitted together in a logical way and constituted a coherent map of behavior for employers and for workers. This map has been erased, and this erasure explains why—even in the face of some good economic news—the sense of unease is so widespread. The erosion of the old rules also helps explain why some outcomes we dislike are becoming increasingly common.

If the old institutional structure is gone, what is replacing it? One possible conclusion, to which many people jump, is that the old system constituted a set of "unnatural" constraints on market forces and that we are moving into an era in which market forces are unfettered, in which, as Bob Kuttner has observed, "Everything [is] for Sale."[3] There are strong views pushing toward this conclusion. Chief executive officers, even those whose firms are laying off employees and losing sales, justify their compensation, as did Gilbert Amelio of Apple, who explained his $2.5-million-dollar salary with the comment, "It is a market-determined figure."[4] Liberal business organizations, such as the National Alliance of Business, support policies to help employees improve their skills but argue against any significant constraint on an employer's actions.[5] In the academic literature the firm is reconceptualized as a "nexus of contracts" with the implication that nothing more than cold market calculus holds it together.

There is much that supports this broad interpretation. The power of the market seems evident in the impact of newly energized stockholders as they seek higher performance from firms in their portfolio. This quest for better returns has led to some of the layoffs and restructuring that have undermined the old system. The image of an irresistible market is reinforced as firms in nations such as Germany increasingly behave like American companies, shedding employees and moving to regions with cheaper labor.

There is no question that market forces are one of the prime movers behind the changes we observe. It does not follow, however, that the labor market will settle down into the bourse celebrated in economic theory. The fundamental fact is that a truly unbridled market is not politically or socially acceptable. The market is not irresistible. It will be resisted; the question is what form this resistance will take and how different interests will be weighed.

The ultimate unacceptability of the unrestrained market was established in the social science literature in Karl Polanyi's classic book *The Great Transformation*. He showed how the spread of the market destroyed the structure of traditional society and then described the constant efforts by society to reconstruct itself and to push back against the market. In the end, people do not want their lives governed by impersonal and atomistic forces, and they eventually seek to limit the scope and power of those forces. Sometimes the market may have the upper hand, and other times it is in retreat. However, in no circumstances is the triumph of the market complete or permanent, nor should we expect or desire it to be. This constant tension takes on special force in the arena that most directly touches people, the labor market.

The choices, however, are far from clear. There are several reasons why it is very difficult to determine where we want to go. First, although the language of the market is used as a weapon in the ongoing struggle over the shape of the new labor market, not all the claims are purely rhetorical. New economic realities do limit choices in novel ways. Many firms, particularly those normally regarded as leaders, unquestionably face fierce competition that constrains what is possible with respect to wages and employment. Information technology and other production innovations enable firms to produce with less labor and to shift production in response to relatively small differences in costs, and in fact consumers may benefit. Aggressive institutional investors have a point when they argue that American firms had become top-heavy with management and that "reengineering" could indeed improve performance.

The second reason why it is hard to picture our destination is that some of the alternatives that have traditionally attracted reformers have lost their sheen. What has happened in Germany is paradigmatic. Until recently the standard interpretation of Germany was that in the postwar period an institutional structure was erected that forced firms onto the "high road" of high wages and job security. That institutional structure consisted of strong unions; works councils (employee committees) within firms; high levels of training administered jointly by government, unions, and firms; and cooperative behavior among erstwhile competitors.[6] In effect, market forces were channeled in particular directions, and the success of the German economy in terms of wages, job security, and economic growth seemed to ratify this strategy.

Germany held many lessons for American advocates of enhanced training, job security, and worker representation. However, in recent years this model has been under severe stress, and the problems appear to be much deeper than simply the strains of reunification. Labor costs are high in Germany, and many firms are fleeing to low-wage settings, be they in Eastern Europe, Asia, or South Carolina.[7] In a refrain familiar to American ears but very new to Germany, the new president of DaimlerChrysler has made maximizing "shareholder value" the centerpiece of his program, and this has led to plant closings, reduced purchases of German-made parts, and corresponding increased purchases from Asia.[8] Even friends of the German model believe that the cooperative business structure that was long seen as an asset has come to stifle innovation.[9] Germany, and Europe in general, no longer are attractive models for American reformers.

The third reason why the future seems so uncertain is that new institutional forms have emerged whose current function and future possibilities we do not fully understand. Temporary help firms are a perfect example. The explosive growth of temporary workers is well known (although sometimes exaggerated, as we shall see in the next chapter). We do not, however, have a real grip on the meaning of this development. Early writing about temporary workers tended to view the phenomenon as uniformly bad, a degradation of "normal" wages, hours, and benefits. There is considerable truth to this view, but we also now understand that some employees prefer the flexibility inherent in a temporary job. More to the present point is that temporary help firms are playing a growing role in shaping the operation of the labor market. They are becoming an important labor market institution. For example, they recruit and screen potential regular employees for firms (hence performing a "labor exchange" function), they staff the human resource departments of some firms (they are an outsourcer),[10] and they have linked up with outplacement firms to help find jobs for laid-off workers (a function in principle performed by the public employment and training system).[11] Where all of this will go is unclear, and the uncertainty adds to the difficulty of understanding the choices that confront us.

What is the evidence that alternative outcomes are possible? The international examples that today may seem poor guides nonetheless are evidence that there are viable choices in how labor market institutions are constructed. Throughout most of the postwar period the labor markets of Germany, Japan, and Sweden (to pick the most typically cited examples) performed quite well by American standards. Unemployment was low, earnings were more equally distributed than in the United States, and productivity growth was high. Yet these nations each had substantially different forms of wage determination, worker representation, and skill development than the American model. These overseas examples may no longer be worthy of emulation in their particulars, but the deeper point is that for thirty years quite different structures than ours had considerable success.

It is also instructive to think about the origins of the American postwar labor market framework. The institutional structure with which we are so familiar, and which is now eroding, emerged not simply from the impersonal interplay of market forces but rather from a complex political, social, and economic process. The postwar labor market structure was constructed shortly after World War II as a result of political bargaining around the Full Employment Act of 1946 and a seminal conflict in 1945–46 between Walter Reuther and the United Automobile Workers and General Motors.[12] Since the labor market was in important measure constructed in the past, the implication is that a new framework can be debated today as a matter of policy.

One reason why it is difficult to recognize that alternative policies are feasible is that the rhetoric of the market carries with it the idea that only one outcome is possible. Much as the "law of one price" implies (incorrectly, at least in the case of labor) that markets converge to uniform outcomes, so the notion that current developments are market-driven carries with it the implication that the organizational outcomes that result are preordained, or at least that efforts to shape them must have substantial costs in terms of economic efficiency. The better way to think about the problem is to recognize that market forces may limit or constrain options but that options still exist.

What Is the Problem?

Why worry about these changes? What is wrong with the labor market that needs to be fixed? Chapter 3 will describe in considerable depth how people are faring in today's labor market. A summary would include:

- Employment security is declining, and the consequences of being dislocated are severe. This is not simply analogous to a firm cutting off its contract with the paper clip supplier. Most workers, particularly most middle-aged work-ers, took their jobs on the basis of an implicit contract. The terms of that implicit contract were set under the old labor market structure, and hence the expec-tation was a considerably higher level of mutual loyalty than is practiced today. On the basis of this expectation workers made personal plans, and they also made commitments to their employer, for example, in terms of investments in training that they expected would pay off over time. These implicit con-tracts have been broken, and employees may reasonably expect some degree of indemnification.

▪ At the bottom of the labor market the situation of many people has dete-riorated. Wages have fallen, economic mobility rates are low, and many people remain trapped in poverty or in near-poverty circumstances. Racial differentials have been unacceptably slow in narrowing. More generally, the growth in earnings inequality is troubling.

▪ New employment forms, for example, the rise in various versions of con-tingent employment, leave many people in jobs whose quality is well below what they desire. Although contingent employment meets the needs of some people, for others it is clearly substandard.

These problems are serious and amply justify some degree of interven-tion. There is, however, a difficulty with this litany that is important to address early in the book. Perhaps it is the case that some people are doing poorly, but is it not also true that many people like the new labor market? Many employees find that the new work systems and organizational forms give them greater opportunities to exercise their creativity, and they are not bothered by the lack of security. They are confident in their own abilities and in their capacities to make their way in the world. The security and lifetime employ-ment in the old system are seen as not relevant or not particularly desirable, and the old system's emphasis on limiting market wages in favor of inter-nal equity is viewed as a way of preventing people from enjoying the rewards of their work.

It would, however, be too easy to say that these positive responses to the new regime are limited to the 20 percent or so of the labor force who have done well in terms of wages in the past decade and a half. This is too facile because, just as many working- and middle-class people don't want to "soak the rich" because they think that they or their children will someday also be rich, so many people who are having difficulty in the new labor market may well nonetheless believe that its features are desirable and that they (or their children) face a bright future.

There is no opinion poll or survey that can enable us to discern what fraction of people fall into one or another of these camps. However, that is not the essential point. Thinking about matters in these terms suggests that it is important to distinguish policies that are aimed at people who, in some sense, come from the "old world" and those that are directed more toward the "new world." The former set of policies would be intended to compensate for losses suffered because people made plans and investments based on a set of assumptions that , owing to no fault of their own, are no longer valid. The latter set of policies would be directed to the central question of this book: What do we want the new labor market to look like?

With respect to the "old world" one possible conclusion is that firms should provide compensation (golden parachutes) to all employees, not just to those at the top. A milder implication points to policies aimed at easing the transition for dislocated workers, providing some level of income support, and retraining. I think that this is right and that public policy has a responsibility to compensate people for these losses. The current form this discussion takes is how workers who are adversely affected by trade should be treated, but the issue is broader. However, it is important to understand that the plight of today's dislocated workers does not necessarily justify fundamental efforts to alter the direction in which the labor market is evolving. This is because new employees who are entering employment are presumably well aware of the new terms under which they labor. They will make their plans, investments, and commitments on the basis of this new world. Broken commitments and sunk investments are serious concerns for today's generation, who indeed deserve assistance, but to make the case for a deeper set of policies we have to look elsewhere.

What is the case for policy in the "new world?" This is a difficult argument to construct because there really is nowhere to see the "new world" in its pure form and hence we cannot be sure what it will be like or what features are problematic. There is, however, enough scattered evidence so that we can make educated guesses about where the labor market is going. A good initial way of thinking about this is to examine in a bit of detail the labor market in the Silicon Valley, an area that exemplifies as well as any other what people think about when they consider the future of work.

The Silicon Valley, an area whose employment in 1996 numbered 1.13 million,[13] is a useful laboratory because its economy is driven by the new businesses of the information technology age. These firms are by and large young, were founded by people who explicitly rejected old bureaucratic or manufacturing organizational models, and seem to be tremendously successful. At the heart of our image of the Silicon Valley is a community of enterprises that sometimes compete and sometimes cooperate. The production side of the Silicon Valley involves firms with very porous boundaries in which supplier relationships and technology sharing are essential elements. The labor market seems to be organized analogously with a high degree of mobility in which people easily move between employers without any negative consequence. This is taken to be a new model, as Annalee Saxenian wrote in her economic history of the valley:

> Traditional corporate hierarchies, with internal job ladders that defined predictable career paths, were far less prevalent or meaningful in Silicon Valley than elsewhere. . . . Without fully recognizing the consequences, Silicon Valley's pioneers were creating the foundations of a decentralized industrial system that blurred the boundaries between social life and work, between firms, between firms and local institutions, and between managers and workers.[14]

Elsewhere Saxenian comments that "the region's engineers developed loyalties to each other and to advancing technology, rather than to individual firms or even industries," and she goes on to quote John Scully, former CEO at Apple, who said, "When someone is fired or leaves on the East Coast, it's a real trauma in their lives. When they are fired or leave here it doesn't mean much. They just go off and do something else."[15]

There is a great deal of accuracy in this image. A striking illustration was a recent trade secrets case dismissed by a judge because, as the district attorney commented, "the problem is that the computer industry is incestuous, with people working in one place today and another tomorrow."[16]

This labor market strikes many observers as exemplary of the future both because of the cachet of high technology and because it seems to work well. The absence of important government support is appealing to current political sensibilities along with what is sometimes taken to be a strong element of individualism. This latter point is something of a misunderstanding, since the labor market, and indeed the economy, seem rooted in a complex social system of interdependencies among firms, a social system that often goes by the term "industrial district" in the academic literature.[17] Furthermore, even in this citadel of modernity, traditional social relations remain important. For example, ethnic networks play a big role in linking people to jobs even for those with the highest skills.[18]

There is no question that in recent years the Silicon Valley has been successful, although by perhaps not quite as big a margin as is sometimes supposed. In recent years employment growth has been strong (increasing by 11.7 percent between 1992 and 1996, compared with 7.4 percent for the country as a whole). Average earnings in the valley in 1996 were $41,400 annually, compared with $28,000 in the nation as a whole; and, compared with the stagnant U.S. wages, real valley wages rose by 7.2 percent between 1992 and 1996.[19]

However, if we probe more closely, there is reason to believe that these impressive figures are generally limited to highly educated people whose skills and scarcity give them considerable market power. This group is not representative of the American labor market, where roughly three-quarters of employees lack a four-year college degree, where nearly half of current high school graduates do not continue to further education, and where even those with a college degree rarely find themselves in an overheated job market like that of high-tech engineers.

The earnings data and other indicators do, in fact, support these concerns. Inequality seems to have increased quite substantially in the valley. In San Jose, the largest city in the valley, in 1979 the ratio of the earnings of the top tenth percentile of the earnings distribution to the bottom tenth percentile (the so-called 90/10 ratio) was 3.89, and the ratio of the top 25 percent to the bottom 25 percent (the 75/25 ratio) was 2.04. Both ratios are higher in 1996, indicating worsening inequality. The 90/10 ratio in 1996 was an eye-popping 5.20, while the 75/25 ratio increased to 2.41. Equally startling, in San Jose only the top 10 percent of people in the wage distribution experienced wage gains between 1989 and 1996.[20]

Racial economic inequality also appears significant. A recent study of the janitorial services industry in the valley found a substantial shift to outsourcing largely to firms heavily staffed by legal and illegal Mexican and Central American immigrants.[21] Within Santa Clara County the percentage of residents without health insurance in 1997 was 7.1 percent for whites and 24.7 percent for Latinos.[22]

These concerns are not meant to gainsay the very substantial achievements of the Silicon Valley. Indeed, if one asked the Rawlsian question in which you had no control over your personal characteristics (e.g., race, gender, education) but could only choose where to live, the Silicon Valley would not be a bad choice. Nonetheless, the outcomes in that labor market do not make a convincing case against policy. The Silicon Valley is a white-collar craft labor market in which very skilled workers move easily from place to place aided not by craft unions but by informal networks. The useful lesson to draw from the valley is that in a labor market characterized by job turnover highly skilled people whose capacities are in short supply will do fine. They will construct their own job-finding networks and, fueled by the strong demand for their abilities, make their own way. However, just as no one believes that the labor market for sports stars or Hollywood actors typifies the circumstances of most Americans, nor should we believe that the success of one stratum in the Silicon Valley presages success for everyone. For most people problems of inequality and blocked mobility seem as real in the valley as they do elsewhere in the nation.

What We Should Try to Build

What do we want the new labor market to look like? In constructing the labor market we should recognize that there are various outcomes and that sometimes they compete against one another. We need to identify these outcomes, think about how they can be accomplished, and decide what tradeoffs we have to make among them. I think that the following principles or objectives stand out:

Efficiency: The labor market should do a good job of allocating people to the firms and to the occupations where they will be the most productive, and the market should provide the appropriate incentives and mechanisms to facilitate this movement as well as to encourage people to obtain the appropriate level of skills.

Equity: Most Americans would agree that equity is an appropriate objective. In a rich nation it is hard to accept that there is no limit to the appropriate gap between the top and the bottom. There may be disagreement about how large that gap should be, but there is broad support for the idea that equity is a legitimate goal of policy and a labor market outcome that should be valued.

Opportunity: The labor market should be structured in a way that permits people to make the most of their abilities and in which everyone has a chance to move ahead. This implies that there are opportunities for learning, and it also implies that the allocation of rewards is fair and not governed by inappropriate standards.

Voice: People spend much of their lives at work, and most want to have some say in how their workplace is organized. Voice is not necessarily the same as power or authority, and there is considerable variation in just where along the spectrum different people and different organizations want to be. However, a real opportunity to be heard and to participate seems fundamental.

Security: No one can guarantee good outcomes for everyone. The economy is dynamic, and conditions change. However, we have long accepted the principle that through a combination of public and private policy some level of insurance should be available to ensure that there is a floor below which no one need fall.

These principles—efficiency, equity, opportunity, voice, and security—are not always internally consistent. Moving a long way on one dimension may undermine others. The debate about the proper balance is what policy making should be about. However, just to accept the legitimacy of each principle should be an important step forward because it implies that pure market outcomes are unacceptable. Beyond this, truly creative policy making would seek to understand what opportunities the new economic realities offer to make progress on each of these dimensions without doing undue damage to the others. This is not to deny that some hard choices and trade-offs will be necessary, but it is also true that in some respects we have new openings for new ideas. For example, the increased openness of internal labor markets means that firms will have a greater need for effective intermediaries. The question is how to build on these new opportunities.

PLAN OF THE BOOK

The goal of this book is to sort through what has happened to the American labor market and what choices are available for its reconstruction. In the next chapter I make the case in more detail that the idea of an "institutional structure" is helpful and that the old system has been undermined. This broad understanding of what has happened in recent years is central to any effort to think through what to do next.

The demise of the old institutional structure has had considerable consequences for the careers of workers. Some of these changes are positive. For example, for many employees new ways of organizing work have led to broader, more interesting, and more challenging jobs. In addition, some people prefer contingent employment for the freedom and flexibility it provides. Other shifts—stagnant wages, increased insecurity—are clearly negative. I devote chapter 3 to describing the impact of these various changes on individuals. This analysis will employ a variety of data. Drawing the different sources together, I will be able to paint an accurate picture of the consequences, positive and negative, of the changing structure of the American labor market.

The spirit of the book is to treat the pressures on firms and their response as central for understanding what has happened in recent years. This is not an obvious or inevitable choice. For example, it is clear that the declining power of unions is very much part of the story, and one might make this the centerpiece of the analysis. Another choice is the changing political environment that has led to a weakened government presence in the labor market and, sometimes, outright public encouragement of substantial changes in norms and behaviors. Nonetheless, I think that understanding why employers are restructuring their employment systems is the more promising route. The description offered earlier of the old institutional labor market framework and where it is eroding all point to the central role of employers, the pressures they face, and the response they have made.

While employers may be at the heart of the story, it is nonetheless very unclear just what has happened and why. Chapter 4 is devoted to sorting out these questions. The chapter asks how widespread is restructuring (defined as layoffs, contingent work, and outsourcing), whether innovative ways of organizing work (often involving teams) have continued to diffuse in the face of restructuring, and whether gains from these new work systems have been shared with their labor force. This chapter draws heavily from two original surveys of firms that I conducted, one in 1992 and one in 1997, as well as a fairly extensive set of open-ended interviews with employers.

The book then turns to policy. The policy debate around these issues has been confused, to say the least. In part the confusion is due to a failure to understand that any given problem is really one element of the broader phenomenon, the crumbling of the postwar institutional structure of the labor market. As a result, many of the proposed solutions have a piecemeal quality: fix labor law, or improve the job training system, or raise the minimum wage. Many of these ideas are good ones, but taken in isolation, they are incomplete and open to criticism that they ignore much of what is happening. The policy chapters are built around the central themes of the book, mobility and power. In chapter 5 I explain why the widely disseminated case against policy—that intervening in the labor market will only make things worse—is wrong. Then in chapter 6 I develop ideas aimed at facilitating movement in the labor market and reducing the risks people face in the new environment. Chapter 7 takes on the issue of the balance of power between employees and employers.

SUMMARY

To make a discussion of policy plausible, it is important to recognize that the market, while powerful and central, does not dictate any particular result. There is a range of discretion that is resolved through institutional processes, political and otherwise. In thinking about the present-day relevance of this point, it may be helpful to close this chapter with a historical analogy. Many commentators turn to the New Deal as an example of an epoch in which people mobilized against the market. But in fact the market was discredited by the depression, and, at least initially, the architects of the New Deal did not face the problem of overcoming the rhetoric of free market advocates. A better analogy to the current period is the turn of this century. This was also an era in which it seemed that impersonal market forces were sweeping away established institutions. Agricultural areas were buffeted by trusts, railroad rate setting, and the power of distant warehouses. Capital markets, personified by J. P. Morgan and his colleagues, appeared irresistible. Factory workers also felt a loss of control as consolidation and new technology destroyed the old basis of their power. As Robert Weibe noted in his aptly titled *The Search for Order,* "As men ranged farther and farther from their communities, they tried desperately to understand the larger world in terms of their small familiar environment. They tried . . . to master an impersonal world through the customs of a personal society. They failed . . . and that failure to comprehend a society they were helping to make contained the essence of the nation's story."[23]

Today, market advocates urge employees to focus on training, skill, and "packing your own parachute." The analogous ideology at the turn of the century was the social Darwinism of Spencer and Sumner, which applied the idea of survival of the fittest to the human economic and social realm. Popular discourse translated these ideas into a strong emphasis on the importance of "character" in explaining success.

Certainly the turn of the century was an era in which the market, having swept away the old institutional structure of the economy, seemed poised to triumph. Yet it did not. Farmers organized the Populist movement, workers formed strong unions, the middle class engaged in civic reform. From this stew emerged the Progressive movement, which fundamentally was about restraining the market as that market then manifested itself. The Progressives did not repeal the laws of supply and demand. Indeed, under some interpretations they set the stage for the emergence of the market in a different guise. But they enacted railroad regulation, created the Interstate Commerce Commission and the Federal Trade Commission, passed antitrust legislation, created the Federal Reserve System, and, perhaps most important, firmly established the idea that the central government would have a major say in the workings and regulation of the economy. The views of the Populists, labor movement, and civic reformers were hardly consistent, and each had to contend with a powerful financial establishment defending its prerogatives. Nonetheless, the Progressives indisputably engaged distant and impersonal market forces and created a new framework within which those forces had to play themselves out. This is the challenge we too face.

————

The Changing Structure of
the American Labor Market

UNTIL THE LAST DECADE or so, the American labor market functioned according to a set of rules and norms put into place after World War II. These constitute what I term the institutional structure of the labor market. Although there was much to dislike about some aspects of this structure (issues of race and poverty loom large here), it was nonetheless the case that the behavior of firms was predictable and understandable and that people could make their plans—plans for their education and training and plans for their careers—with some reasonable sense of certainty about the relationship between actions and consequences. This institutional structure has been blown apart in the past decade, and with it has gone the sense of order that undergirded people's notions of the economy. The loss of order is what explains the unease that persists even in the face of good economic news.

In this chapter I develop the idea of the postwar institutional structure and demonstrate that it has been undermined. We shall see a greater willingness of firms to lay off employees even when times are good and, related to this, that job security has eroded and that the length of time an employee can expect to stay with an employer has shrunk. I also demonstrate how changes in wage-setting practices have undermined the older norms that emphasized fairness and equity in compensation. The rise in various forms of contingent employment has made it much less certain what it means to have a "job." In these and in other ways the rules that structure work have been transformed, and while we may not yet be sure of the new rules, we can be certain that the game has changed in significant ways.

THE POSTWAR INSTITUTIONAL STRUCTURE

It is important to understand at the outset that the notion of an "institutional structure" is not a self-evident idea. For example, most economists are trained to think as follows: the legal system (contract law, regulations, and the like) provides a framework within which the laws of supply and demand operate. Outside these legal restrictions the market rules supreme. Hence the only meaning attached to the idea of an "institutional structure" is laws and regulations, and, although they are consequential, their existence and importance are hardly an earthshaking idea. Some economists would go even further and deny, or at least minimize, the independent importance of laws and regulations. They view laws as emerging endogenously from the economic system. For example, they might argue that child labor was abolished only when it became economically efficient to do so.[1] In other cases, market mechanisms subvert and render laws irrelevant. For example, price. controls can be sidestepped by side payments and a black market.

The intellectual history of theorizing and research about the labor market can be understood as an ongoing debate between those who believe that the concept of structure is important and those more interested in traditional market forces.[2] During the depression and World War II, a distinguished group of labor economists were intimately involved in wage setting and collective bargaining. They emerged from this experience struck by how different the actual labor market was from the models and theoretical descriptions they had learned from the academic profession. They wrote about this and launched an important series of studies to document them.[3] These scholars were influential voices but were soon challenged by more traditional economists who centered their work on supply and demand and the various extensions of this paradigm. This latter group spoke in terms that resonated with how the rest of the economics profession thought about the world, be that world the market for pork bellies or exchange rates, and by the end of the 1960s mainstream economic thinking was triumphant. What might be termed "institutional labor economics" still had adherents, but these scholars retreated from economics departments into business schools, schools of industrial relations, and public policy institutes. Be that as it may, the older institutional tradition offers important clues as to how best to understand current events.

What, then, is the "institutional structure" of the labor market? One difference between labor markets and markets for other commodities is that "imperfections" seem to play a more prominent role in the labor market. Two examples are imperfect information and mobility costs. Imperfect information arises because the market is very dispersed and job seekers may not know with certainty the full range of job offers and wage rates that are available. Mobility costs mean that workers will not easily switch jobs or locations in response to small differences in economic opportunity. These "imperfections" distinguish the market for labor from the market for commodities and have been used by theorists as levers to explain why the labor market seems to operate differently than other markets.

It is certainly true that imperfect information and constrained mobility are important characteristics of the labor market. In themselves, however, these considerations complicate the analysis but do not render the labor market different in any fundamental way from other markets. For the labor market to be different we need to argue that the underlying motives and behavior of participants differ from those of participants in other commodity markets.

One distinctive characteristic of the labor market is that strong norms and expectations arise concerning what is proper behavior, and for long periods of time these norms have considerable force. As sociologists have long recognized, norms can take on a life of their own, influencing the choices organizations make independent of whatever rational calculation led to their initial establishment.[4] Norms are particularly important in the labor market because of the human tendency to avoid making purely rational or economistic judgments about how to treat people in work groups.

In the labor market what people think of as "proper" frequently does not imply seeking the maximum possible advantage but rather balancing economic gains with social values. In addition, the strength of these norms, or rather the strength of the view that employees should not be treated in a fashion parallel with pork bellies, is such that laws and regulations also come to embody them. These norms are (or, rather, were) important in shaping the relationship between employees and firms with respect to careers and with respect to wages. These, then, are a good place to begin a description of the postwar labor market structure.

The Firm as Family

One way of thinking about the evolution of employment relations during most of the postwar period is to conceive of two competing models. One of these, the industrial union model, was best typified by the employment practices that emerged in the automobile industry, an employment system that was strongly shaped by bargains between the United Automobile Workers and the Big Three auto firms. This was a system in which seniority, not individual merit, played a key role in wages, in which job duties were tightly specified by contract, and in which the firm was free to adjust employment levels by layoffs, although most layoffs were followed by recall.[5] These patterns were not only extended throughout the union sector but were also widely imitated by many large nonunion employers.

The competing employment model was the aggressively nonunion approach perhaps best typified by IBM. Under this system the firm sought to establish direct relations with employees via numerous communications programs and employee surveys. Wages had a larger individual component, and job descriptions were flexible. At IBM there was a strong implicit job security commitment. IBM was one of the most powerful and most successful firms in the nation, and not many firms could imitate it in all respects. However, IBM was consistently cited as one of the most admired employers in the country, and among those firms that sought to avoid unions or unionlike employment systems the IBM model was the target to be chased.

While it is true that at some level these were two competing systems, my point is quite different. In a deep sense the IBM and the Big Auto systems shared a great deal in common. They were both premised on the assumption that the firm and the employee had long-term attachments to each other and that a web of mutual obligations existed between the two parties. Both models accepted the idea of a firm as a coherent organizational form with relatively fixed boundaries and relationships. They weren't the same kind of family in all the details, just as real families may differ in how the members get along, but they shared a deep underlying assumption about stable relationships and long-term attachments. Since these were the two dominant employment models in the postwar period, it seems fair to say that their commonalities fundamentally define what was the core of the postwar employment model.

The notion that IBM and the unionized model were at least in some ways two manifestations of the same underlying set of ideas may strike many people as strange. After all, IBM and its imitators were fanatically opposed to unions and devoted a great deal of effort to keeping them out. By the same token, protections that unionized employees fought hard for and won—for example, third-party arbitration of shop-floor disputes—were never available to employees in the nonunion sector. These differences were important and should not be minimized. However, it is nonetheless true that both systems did share a common view about long-term attachments between employers and employees, and therefore both accepted the idea that employees would ideally make their careers within the enterprise. Both models also accepted the idea that the firm incurred obligations to its workers that extended beyond the daily paycheck. It is only as these assumptions break down, which is what is happening now, that we can see how much such a diverse group of employers had in common under the old system.

In important measure what IBM and the union model shared in common was grounded in the academic literature termed the Human Relations School.[6] This line of thought, which began with Elton Mayo and was elaborated by numerous management theorists, reached the peak of its influence in the postwar period. The central idea, as Mauro Guillen points out, was that "neglecting the morale, sentiments, and emotions of both the worker and manager would set limits to the firm's productivity and profitability."[7] This perspective, very different in spirit from the engineering-oriented scientific management approach to boosting performance, led to the diffusion of human resource practices such as morale surveys, suggestion systems, and various communication techniques. More to the point, Human Relations reinforced the view that ideally the firm should make a long-term commitment to its labor force.

It is not easy to prove this assertion because opinion polls of representative samples of senior managers are not available. Guillen offers a content analysis of business publications that shows that the Human Relations School was dominant during the decades following World War II, and he also documents the spread of specific human resource practices associated with this perspective. Another sort of evidence is provided by asking what management "gurus" were telling their listeners. In 1982, just as the postwar model was beginning to fray, Peters and Waterman published their phenomenally popular *In Search of Excellence,* which was a cookbook distilling the "keys" to the success of those firms that had prospered during the past several decades. The authors were explicit in their debt to Human Relations theorists.[8] Peters and Waterman were, however, much more open than Human Relations scholars in arguing for employment continuity. The countless managers who read this book learned that "many of the best companies view themselves as an extended family" and that "when we look at excellent companies . . . we see . . . full employment policies in times of recession."[9] Clearly, the conventional wisdom, the ideology, of this period was that employment security was a desirable objective and that best practice was to view the workforce as a community and to maintain that workforce in place whenever possible.

Internalized Careers

A corollary of the foregoing argument is that the postwar period was characterized by a particular system for shaping careers. For most people, the typical career pattern was to enter a firm at the bottom of a job ladder and to move up that ladder over time. This system implied a fairly high degree of job security because both individuals and firms made mutual investments in each other (particularly in training) and were loath to lose those investments. Indeed, early in the 1980s researchers comparing American and Japanese workers were surprised to discover that the Americans seemed to enjoy nearly as much job stability as the Japanese despite the much ballyhooed Japanese system of lifetime employment.[10]

It was never the case that this relatively secure closed system was universal. Some people held good jobs but under different arrangements. An example is craft workers who moved from employer to employer, or work site to work site, but who were protected by their high level of skills. Other people were trapped in a low-wage casual segment of the labor market, unable to break into the security of the more protected sector. However, despite these exceptions, the dominant image and paradigm of postwar employment was very much the "organization man" who lived his (and sometimes her) life within one organization.

Even during the golden years of American economic dominance, the economy ebbed and flowed, and firms needed to adjust their labor force. How they did so, however, was played out in the context of the internal career structure outlined above. Managers and other senior white-collar employees faced very little employment risk. They were treated as a fixed factor of production, and their layoff rates were very low. Blue-collar workers were laid off, but most typically these were temporary layoffs that were followed by recall.

Institutional economists treated these closed and relatively stable internal career structures as central to the structure of the postwar system. In 1972 Peter Doeringer and Michael Piore wrote their widely read *Internal Labor Markets and Manpower Analysis,* which described these career systems in great detail for blue-collar work. This book, which drew on an earlier stream of research by the postwar generation of institutional labor economists, came to be seen as describing the quintessential characteristics of manufacturing employment in America. There was no equivalent unified treatment of white-collar work, but numerous accounts, ranging from the popular *Organization Man* to the more scholarly treatment of employment by Ann Howard and Douglas Bray of the old Bell System,[11] made it clear that managers and white-collar workers expected and experienced long-term attachments to their employer.

The academic debate revolved not around whether these stable blue- and white-collar employment structures were typical but rather why they had emerged. Characteristically, many economists developed models that explained stable career structures as optimal solutions to problems of training, monitoring employees, and providing appropriate behavioral incentives.[12] Other researchers sought the origins of these systems in the interaction of union bargaining, government intervention, informal employee power, and economic considerations.[13] Everyone agreed, however, that stable careers typified the postwar system.

Wage Setting

Nothing is more central to our understanding of how the labor market works than wage determination. How wages are set is one of the key elements of any theoretical picture of labor markets, and to show that there was indeed an identifiable postwar institutional structure, it is important to be able to characterize the process of wage determination convincingly.

Standard economic models provide a useful foil against which one can judge the nature of the wage-setting regime. According to these models, relative wages (i.e., the relationship of the wages of different occupations to one another) are set by the forces of supply and demand. Behind the supply curves are people's choices between work and leisure, the skills they bring to the workforce, and their assessment of the desirability, or lack thereof, of different kinds of work. Underlying the demand curves are the productivity of each type of labor and the technological possibilities of substituting one kind of labor for another. Supply and demand interact to set the wages of each occupation, and the movement of employees from one firm to another enforces this process. From the firm's viewpoint the wage is given: the firm must pay the going wage or else be unable to recruit, and, of course, no rational firm would pay more than the going wage. Hence there is no such thing as a "wage policy" for a given employer.

This model of wage setting is to some extent a straw man, and no one, even the most orthodox economist, believes that it is accurate at each point in time. It does, however, capture the essential spirit of wage setting as understood by standard models. More sophisticated variants maintain some of the basic assumptions. For example, in recent years some scholars have argued that firms may be willing to pay above-market wages (so-called efficiency wages) because these induce employees to work harder for fear of losing these premium jobs and being forced into the market. This formulation permits wage dispersion, that is, the wages of the same occupation can vary from firm to firm. However, at its core the model maintains the traditional assumption that the firm is focused on the wages of an individual and no attention is paid to group processes or politics.

In sharp contrast to these theoretical models, people who studied actual wage setting in the postwar period discovered very different forces at work. These muted market forces and pushed strongly in the direction of a wage structure that was fairly stable and that was biased toward wage compression (i.e., relative equality). The key processes that underwrote this structure were the following:

High valuation of internal equity in the firms' wage structure. Sociologists studying the shop floor discovered that employees, particularly those in stable work groups, developed norms about the relative wage structure.[14] These norms, which were couched in the language of fairness, dealt with the relative pay of different jobs as well as the weight that should be given in wage setting to personal characteristics such as skill and seniority. Even in the absence of collective bargaining, these norms could be enforced by collective withholding of effort by employees. Firms in turn recognized the importance of these norms in their own approach to pay administration. A great deal of care was devoted to developing job evaluation procedures (typically the awarding of points to jobs based on their skill, responsibility, and so on) were used to rationalize and stabilize the internal pay structure. Merit pay, which on its face appears to emphasize individual differences, was typically administered in a way that led to everyone receiving relatively equal raises. Researchers referred to the importance of "customary standards of equity" in pay setting.[15] Accounts of wage determination demonstrated that firms paid much more attention to internal administrative pay-setting procedure than to attempts, for example, via community surveys, to learn about going wages in the labor market.[16] A crude verification of this observation is that the leading compensation textbook devoted 155 pages to an exposition of internal job evaluation schemes and only half that to community wage surveys.[17]

A stable set of pay relationships among firms and industries. Researchers also observed that a stable and predictable relationship existed among the wages of diverse industries and firms. This observation led writers to coin phrases such as "pattern bargaining" and "wage contours" to describe the phenomenon. In pattern bargaining the wages of workers in one industry, for example, agricultural implements, were tightly connected to those in another industry, such as automobiles. Although the word "bargaining" strongly points to the role of unions, it was also accepted that via spillovers and imitation the patterns were often extended into the nonunion sector. Researchers set about showing that the dollar value of wage agreements in one industry was imitated (plus or minus a stable markup or markdown) elsewhere even though "objective" economic conditions such as unemployment or product market developments might have implied a different outcome.[18] In a similar spirit, wage contours or orbits or coercive comparison referred to the interrelationship of wages within a community and the linkage between the wages in one job and another.

The importance of ability to pay. An additional element in pay setting in the old regime was the important role played by the firm's financial capacity. Virtually all observers noted that a key consideration was the company's balance sheet: when times were good, employers shared the profits with their employees.[19] There was an asymmetry to the system given that in bad times wages may have been held down but they did not fall in nominal terms. Nonetheless, whatever the level of conflicts that might emerge in the workplace, the role of "ability to pay" created some degree of shared community interest.

Taken as a whole, what did this picture of wage setting add up to? To begin, these considerations did not necessarily suggest a coherent theoretical structure, and in particular "ability to pay" poses problems. The pattern bargaining and wage contours of institutional theory have difficulty accommodating "ability to pay" because different firms within the pattern or contour may be at different points in their profit cycle. The thrust of patterns and contours is to push for uniformity, while "ability to pay" can create centrifugal forces in the wage structure.

What this account of wage setting does clearly suggest is that the wage structure of the economy was very sticky, that is, slow to adjust to conventional economic forces. The source of this stickiness was a set of considerations—particularly the role of equity, custom, and comparisons—that have no place in simple market-oriented models or in their more sophisticated extensions. These factors meshed very well with the broader picture of stable employment relationships described earlier and created an overall system for wages and careers that placed a heavy emphasis on continuity and fairness.

The Broader Context

This postwar system of careers and wages did not emerge in isolation, nor was it sustainable without a broader set of supports that were consistent with it. One of these elements was a secure and influential industrial relations system. Unions, while never representing a majority of the labor force, played an important role in structuring the labor market. Many of the practices and norms regarding how employers behaved and what employees could expect were derived from union-management agreements.

At their peak, unions represented 35.5 percent of the private sector labor force (in 1945). The influence of unions, however, extended beyond the firms and industries in which they were strong. Unions played a central role in structuring the postwar labor market. They did so in several ways. Nonunion firms typically organized work and paid wages in line with the union standards, and they did so for two reasons. The first was fear: owing to what the industrial relations scholars termed the union "threat effect," the nonunion sector sought to match union patterns in order to avoid being organized. In an important sense the unions established a "minimum wage" for significant regions of the labor market.

Perhaps as significant was the impact union models had on other firms' images of what was the "right" or "accepted" way of structuring themselves. The unionized system of seniority, job classifications, and temporary layoffs followed by recall was widely influential even in the nonunion manufacturing sector. A good example of this is my experience in Digital Equipment Corporation, a militantly antiunion company. When DEC began its first round of layoffs in the 1980s, I happened to be conducting interviews in the firm, and it turned out, much to my surprise, that the basis for the blue-collar layoffs was employment date, that is, seniority.

If the industrial relations system helped support the postwar system from the perspective of the shop floor and office, another important contextual feature was the nature of corporate governance. American corporate law gives the owner of stock primacy in the governance of the firm, and maximizing the welfare of the stockholder is supposed to be the guiding objective of managers. However, as Adolf Berle and Gardiner Means observed as far back as 1933, the reality was that executives enjoyed a great deal of autonomy.[20] The ownership of stock was widely dispersed, and boards of directors provided very little effective oversight.

The important question, therefore, is what were managers trying to achieve, and there is a great deal of evidence that they placed substantial value on maintaining, indeed growing, employment and on sharing profits not only with stockholders but with the broad employee base. This was not necessarily because managers had humanitarian values. The strongest correlate of executive pay during this period was the size of the firm, and hence there was a clear incentive to grow. Furthermore, it is simply more pleasant to manage in a situation in which people are treated well and conflict is lower than in other circumstances. Managers also enjoyed being considered good corporate and community citizens and were willing to expend stockholder resources in order to achieve this. It was also true, as noted earlier, that managers had been schooled in the human relations perspective, and their relative freedom from oversight gave them the slack necessary to implement these policies even when the immediate payback was hard to demonstrate.

The third element in the broader context was the role of government. In some European nations public institutions play an important role in shaping labor markets. In Sweden, for example, the employment service long enjoyed a monopoly on job placements, while in Germany the youth apprenticeship system—jointly run by firms, unions, and the government— is the most common way young people obtain their skills and enter the labor market. The role of government in the U.S. labor market is more complicated and shaded.

On the one hand, in many respects the government does exert a powerful influence on the labor market. There has been a growing volume of regulations and laws, ranging from health and safety to equal employment opportunity to the Americans With Disabilities Act, which have significant impacts on employment practices. In low-wage labor markets immigration policy and minimum wage legislation are important. The expansion of public education, notably the by now largely vocational community colleges, has shaped both labor supply (the decisions of young people about when to enter the labor force) and the characteristics of that supply, notably their knowledge and skills.

By contrast, what in Europe would be called "active labor market policy" has not been important in America. Institutions, other than schools, explicitly aimed at either providing vocational skills or facilitating the flows of labor are generally weak and ineffective. Specifically, the job-training system has been small and limited to serving marginalized poverty populations. The Employment Service similarly has been generally ineffective and unimportant in the calculations of most firms and people (more will be said on both of these institutions in a later chapter).

There was an effort shortly after World War II to construct a more active employment policy and a set of public institutions to implement it, but that effort failed, as Margaret Weir has shown,[21] because of the opposition of southern politicians, who feared any interference with their then semifeudal labor markets, and the powerful ideology of Keynesian economists who saw no need for microeconomic interventions once fiscal and monetary policy was properly tuned. To these explanations might be added the observation that in a world of relatively closed internal labor markets, in which mobility is not great and in which firms do their own training, neither companies nor unions will feel any pressing need for an active labor market policy.

THE COLLAPSE OF THE POSTWAR STRUCTURE

The institutional structure that shaped the postwar labor market is disappearing. Each of the symptoms of labor market distress—stagnating earnings, heightened insecurity, uncertainty about what it means to hold a job—reflects this collapse. In this section I provide evidence that the rules, norms, and behaviors that guided the postwar market are no longer operative.

Before turning to the evidence that the postwar structure has eroded, it is worth pausing to think about why this transformation occurred. The idea of the market dictating particular outcomes may be in part a rhetorical weapon, but what gives it power is that there is an important underlying truth to its claims. We do have choices, and in this sense the market metaphor is being misused. But it is also true that firms are under tremendous pressure, and this must also be acknowledged. It is important to understand these pressures because they shape the varied nature of the responses. What, then, are the possible explanations of why so much change has occurred?

Times are tougher, and competition has increased. For a variety of reasons many firms are operating in a tougher environment than before. In some industries, such as telecommunications, deregulation and the emergence of new competitors have radically changed the game. The scale of layoffs in the Regional Bells as well as AT&T is therefore not surprising. Changes in interstate banking laws have triggered fierce competition, mergers, and lay-offs in institutions such as Chase, Chemical, Fleet, and Citigroup.

Deregulation is not the only source of more difficult times. The insurance industry, for example, faces numerous challenges. Large firms are increasingly self-insuring, banks are going after easy business such as workers' compensation, and nimble smaller firms are offering new products that old multiline insurers find hard to match.[22] The consequence has been restructuring in firms such as Prudential, Travelers, and Aetna.

The foregoing examples are driven by largely domestic considerations. It is important to see this because so much attention has been devoted to issues of trade. Nonetheless, while not the whole story, trade clearly adds to the list of reasons why life is tougher, as the auto, steel, and textile industries can attest.

Evidence of tougher competition is real and could be multiplied many times. In some sense, however, the point is too facile. Firms have always faced competition and have responded by cutting prices, laying off employees (historically blue-collar ones), and innovating new products. However, only recently have fundamental organizational structures been called into question. If firms had been optimally organized before, then the presence of competition should stimulate the traditional responses but not necessarily lead to radical rethinking of the organization itself. Something else must be at play that enables a more far-reaching response than was possible in the past or that overcomes past political and social obstacles to such a response. This is a crucial point because it gets us beyond overly simple appeals to tough competition as an explanation for changes in employer organization and strategy.

Technology, hard and soft. Alfred Chandler, the dean of business historians and chronicler of the traditional American bureaucratic firm, likens the spread of microcomputers and chips to the extension of the railroad. The railroad created the modern corporation by enabling mass markets, and analogously the microchip enables new forms of management and control. With more than 40 percent of new capital investment spent on information technology and with a 6,000 percent quality-adjusted price decline in computers over the past thirty years, this argument is more than plausible.[23]

At a crude level computers can substitute for labor, permitting more to be produced with less. There has been considerable academic dispute about the size of this effect, although the weight of recent evidence is that computers do indeed replace both managerial and blue-collar labor, at least for a given amount of output.[24] However, the more interesting impact is deeper because computers enable new systems of management and control. A great deal of energy within firms and business schools is spent thinking about how to use computers to change business processes radically. Classic examples include combining steps in customer service and order entry or streamlining backroom processing of financial records in banking and insurance. The downsizing and restructuring that follow—as when GM recently announced that five thousand engineers would lose their jobs because of innovations in how car design is linked to manufacturing[25]—are really by-products of the use of microprocessors to alter the nature of the firm.

It is important to understand that exactly how information technology is used within an organization is determined by decisions that organization makes, not by some irresistible imperative of the technology itself. Indeed, a major theme of recent social science research on technology is the contingent nature of its impact. These technologies can be used to decentralize knowledge and decision-making power to employees, or they can be used to centralize information in the hands of people at the top and eliminate the need for managers in the middle to process and analyze data. Because the outcome is an organizational decision, it is influenced by the values of the firm, the balance of power between different constituencies, and whatever external constraints the environment places on decisions.[26] Be all this as it may, it cannot be denied that IT has opened the door to new organizational designs with radical implications for both the shape of the organization and how it conceives of its employees. Given this option, we can understand how the much tougher competitive environment of recent years interacted with technology to yield substantial shifts in the nature and behavior of the firm.

As impressive as the impact of microprocessors is, it is crucial not to overlook the importance of a "soft" technological innovation: new ideas about organizational design. These new ideas, which have become broadly accessible to the managerial community in recent years, have implications that may well equal or exceed more traditional technological change. The spread of these new ideas was stimulated in the 1980s by the success of the Japanese economy and by what seemed to most observers to be the link between that success and how firms were organized. Although perhaps arbitrary, the list of these central organizational ideas would include (1) the Japanese approach to quality, which shifted quality from being the province of a separate unit and instead diffused accountability throughout the production process; (2) devolution of increased responsibility to ordinary workers (white and blue collar) to come up with new ideas and processes and the related organization of the workforce into teams with substantial training and job rotation; (3) the notion that some workers are core to the organization, whereas others are peripheral and can be managed with quite different sets of rules and expectations; (4) production process innovations, notably just-in-time systems of inventory; (5) long-term and intimate relationships with suppliers and hence a considerable interpenetration between what others might perceive as distinct organizational units.

These ideas spread in American business circles through many channels. Academics wrote books laying out Japanese principles and providing evidence of their positive impacts. Consultants and the business press were aggressive in more popular presentations of the same point. Many American firms sent delegations to Japan to observe and to learn. By the early 1990s most large and many smaller American firms had adopted variants of these ideas.

Although these organizational innovations quickly became part of American business vocabulary, it is important to understand that they played out in different ways in different settings. Even within one industry there is substantial variation: consider the uneven but generally successful partnership between the union and the firm at the General Motors Saturn operation, and contrast that with the conflict and struggle described by Joseph and Suzy Fucini in a Mazda plant.[27] Furthermore, in many firms it is doubtlessly the case that the vocabulary has been adopted with little real change in practices. Just how deeply these practices have actually penetrated will be at least in part illuminated when I turn in chapter 4 to several surveys I have conducted.

However, even with these qualifications in mind, it is clear that these new organizational ideas present firms with opportunities similar to those offered by information technology as they seek ways to respond to competitive stress. There is perhaps even more scope for values, external constraints, and internal power/politics to shape just how these opportunities are used, but their far-reaching implications seem undeniable. The very boundaries of the firm are placed into question, the flow of work is again open to reconsideration, and fundamental issues arise regarding to which set of workers the firm is willing to make any degree of commitment.

Capital markets are calling the tune. Informational and organizational technology are tools offering firms new ways to respond to competitive stress. The capital market explanation is different in that it looks outside the organization and calls attention to the role of the financial community in influencing the motivation and objectives of firms. There are basically three lines of argument. The first is that the institutional investors currently place much greater pressure on firms to perform than they faced in the past. The second is that in general the stock market undervalues "soft" investments in people. This might happen because these investments are hard to observe and hence are subject to the suspicion that they really represent managerial featherbedding. Another possibility is that analysts simply don't believe that such investments pay off. The third argument is that the stock market places unreasonably short time horizons on firms, which must then manage for quarterly performance and not long-term growth.

The stories summarized above suggest two related but distinct hypotheses. The first is that capital markets are making firms more performance-oriented than in the past. This might help explain the rapid adoption of the new organizational and IT technologies. The second argument is that capital markets bias firms away from investments in people and that this bias is increasing. I want to defer a careful assessment of these hypotheses until the discussion of corporate governance in chapter 7. However, it is worth making a few points. First, for capital market explanations to hold water, it must be the case that firms were either suboptimally structured in the past or else, absent capital market pressures, they would be too slow to take up the opportunities offered by the "hard" and "soft" technologies described above. If firms were doing their best in tough circumstances, then capital market participants would have no incentives to pressure managers. From the viewpoint of capital markets this suboptimality can take two forms: either managers are simply making bad decisions and need to be set back on course, or managers are doing fine on their own terms but are pursuing somewhat different objectives than simply maximizing stockholders' returns. For example, if managers placed a positive value on loyalty to long-standing employees, this might be seen by the investment community as wasteful spending. This is certainly the perspective of finance theorists such as Michael Jensen who celebrate the rise of corporate raiders as a technique for eliminating "excess capacity."[28] The trick in assessing claims regarding the impact of capital markets lies in distinguishing between firms that really need a wake-up call and cases in which capital markets are simply struggling for a higher share of profits at the expense of employment and wages.

A second qualification is that some of the capital market stories are inconsistent with fundamental economic ideas of efficiency. For example, the short-time horizons argument does not fully make sense. If an action by a firm has a short-run cost but a large long-run payoff, then the capital markets—interested in the present discounted value of investment—should be willing to await the payoff.

These qualifications and amendments aside, the interaction of heightened competition and shifting capital market constraints is most likely an additional source of pressure on firms. Although the complaints of incumbent management probably have a strongly self-serving element (attacks on "impatient" investors may be simply pleas by management to retain their unchecked and poorly utilized discretion), observation of managerial behavior does suggest that, for good reasons or bad, concerns about capital markets are shaping behavior in ways that were not true in the past. Michael Useem, in his study of the impact of institutional investors, concludes, "Management has been responding. In reviewing executive compensation plans . . . general counsels often review the plans privately with activist pension funds. When considering . . . an acquisition chief executives turn to investor specialists for a prediction of how the markets will react. Whether in setting strategy or selling divisions, investor preferences now unite with regulatory constraints and legal risks as part of the operating environment that executives no longer ignore."[29]

EVIDENCE OF CHANGE

The erosion of the postwar system for organizing labor markets can be seen along the dimensions of norms, career patterns, wage determination, shifts in the external context that governs the labor market, and changes in the structure of the economy itself. I now take up each of these in turn.

Norms

It is difficult to demonstrate conclusively that the norms regarding appropriate treatment of employees have shifted in the past several decades. No opinion polls of business leaders are taken, and in any case the value structure that undergirds decisions may be too elusive to measure accurately. Because of this I have to rely on a series of indirect indicators to make the point plausible.

Perhaps the strongest impression held by observers critical of the current scene is that today, unlike in the past, healthy companies are laying off employees. Obviously layoffs per se are nothing new, but the issue is whether previously they reflected distress whereas today, with the inhibition against firing members of the "family" weakened, firms now discharge large numbers of employees even when times are good. This impression is reinforced by headlines such as "Earnings Up, Workers Down," which referred to an MCI layoff,[30] and by statements such as the following by Edwin Artz, chairman of Procter & Gamble: "We must slim down to stay competitive. The consumer wants better value. Our competitors are getting leaner and quicker, and we are simply going to have to run faster to stay ahead. The public has come to think of corporate restructuring as a sign of trouble, but this is definitely not our situation."[31] In a similar vein, a spokesperson for Xerox commented, "I know it can sound very heartless when you're making these decisions when individual's careers are affected, especially when you are making money. But I think it's a new reality."[32]

Is this reality really new? A natural test is to compare layoffs in the current period with those in the past and see if the underlying reasons have shifted. The question is not whether layoffs have become more frequent but rather whether the reasons for layoffs have changed. To pursue this we searched the *Wall Street Journal* for the entire year 1994, collecting all announcements of layoffs.[33] It is important to understand that a layoff announcement is not exactly equivalent to an actual layoff because plans may change. However, it is not practical to contact every firm that announces a layoff to learn what actually happened. In compiling this list we recorded multiple announcements by a company, but in the actual classification reported below each firm is counted only once. The *Wall Street Journal* for 1994 is accessible via computer, and hence the search of the entire year, using keywords, was feasible.

However, to see if patterns have shifted, we decided to do an equivalent search for 1972, which was comparable in terms of the business cycle, and this search had to be done "by hand," looking at each issue of the newspaper. Because it was not possible to search the entire year, we chose to record and classify layoffs for the months of January, February, and March.

We read each story and classified the layoff into one of three categories: layoffs due to poor current results, layoffs in which the firm's current results were good but there was anticipation of future competition or structural change, and layoffs in which the reasons were unclear or that we could not classify. Two of us independently made these classifications, and then we compared the results and discussed cases in which we differed.

The results of this exercise are shown in figure 2.1. The first interesting finding is that well over half of the layoff announcements in 1994 were due to structural change and not to poor current results. This is "hard" evidence for the widespread public intuition that layoff announcements are not simply due to weak firm performance. Perhaps surprisingly, the 1972 data suggest that layoffs in response to considerations other than weak performance are not new; a substantial fraction of layoffs in the earlier period were also of this nature. However, the proportion of layoffs due to weak performance

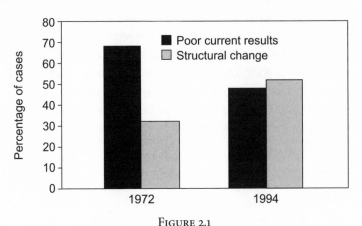

FIGURE 2.1
Reasons for Layoffs
Source: Wall Street Journal.
Sample size for first quarter
of 1972 is 47; for 1994, it is 192.

was notably higher in 1972 than in 1994, and this does suggest that something of a shift has occurred. In short, these patterns, for all the reasonable caveats that apply, do support the view that firms are more willing to fire people for reasons that differ from those in the past.

The rhetoric of management also has changed in a direction that supports the argument that underlying norms have shifted. Recall that the prototypical best-selling business book in the earlier epoch was *In Search of Excellence*, with its Human Relations–inspired rhetoric about the importance of treating employees like family. In the current era, the analogous best-seller is *Reengineering the Corporation*, whose tone is decidedly different. The emphasis is on using information technology to obtain substantial cost savings via improvements in business processes such as order processing, inventory management, supplier relations, and the like. Business success comes from these savings, not from "soft" concepts such as culture- or employee-oriented values, and the savings in turn come partly from the downsizing that the new processes permit. James Champy, one of the authors of *Reengineering the Corporation*, commented that "to prevent or discourage companies from undertaking layoffs would ask them to be noncompetitive and potentially go out of business. It could mean not just fewer jobs but no jobs."[34] Coauthor Michael Hammer, writing in the *Wall Street Journal*, defended large-scale downsizing as resulting from process improvements that are driven by customer demands.[35] Whether Champy and Hammer are right or wrong is not now the point (I return to the reasons for downsizing in a subsequent chapter). Rather, the point for now is the dramatic change in popular managerial rhetoric. Today the position of business is best represented by Robert Eaton, CEO of Chrysler, who commented that "downsizing and layoffs are the price of being more competitive."[36]

THE DECLINE OF INTERNAL LABOR MARKETS

Recall that a central element of the postwar structure was protected career structures internal to firms. People constructed their careers within one or a small number of organizations, with white-collar employees nearly inoculated against layoffs and blue-collar workers living in a regime in which layoffs were followed by recall. One of the central elements of destruction of the postwar system is the erosion of these secure career structures.

There are several ways to see how these internal structures are unraveling. I begin by reviewing data from a variety of sources on job security and layoffs. I then turn to a description of the rapid rise of temporary, or contingent, work. This is a form of employment that is the antithesis of stable orderly careers within a well-defined enterprise.

In addressing these questions, much of the rest of this chapter, as well as the chapters that follow, will periodically use data taken from several national surveys. Two of the surveys, the National Establishment Surveys, were designed and organized by me and focus on employers. Other surveys of individuals are organized by the Census Department and the Bureau of Labor Statistics. Yet another, a longitudinal survey of employees, is federally funded but executed by the University of Michigan. In order to facilitate the flow of the discussion, an appendix to this chapter describes the essential features of each of these surveys.

Employment Tenure

A natural implication of the notion that jobs have become less secure is that if we could collect data on the distribution of employment tenure (i.e., the number of years a worker has remained with an employer), we would see that the distribution would shift over time as people lost previously secure jobs. Hypothetically (if other factors such as entry and exit rates remained constant), one might expect that the fraction of the labor force with job tenure of more than, say, ten years would be smaller now than it was fifteen years ago. If this was true, it could be taken as evidence that job security has truly worsened.

The Bureau of Labor Statistics, as part of the Current Population Survey, periodically asks people the number of years they have worked for their employer, and hence it is possible to see how these distributions shift over time. It is very important in looking at these data to control for age, since otherwise the average tenure in the labor market could fall simply owing to the entry of more young people. Figure 2.2 shows the median tenure for men and women in different age groups over time, and figure 2.3 shows the frac-

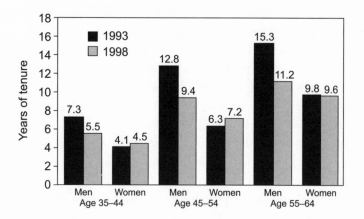

FIGURE 2.2

Median Years of Job Tenure for Men and Women, 1983 and 1998
Source: U.S. Bureau of Labor Statistics, News Release:
"Employee Tenure in 1998," 23 September 1998.

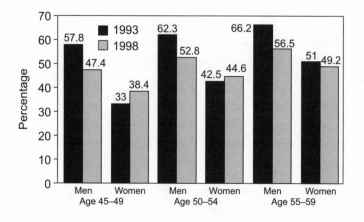

FIGURE 2.3

Percentage of Men and Women with Ten or More Years' Tenure, 1983 and 1998
Source: U.S. Bureau of Labor Statistics, News Release: "Employee Tenure in
1998," 23 September 1998.

tion of men and women within different age groups with ten or more years of tenure. This latter figure is valuable because it gets directly at the question of whether long-term jobs are becoming scarcer.

When the data for both sexes are combined, there has been a mild yet perceptible decline in job tenure, but this decline masks divergent trends for men and women. For men the decline has been quite sharp across all age groups, whereas for women below the age of 55 job tenure has steadily increased over the period. The differing outcomes for men and women are consistent with other patterns, particularly the fact that women's wages have mildly increased while men's have declined. It is tempting to conclude that, although longer tenures for women in part reflect forces on the demand side, they are largely driven by the growing attachment of women to the labor force and their increased disinclination to quit jobs to return to family duties.

In assessing whether internal labor markets have unraveled, it is not obvious whether to focus on the data for the entire labor force, which reflect all the jobs, or to look at the more dramatic male data on the grounds that the increased tenure of women is likely to reflect supply decisions as well as actions by firms. In either case, however, the conclusion is that there is some loosening of internal ties. However, it should also be understood that there are a series of technical problems that complicate the use of these data. Some of these issues are described in the box entitled "Data Problems." However, when more sophisticated adjustments are made, the conclusion that job tenure has declined still holds.

Quits

The fact that these data, particularly for women, probably reflect supply- as well as demand-side considerations points to a problem with using tenure to measure changes in internal labor markets. Job stability in reality is determined by two events, whether the person has lost his or her job involuntarily (a layoff) or whether he or she quit. It is quite possible that the chances of being laid off have increased but that quits have declined as people choose to avoid risk by remaining with their employer. In this scenario economic insecurity has increased, but this is not reflected in job tenure data

TABLE 2.1
Distribution of Reasons for Unemployment

	1979	1989	1998
Quits	.250	.241	.206
Temporary layoff	.245	.208	.234
Permanent layoff	.504	.549	.559

Source: Employment and Earnings, January 1980, January 1990, November 1998.
Note: The data include people over the age of 20. Entrants and reentrants are omitted from the calculations.

because what is being picked up is increasing layoffs offset by declining quits. The solution to these complications lies in studying the pattern of quits and layoffs over time. Layoff data will be taken up shortly. When it comes to quits, data are not available for the entire workforce. What is available are data on why people who are unemployed lost their job, and table 2.1 displays these. This table includes data for three years, two business cycle peaks (1979 and 1989) and 1998, a year that, while not an official peak, is surely near one.

These data show that over time, and controlling for the business cycle, the pool of unemployed is increasingly made up of those who were laid off and, correspondingly, decreasingly made up of those who quit their jobs. Furthermore, among those who had experienced layoffs, a growing fraction were victims of permanent, as opposed to temporary, layoffs. Therefore, these quit and layoff data support the view that job security is weakening, and the conclusions do not change when the data are disaggregated by gender.[37]

Longitudinal Surveys

Another strategy for determining how tenure patterns have shifted is to take advantage of several longitudinal surveys of the workforce. In an important research project Annette Bernhardt, Martina Morris, Mark Handcock, and Marc Scott worked with two separate panels of the National Longitudinal Survey of Youth. The first panel followed young men as they entered the labor force in the years 1966–81. The second tracked a different cohort as they entered in the years 1979–94. By comparing the experience of these two cohorts the researchers were able to describe how the labor market changed between those two time periods, periods that correspond well to the old and the new labor market that I have described.

The authors found, as the foregoing argument would suggest, a substantial increase in job turnover. In their words: "We calculate that the odds of a job change are 34% higher for youth in the recent cohort as compared to the original cohort, after adjusting for basic factors such as age, education, work experience and tenure, attrition and local unemployment rates. . . . A significant and unexplained difference in job stability remains after all controls, even for youth who have permanently entered the labor market and 'settled down.'"[38] Clearly these findings strongly reinforce the implications of the tenure and the quit data described above: job turnover has increased, and job tenure has fallen.

Evidence from the Dislocated Worker Data

One of the best sources of information on employment security is the dislocated worker surveys that have been conducted every two years by the Bureau of Labor Statistics. Using these data, we can track how the risk of dislocation has shifted over time both for the labor force as a whole and for various subgroups.

In each survey year people were asked whether they had lost a job over a specified time period and, if so, why the job was lost. Six possible explanations are recorded: plant closing, large-scale layoffs, slack work, loss of a seasonal job, loss of a self-employment job, and other. In the charts in figure 2.4 I count as dislocated those people who gave any of the replies except loss of a self-employment job. It is not clear what it means to be dislocated from such a job.

Before turning to the results, it is also worth noting that these data understate the rate of dislocation and, very probably, also understate the extent to which dislocation has increased over time. The rate of dislocation is understated because only one spell of dislocation is recorded; thus, if someone experienced multiple spells, that does not show up in the data. Second, in a variety of ways—ranging from maltreatment to early retirement plans—firms can induce people to leave. These "voluntary" departures do not show up in the dislocated worker data. The use of early retirement plans has increased in recent years.

DATA PROBLEMS

The discussion in this section centers on two sets of data, surveys that ask people about job tenure with an employer and surveys that ask about layoffs and dislocation. As is always the case, there are conceptual worries that need to be taken seriously. For example, as noted in the text, at first glance job tenure seems the right measure, but on reflection we see that it is determined by both quits and layoffs, and we probably should be most concerned with layoffs. This leads us to the dislocated worker data that focus only on layoffs, but even here there is a problem because these data do not capture those quits that are forced or encouraged.

However, and discouragingly, even beyond these conceptual problems there are a set of technical issues that require us to be very careful in interpreting the data. In the tenure surveys one key issue is controlling for the effect of the business cycle, since this can influence turnover. However, there is no generally accepted way to do this, and different approaches yield somewhat different answers. Second, research shows that people tend to round off their answers and to think about their tenure in five-year intervals. It is also important to make corrections for these problems. When David Neumark, Daniel Polsky, and Daniel Hansen, researchers who have worked most closely with these data, make these various corrections, they find that the raw data shown in the text overstate the decline of tenure, but they also conclude that for midcareer workers the probability of holding on to a job has indeed fallen in the 1990s.[39] However, there is reason for concern that they are "overcorrecting," and it remains quite possible that the even stronger message in figure 2.2 is correct.

The dislocated worker surveys also have a series of problems. Over the course of the survey the wording of the question changed three times. In addition, until 1994 the respondent was asked about layoffs over a five-year period, whereas in 1994 and 1996 the question referred to a three-year period. This creates technical problems that cannot be resolved simply by looking at the last three years of the five-year intervals (in the data I report I use a correction Henry Farber has developed to deal with this, but the correction is at best an approximation).[40] In addition, the survey asks about only one layoff, but many people have experienced more than one.

When all this is considered, it is probably best to think of these various surveys as clues or pieces of a puzzle. No single data source will answer the question, and we need to look for a broadly consistent pattern among them.

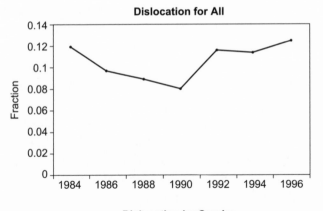

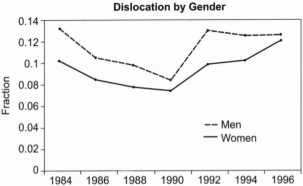

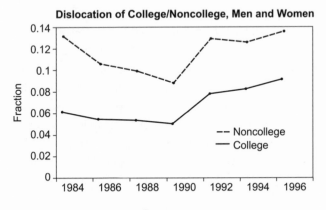

FIGURE 2.4

Dislocation Rates

Source: Dislocated Worker Surveys.

Dislocation rates are presented in figure 2.4, which shows for all people between the ages of 20 and 64 the fraction of the employed labor force who reported dislocation over the past three years at each of the survey dates. For example, in 1986 just under 10 percent of employed people reported that in the years 1983–85 they had been dislocated at least once from a job they held.

The pattern is quite striking. The rate starts relatively high, reflecting the recession at the beginning of the 1980s. It then declines, as would be expected during the expansion that ran from 1982 until 1990. Again, as we would expect, it rises during the brief recession of 1990–91. The big surprise is what comes next. Despite an improving economy in the 1990s, the rate of dislocation has clearly trended upward. This is not a pattern that would be expected in good times and does indeed suggest that firms have altered their behavior in some important ways. Although these data end in 1996, preliminary analysis of an even more recent survey suggests that the problem continues.[41]

When I look at the patterns separately for men and women, an important difference between the two sexes is apparent. Throughout most of the period women experienced a rate of dislocation below that for men; however, by the time of the most recent survey, they had the dubious distinction of having caught up. It remains striking that the male rate failed to decline during the recent strong economy, but it is even more startling that the female rate rose so sharply.

The final issue is whether in recent years the situation of college-educated people has worsened. This is certainly the popular perception as the risk of restructuring has extended into the ranks of groups such as managers and professionals who had previously been exempt. The data show that college-educated workers have always been much more secure than their less-well-educated colleagues but that in recent years the gap has slightly closed. For this reason the psychological impact of the past few years may well have been greater on college-educated workers. The facts are, however, that while their relative situation has slightly deteriorated they are still much better off than others.

ARE LABOR MARKETS SECURE?
A SAMPLE OF LAYOFFS IN 1998

- "Owens Corning said today it would dismiss 2,300 people, or 9 percent of its workforce ... because intense competition in the home-insulation business had caused prices to fall." *New York Times,* 10 January 1998, B2.
- "The Raytheon Company said today that it would cut 10 percent of its military related work-force, or about 8,700 people." *New York Times,* 24 January 1998, B1.
- "AT&T Corp. chief executive, C. Michael Armstrong, will slash up to 18,000 jobs, or 14 percent of the work force.... Armstrong told analysts and investors that AT&T is prepared to fire workers if 15,000 to 18,000 don't take early retirement." *Boston Globe,* 27 January 1998, C1.
- "J. C. Penny, hobbled by high costs and weak sales, said it plans to close 75 of its 1,200 department stores and lay off 5% of its managerial workforce." *Wall Street Journal,* 28 January 1998, A6.
- "Last week another financially healthy company, the Xerox Corporation, said it would eliminate 9,000 jobs or roughly 10 percent of its labor force." *New York Times,* 15 April 1998, D4.
- "The Boeing Company said yesterday that it would eliminate 8,200 jobs by the turn of the century as it consolidates its North American operations." *New York Times,* 21 March 1998, B1.
- "Ameritech Corporation said yesterday it would eliminate 5,000 jobs this year. The layoffs ... amount to 7 percent of the company's workforce.... [Analysts said] with more competition, they will ... do things to try and improve margins, like cutting cost." *New York Times,* 15 April 1998, D4.
- "As many as 15,000 Digital Equipment Corporation employees, more than one in four, will lose their jobs when Compaq Corporation completes its proposed buyout.... On March 19 a special committee of Digital's board adopted a severance plan for key employees. Under that plan, chairman and chief executive Robert B. Palmer, 57, will receive $6.45 million in severance pay.... Palmer's top deputies will receive severance equal to twice their annual salaries and bonuses. ... About 250 vice presidents and other key executives will also receive severance packages ranging from one to 1.5 times their annual salaries. ... By comparison, Digital's rank and file employees are entitled to severance benefits of between eight and 39 weeks' pay." *Boston Globe,* 7 May 1998, A1.

- "The Sunbeam Corporation stunned employees yesterday by announcing a plan to eliminate 6,400 jobs, or 40 percent of its work force, and to close 8 of 24 plants." *New York Times*, 12 May 1998, D1.
- "Motorola, Inc. announced today that it would eliminate 15,000 jobs, or 10 percent of its workforce." *New York Times*, 5 June 1998, C1.
- "Faced with sluggish cookie and cracker sales, Nabisco Holding Company said it will close plants and cut 3,500 jobs, or 6% of its workforce." *Wall Street Journal*, 9 June 1998, A4.
- "Texas Instruments is eliminating 3,500 jobs worldwide . . . about 8 percent of its payroll." *Boston Globe*, 19 June 1998, C2.
- "Citing the loss of two important government contracts, the Lockheed Martin Corporation said it would eliminate up to 2,500 jobs." *Wall Street Journal*, 22 June 1998, A6.
- "The Rockwell International Corporation . . . suffered a setback today when the company announced that it would . . . cut 3,800 jobs." *New York Times*, 30 June 1998, D1.
- "The Russell Corporation . . . said today it would close 25 of its 90 plants . . . and dismiss about 4,000 or 22% of its workers." *New York Times*, 23 July 1998, D4.
- "Unisource Worldwide Inc. said it will cut 1,500 jobs, or 10% of its workforce . . . as part of a sweeping restructuring." *Wall Street Journal*, 30 July 1998.
- "TRW Inc., one of the most successful companies in the auto parts industry, said it is undertaking a substantial restructuring involving plant closings and elimination of 7,500 jobs." *Wall Street Journal*, 30 July 1998, A3.
- "British Petroleum PLC is buying Amoco Corp. . . . BP Chief Executive Sir John Brown told a news conference in London that the combined company would slash 6,000 jobs, with most of the cuts coming from operations in Cleveland and Houston." *Boston Globe*, 12 August 1998, C1.
- "Northrop Grumman Corp. said yesterday that it would reorganize its businesses and cut its work force by an additional 2,100 jobs." *Boston Globe*, 25 August 1998, D2.
- "Harnischfeger Industries said today that it would cut about 3,100 jobs, or about 20 percent of its labor force, because a glut of paper was reducing demand for its products." *New York Times*, 27 August 1998, D23.
- "Take Citicorp's merge with Travelers Group Inc. . . . The two financial giants plan significant reductions in their combined workforce of 160,000—layoffs of up to 5%." *Business Week*, 5 October 1998, 40.
- "Once, investors saw consumer products companies as a good bet in hard times, but Gillette Co.'s announcement Monday that it plans to lay off

4,700 workers is a sign that the rules have changed." *Boston Globe,* 30 September 1998, E1.

- "Thermo Electron Corp. of Waltham yesterday named a new president and said it will lay off more than 700 employees in three subsidiaries." *Boston Globe,* 30 September 1998, E1.

- "Raytheon Co. stepped up layoffs and plant closings in its core defense business. . . . Layoffs will total 14,000 employees, or 16% of the unit's workforce." *Wall Street Journal,* 8 October 1998, A3.

- "Packard Bell NEC Inc., the world's number five personal computer maker, will cut as many as 1,000 jobs, or about 20 percent of its U.S. workforce, to lower costs and try to compete better with rivals." *Boston Globe,* 9 October 1998, C2.

- "Merrill Lynch & Company, the nation's biggest brokerage firm, said yesterday it would eliminate about 3,400 jobs, or just more than 5 percent of its work force, because of global economic turmoil." *New York Times,* 14 October 1998, A1.

- "Monsanto Co. said Wednesday it would pay for recent seed company acquisitions with new issues of debt and equity, the sale of some businesses and a restructuring that will cut as many as 2,500 jobs, or about 9 percent, of its global workforce. The company said it would raise up to $4 billion to fund the acquisitions and that 700 to 1,000 jobs would be cut as part of the restructuring, with another 1,300 to 1,500 jobs taken off the Monsanto payroll through business divestitures." Reuters, 12 November 1998.

- "International Paper . . . in a nationwide restructuring plans to whittle about 1,500 employees." *Wall Street Journal,* 18 November 1998, A2.

- "Texaco Inc. said Wednesday it will slash 1,000 jobs in an effort to remain competitive in the current low-price oil environment, three days after telling Wall Street that 1998 spending will come in 20 percent below earlier estimates. The White Plains, N.Y.–based oil producer and marketer estimates the reorganization, expected to be complete early next year, will save $200 million a year." CNN Financial News, 1 December 1998.

- "Deutsche Bank formally announced its plan for a 10.1 billion takeover of Bankers Trust and said the acquisition would result in the loss of 5,000 jobs, mostly in New York and London." *New York Times,* 1 December 1998, A1.

- "Volvo A.B. . . . said today it would lay off more than 7 percent of its workforce . . . including 1,000 jobs in the United States." *New York Times,* 1 December 1998, C2.

(continued)

- "Exxon, the nation's largest oil company, agreed yesterday to buy Mobil. . . . About 9,000 workers . . . are likely to find themselves without jobs, the companies said." *New York Times,* 2 December 1998, A1.
- "The Boeing Company said yesterday the economic downturn in Asia was forcing it to scale back . . . and to cut more jobs over the next two years— perhaps as many as 20,000—than it had indicated in June. . . . Boeing had previously estimated that it would eliminate as many as 28,000 jobs by the end of next year." *New York Times,* 2 December 1998, D1.
- "ITT Industries said yesterday it plans to streamline its manufacturing operations, cutting up to 1,200 jobs." *New York Times,* 3 December 1998, C7.
- "In a widely expected move intended to help revive its ailing cereal business, the Kellogg Company said yesterday it would dismiss 525 salaried employees . . . and would eliminate 240 . . . contracted positions." *New York Times,* 3 December 1998, C7.
- "The B. F. Goodrich company . . . said yesterday it would close four plants [that] employed a total of 775 workers." *New York Times,* 3 December 1998, C7.
- "Johnson & Johnson . . . announced yesterday it would . . . close 36 plants and cut 4,100 jobs. . . . Eleven of the plants are in the United States." *New York Times,* 4 December 1998, D1.
- "Weirton Steel said it will lay off 415 employees two weeks before Christmas, blaming underpriced, imported steel. Last month the Weirton, W.Va.–based steel maker laid off 342 workers." Associated Press, 4 December 1998.
- "New York–based securities firm D.E. Shaw & Co. said it was eliminating 264 jobs, or nearly 25 percent of its work force, in a restructuring related to BankAmerica Corp.'s $43 billion merger with NationsBank Corp." Associated Press, 4 December 1998.
- "The newly combined MCI WorldCom Inc. is moving to cut . . . expenses . . . by undertaking a sweeping cost-cutting program expected to include as many as 3,750 layoffs. . . . Partly in anticipation of such cutbacks, MCI WorldCom's stock has doubled in the past year." *Wall Street Journal,* 10 December 1998, A3.
- "Citigroup Inc., the newly formed financial services giant that is wrestling to integrate its businesses, said on Tuesday it would cut 10,400 jobs, or 6 percent of its global work force, and take a restructuring charge of $900 million." Reuters, 15 December 1998.
- "With Christmas just around the corner, 6,400 local R. J. Reynolds Tobacco Co. workers are nervously waiting to find out if they are among the

1,000 domestic employees the company intends to release." Associated Press, 15 December 1998.

- "Levitz Furniture, the number two home furniture retailer, will close 27 of its 90 stores and cut 1,000 workers or a quarter of its workforce, to focus on its most lucrative markets." *Boston Globe,* 22 December 1998, C3.
- "Case Corp., saying demand for its agricultural equipment is dropping even more precipitously than previously forecast, disclosed production cutbacks that will slice an additional 1,300 workers from its payroll." *Wall Street Journal,* 22 December 1998, A3.
- "Auto parts maker SPX Corp. said Monday it will eliminate 1,000 jobs, close 25 of its newly acquired General Signal offices, and take a restructuring charge of as much as $250 million in the fourth quarter." Reuters, 22 December 1998.
- "Cooper Industries Inc. said Monday it will cut 1,000 jobs and close 12 plants worldwide in an attempt to cut costs and improve profits following the recent sale of its automotive products business." Reuters, 22 December 1998.

This section pulled together data on job tenure, quits, and layoffs. None of these data sources or the underlying concepts are perfect, but they do complement one another and point to a consistent story. Job tenure is falling, modestly for the entire labor force and sharply for men. Quit rates have not increased, even though the labor market superficially seems stronger. The longitudinal data on youth show an increase in mobility and a decline in job tenure over two cohorts. Dislocation has increased, also in the face of a strong labor market, and some groups, particularly people with a college education, find that the risks they face are rising even more quickly. When these data are taken as a whole, then, it is safe to conclude that job security has worsened and that internal labor markets, while not disappearing, are fraying.

Not only does mere statistical evidence point to an increasingly turbulent labor market. So does that most American of indicators: television advertising. New York Life recently ran a national ad in which an executive sitting at his desk is suddenly upended. The voice-over says that if you are unemployed everything looks upside down and it may take time to get your world looking right. That's why, the ad tells us, New York Life is the only company to offer easier access to annuities to people who are unemployed. When the insurance industry ratifies a shift in statistical outcomes, we can be sure that something indeed is new.

The Rise of Temporary Work

Throughout the postwar period there was a common understanding of what it meant to hold a job. A job represented an attachment to a single employer. Employment law was premised on this idea (as witnessed by the nature of the unemployment insurance system, which requires a period of stable relationship to a single employer to establish eligibility). So was the American system of social welfare. For example, health and pension systems are built around a presumed stable employer. Although it is clearly true that not everyone managed to get jobs that fit this ideal, it is nonetheless true that we all understood what a real job meant.

This understanding has been undermined. One reason is an increase in job changing and the fact that more and more people have to construct their careers by moving across different employers. This weakening hold of internal labor markets was documented in the material just above. The other related trend, which has garnered even more attention, is the sharp increase in what has come to be termed "contingent work," that is, various kinds of temporary jobs obtained via temporary help agencies or other channels. These jobs represent a deep challenge to the conventional model of employment because employees typically work on the site of one firm but under different terms than others with whom they work, often side by side. Hence the linkage between the content of the work and the structure of employment and career paths is sharply attenuated.

In the next chapter I describe the implications of contingent work for the economic welfare of employees. For now, however, it is worth noting that two images dominate popular interpretations of this kind of employment. One is largely negative. In the words of the *San Jose Mercury News*, the paper serving the Silicon Valley, where the use of temps is probably more intense than anywhere else in the nation, these workers are "America's new migrant laborers," moving from job to job without security and without benefits. Set against this is the image of the independent contractor choosing temporary work because of the freedom and flexibility it provides.

The term "contingent employment" does not have a precise meaning, and because of this there has been some confusion about what is meant. My usage will refer to an employment situation in which an essential characteristic of the job is that the employee lacks the level of job security that a given employer makes available to "regular" workers. I shall define the types of contingent work more precisely below, but for now think of employees at temporary help firms or workers a firm might hire on the understanding that they have limited-length contracts or can be terminated more easily than the regular workforce.

In contrast to this relatively tight meaning, some writers have preferred to combine contingent workers as defined above with other categories of "nonstandard" employment, including part-time work. When this is done, the numbers become very large but at the cost of precision. The problem is that a great many part-time employees have permanent attachments to one firm. For example, the Bureau of Labor Statistics has provided several definitions of contingent work, the most expansive of which (and hence the most generous to the argument that part-timers are contingent) is that persons are contingent if they are wage or salaried workers who, for nonpersonal reasons, do not expect their job to last as long as they wish.[42] Of full-time workers only 3.4 percent met this definition; among part-timers the fraction was 10.8 percent.[43] It is true that proportionally more part-timers are contingent than are full-time workers, but it is also true that the vast majority of part-time workers are not contingent.

A further reason for maintaining the distinction between contingent and part-time work is that the motivation of employers for using the two types of labor is likely to differ, as are the problems facing employers in managing the two different labor forces. The motives may vary if employers use contingent employees as a strategy for buffering their regular workforce with a group who can be let go very easily. Management problems differ because tensions are more likely to arise between contingent and regular employees who work side by side than between full- and part-time workers. As an aside it is also worth noting that part-time employment has not increased over the past two decades as a fraction of the labor force although the fraction of employees who work part-time against their will has grown.[44]

Returning to contingent workers, the reason for the heightened interest in these workers is twofold. First, their employment circumstances support

the broader idea that the nature of work is changing. Second, their numbers have grown considerably in recent years. This impression of growth
is driven by a variety of industry statistics. For example, from 1991 to 1996
the fastest-growing industry group was Personnel Supply Services, that is,
temporary help agencies.[45] In the years 1994 to 1996 the revenue growth
of publicly traded staffing firms averaged an annual increase of 24.5 percent.[46] Another indicator is that in 1996 thirty-four of *Inc. Magazine*'s list
of the five hundred fastest-growing private companies were staffing firms.
Finally, census data show that of the net new jobs created between 1988
and 1996 fully 22 percent were in business services and engineering/man-
agement services—the two sectors that supply contract and contingent
labor.[47]

In recent years the industry has matured and become more central to a
wider range of employer activities. Increasingly temporary help firms take
responsibility for an entire work function, for example, call centers that han-
dle customer relations. Illustrative of this trend is a recent agreement
between Manpower Inc. and Ameritech. They plan to seek call center business jointly, with Manpower supplying the people and Ameritech providing the technology. Call center outsourcing is growing at a rate of between
20 and 40 percent a year, and, according to one source, all types of vendor
on premise agreements grew from 2 percent of total temporary help agency
revenues in 1992 to 11 percent in 1996.[48]

Another innovation of growing importance is national contracts in
which a large employer with branches across the nation signs a master
agreement with one agency, for example, Manpower, Olsten, or Kelly Services, to provide temporary workers in all locations. Examples of these
accounts are agreements between Manpower and EDS and Hewlett-Packard,
Olsten with Lexmark and Chase Manhattan, and Kelly Services with Johnson & Johnson. These agreements also underwrite another emerging tendency in the industry: the development of subcontractor networks and
supplier tiers within the temporary help industry. Increasingly, large temporary help firms are establishing subcontracting relationships with local
agencies to provide specialty employees when the larger firm cannot meet
the demand.

Another striking characteristic of contingent work is its penetration
into a wide range of occupational categories. The old image of temporary

TABLE 2.2

1996 Revenue by Type of Sector in Staffing Industry
(in billions of dollars)

Medical	4.0
Professional	4.8
Technical/computer	11.4
Office/clerical	13.7
Industrial	11.2

Source: *Staffing Industry Report* (Staffing Industry Analysts,
Los Altos, Calif.) 7, no. 14 (1996), 10.

office work is no longer accurate. Table 2.2, which is taken from a leading
industry publication, provides a good sense of this diversity. Industrial
work is essentially as important as clerical/office work, and there is also a
strong representation in relatively higher skill areas.

How Many Contingent Employees Are There?

The foregoing material suggests that, compared with, say, 1979, contingent
work has increased substantially. However, data of this sort are not very useful for knowing just how many such workers there are or whether the
growth rate is accelerating. This is because much of the data are based on
impressionistic or unrepresentative and narrow sampling of the workforce
and, second, because the impressive percentage gains may still translate into
small numbers. There are, however, other and better sources for estimating
how widespread the use of contingent employees is. One such source is the
Current Population Survey, which in 1995 and 1997 asked employed people
about the nature of their work. Another source is the two nationally representative surveys of establishments I conducted that asked employers
about their use of contingent employees.

Tables 2.3 and 2.4 are based on the definition of contingent work developed above, that is, people who as part of their employment arrangement
lack a steady tie to the employer. In the Current Population Survey several
categories of these workers are identified, and I report data on four of
them. The definitions below are those used by the census:

58

SECURING PROSPERITY

TABLE 2.3
Fraction of the Labor Force Accounted for by
Different Types of Contingent Workers

	1995	1997
Independent contractor/freelance	6.7%	6.7%
On-call	1.6%	1.6%
Agency temporaries	1.0%	0.9%
Contract workers	0.6%	0.5%

Source: 1995 and 1997 Current Population Surveys.

- *Independent contractors:* Workers who were identified as independent contractors, independent consultants, or freelance workers, whether they were self-employed or wage and salary workers.
- *On-call workers:* Workers who are called to work only as needed, although they can be scheduled to work for several days or weeks in a row.
- *Temporary help agency workers:* Workers who were paid by a temporary help agency, whether or not their job was temporary.
- *Contract workers:* Workers provided by contract firms who are employed by a company that provides them or their services to others under contract, and who are usually assigned to only one customer and usually work at the customer's work site.

My survey asked a random sample of private sector establishments (with fifty or more employees) about only two categories, temporary help agency employees and on-call workers.

Both surveys tell essentially the same story (the differences in the surveys are small and can easily be explained by the limitation of the employer-based survey to establishments with more than fifty employees). While the frac-

TABLE 2.4
Employment of Contingent Workers in Sampled Establishments

	1992	1997
Agency temporaries	2.6%	3.3%
On-call	1.1%	1.1%

Source: 1992 and 1997 National Establishment Surveys.

tion of employees who are contingent has doubtless grown since the early 1980s, nonetheless as a proportion of the labor force the numbers are not very great. This should not be a big surprise, given that even small percentage changes can lead to large absolute numbers in an economy as large as ours and hence can catch people's attention.

Although these absolute numbers are relatively small, it is important to remember that they represent the stock of employees who, at any point in time, are contingent. Because contingent assignments are often short term, it is very likely that a larger fraction of employees are contingent at some point over a year. In my 1997 National Establishment Survey I found that the median duration of a contingent or temporary job was five months.[49] Hence, depending on the extent to which the same or different people move through a series of short-term assignments, it is possible that the fraction of employees who are contingent at some point in the year could be up to twice as large as the fraction contingent at any particular time.

Both the census data and the National Establishment Survey suggest that the growth of contingent work has leveled off. This message is reenforced by my 1992 survey, which asked employers what were the most important factors that might limit their use of contingent work. The replies are shown in table 2.5.

Clearly, whatever the attractive features of this form of employment, it seems very unlikely that it will grow to become anything near the dominant form of work. This conclusion is strengthened by the fact that the vast

TABLE 2.5
Considerations Limiting the Use of Contingent Work

Not enough skilled people available	30.4%
These workers not committed to the firm's success	32.0%
Too expensive	20.6%
Turnover too high to build a skilled labor force	20.5%
Inadequate control over these workers	16.7%

Source: 1992 National Establishment Survey.
Note: These are responses to questions that asked about the first and second most important reasons for limiting the growth of contingent work. Hence the responses need not add to 100 percent.

majority of employers predicted in both the 1992 and the 1997 survey that their use of contingent workers would remain the same or grow moderately.

What is the bottom line with respect to contingent employment? On the one hand, it has grown sharply in percentage terms and is very much on people's minds when they think about how firms are reorganizing work. On the other hand, the numbers are not as large as many believe, and the data do not suggest explosive growth. The best way to think about contingent work is that it is one element in a larger set of changes. It has an impact beyond the absolute numbers because regular employees are well aware of contingent employment within their organization and the implicit threat it entails. The growth of contingent work, no matter how modest the absolute numbers, has been sufficiently strong that it is a constant reminder and important aspect of the many other ways firms are rethinking the employment relationship.

Changes in Wage Determination

The central fact about wages in the new era is their rapid dispersion, that is, the sharp growth in wage inequality as well as the sluggish growth of real wages for most people. These developments have been widely noted and have generated a burgeoning literature. However, relatively little attention has been paid to the implications for our understanding of wage setting. Recall that at the heart of the postwar model was a wage system that placed very heavy emphasis on stability and equity. Implicit in the growth of inequality is that these considerations have lost force and that when employers set wages other concerns are now paramount. The postwar wage system was also characterized by de facto profit sharing, yet in recent years the average level of wages has stagnated even in the face of rising profits. Clearly, then, our previous understanding of how wages are set is obsolete, and this signals a radical shift from the old system.

Internal equity considerations play much less of a role in wage setting than in the past. The evidence for this lies in the explosive spread of new systems of pay centered around identifying and rewarding individual performance. These innovations have two main effects. The first is to put employees more at risk by tying their pay to firm performance. Various forms of profit sharing and bonuses are part of this. In many cases these innovations were tied to concession bargaining in the unionized sector,[50] but they had a broader reach. The second set of innovations move employers away from standard across-the-board increases and instead make pay increasingly dependent on the performance and characteristics of individuals. The most dramatic of these are so-called forced distributions, which are the real-world equivalent of grading on a curve. Taken together, these innovations naturally lead to the erosion of stable wage differentials, in part because of the variation across firms in how they perform and in part because of variations across individuals that are no longer dampened by attention to equity. As these new compensation systems spread, the old wage structure was undermined, and inequality surged.

In the 1992 survey I asked about profit sharing (in which a portion of an employee's pay depended on the profitability of the firm), pay for skill (in which the individual receives raises as he or she is certified to have new skills), and gain sharing (in which a work group receives increases if it exceeds some baseline measure of performance). For each of these I inquired whether or not the establishment had the innovation in place and, if so, in what year it was begun. The results are shown in table 2.6.

It is apparent that these innovations were reasonably widespread in 1992 and that they were overwhelmingly new, with the vast majority begun within ten years of the survey.

The 1997 survey took a somewhat different approach; instead of examining specific formal pay approaches, it probed the basis on which people received raises. The following question was asked:

TABLE 2.6
Pay Innovations

Innovation	Percentage of Establishments	When Started
Profit sharing	45.5%	1988–92: 39.4%
		1982–87: 31.0%
Gain sharing	14.4%	1988–92: 58.0%
		1982–87: 26.9%
Pay for skill	31.0%	1988–92: 37.8%
		1982–87: 28.5%

Source: 1992 National Establishment Survey.

Now we would like to get an idea about the importance of different kinds of performance- or merit-based raises for workers. I will ask you about three sources of increases in compensation—first, an across-the-board increase; second, an increase due to individual merit or performance; and third, an increase due to group performance. I will ask you what percentage of a typical worker's raise was due to each of these. The sum must equal 100 percent.

The answers to this question are presented in table 2.7.

Two patterns stand out starkly. The first is that for most employees the performance of the group is the dominant source of pay increase. The survey does not provide a definition of the "group," and hence it may include all employees or else a subgroup. In either case, raises are clearly tied to establishment performance, which means that variation in economic success across firms will be quickly transmitted into the wage structure. The second striking finding is that blue-collar workers are different in their wage determination than everyone else. This is the only occupation for whom group performance is relatively unimportant and for whom across-the-board increases are the dominant mode of pay. This pattern is influenced by union status: in establishments without unions 41 percent of blue-collar pay is based on across-the-board increases; in union establishments the figure is 93 percent. However, even the blue-collar nonunion fraction is much higher than for other occupations.

There are other occupational differences, although they are more muted than the "blue collar/everyone else" divide. In particular, there is virtually no role for individual performance for clerical and service workers, and the

TABLE 2.7
Sources of Pay

	Managers	Blue Collar	Technicians	Professionals	Clerical	Service
Across the board	8.5%	68.1%	6.8%	10.7%	4.5%	26.9%
Group	78.3%	25.8%	84.4%	74.7%	94.3%	68.7%
Individual	12.8%	5.4%	8.7%	13.7%	1.0%	2.3%

Source: 1997 National Establishment Survey.
Note: Employee basis weights are used.

pay determination of service employees looks more like that of blue-collar workers than does that of any other group.

These data, from both 1992 and 1997, show considerable potential for pay-setting practices that break apart traditional stable pay relationships. This is true with respect to both formal practices (e.g., profit sharing) and the actual basis of pay setting. Only blue-collar workers appear to be paid under a regime that promotes stability.

Even within the shrinking orbit of unionized firms, pattern bargaining has dramatically weakened, as witnessed by the end of the Basic Steel agreement in 1986 or the disparate settlements reached by firms within the United Automobile Workers sphere of influence.[51] Within the auto industry, for example, recent contracts between the UAW and the Big Three auto companies have differed in important ways—regarding, for example, the ability of firms to close plants or outsource labor. In addition, compensation has varied across the firms, with Chrysler workers receiving much larger profit-sharing checks than their counterparts at the other two firms. More broadly, Harry Katz has demonstrated that the decentralization of collective bargaining has eroded traditional wage patterns.[52]

The Decline of Unions

It would be a mistake to equate the collapse of the postwar institutional structure with the decline of union power. Even at the height of their power, American unions organized only 35 percent of the private sector labor force, and the norms, ideology, and behaviors that characterized the postwar system extended deeply into the nonunion sector. Indeed, in some respects—for example, commitments to employment security—the nonunion sector, represented by firms such as IBM, Digital Equipment Corporation, and Procter & Gamble, was more advanced than unionized employers. Nonetheless, the erosion of union power is an important element in the destruction of the postwar regime.

That union power has declined is well known and incontrovertible. The impact of this decline can be seen in figure 2.5, which graphs one measure of actual power, namely, the fraction of workdays that are lost owing to strikes. The decline is precipitous.

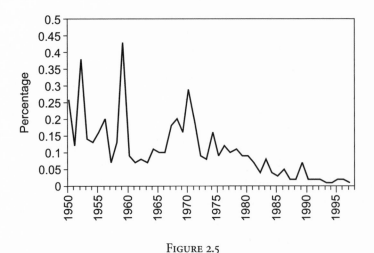

FIGURE 2.5
Percentage of Working Time Lost Owing to Strikes, 1950–1997
Source: U.S. Bureau of Labor Statistics, "Work Stoppage Data," Series WSU002.

As the perimeter of union power has shrunk, the ability of unions to shape employer behavior in both union and nonunion settings diminished. The weakened capacity of unions to influence the behavior of unionized employers, who are now able to be more aggressive in setting wages and working conditions, is obvious. More important, perhaps, is the impact of debilitated unions on the much larger nonunion sector. The earlier generation of institutional economists recognized this broader effect of union power and coined terms such as the "threat effect" or "spillovers" to capture the idea that nonunion employers modified their actions either to avoid unionization or simply out of imitation. Using data drawn largely from the 1970s, Richard Freeman and James Medoff estimated that the wages of employees in large nonunion firms were raised by between 10 and 20 percent as a consequence of these spillovers.[53] Today most employers are free to determine their employment conditions without fear of being organized.

The decline of unions is due to the convergence of many factors, ranging from fierce employer resistance to the failure of many unions to adapt their appeal to an increasingly well-educated white- and pink-collar labor force. The weakened power of unions then becomes part of the explanation for the broader collapse in the postwar labor market structure. However, it is important to recognize that the decline of unions is also a symptom of this shift, not the cause. An important component in the decline of unions is the same transformation in attitudes and norms that underlies some of the other changes I have described. This is illustrated by the substantial increase in unfair labor practice filings coming out of efforts to organize new local unions. An index of unfair labor practices per union member jumped from 95.5 between 1960 and 1968 to 162.9 in 1969–77 to 285.2 between 1983 and 1988. A similar index of employer-sponsored union decertification petitions grew from 158.2 in 1969–77 to 358.0 in 1983–88.[54] More generally, firms are simply more willing to oppose unions. As Thomas Kochan, Harry Katz, and Robert McKersie have shown, a cottage industry of consultants has emerged whose expertise lies in teaching employers how to resist unions.[55]

One of the most emblematic illustrations is the recent strike waged by the strong national United Automobile Workers against the Caterpillar Corporation. Caterpillar had installed work teams and engaged in extensive training, both of which implied that the firm had embarked upon a production system that drew heavily on worker knowledge and commitment. Yet, when faced with a strike, the firm refused to compromise and continued to operate by hiring replacement workers. Many of these replacements were skilled workers who had been laid off in the aerospace industry, demonstrating how weakness in one sector of the labor market is propagated elsewhere.[56] Production quality did not decline, and profits at Caterpillar steadily rose.

Changing Patterns of Corporate Control

Recall that for most of the postwar period managers enjoyed substantial freedom from oversight by stock owners. Although always nominally working to maximize the wealth of those stock owners, in fact managers were free to pursue other objectives, which included sharing profit growth with employees and the kind of employment policies advocated by Human Relations theorists. This all changed in the 1980s.

The difficult competitive environment and fears of declining American competitiveness set the stage and were followed by two important developments in finance. The first was the rise of the leveraged buyout, pioneered by junk bond dealer Michael Milken. This new source of finance suddenly made previously seemingly invulnerable firms potential targets for raiders who felt that financial results could be improved by changing management. The second was the increased concentration of stock ownership in the hands of institutional investors (public and private pension funds, investment funds, insurance companies). As documented by Michael Useem, in 1965 individuals held 84 percent of corporate stock while institutions held 16 percent. By 1990 the proportion held by individuals declined to 54 percent, and the institutional fraction rose to 46 percent. Among the one thousand largest publicly traded firms in 1994, institutions held 57 percent of stock.[57] These institutional investors increasingly demanded higher levels of performance and frequently worked as a group to put pressure on managers to deliver.

Taken together, these two events radically shifted the perspective of senior management. Driven in part by the examples of their compatriots at major firms who lost their jobs because of inadequate performance—Akers of IBM, Stempel of General Motors, Whitman of Kodak, and many others—the rhetoric of shareholder value became the dominant managerial goal. Although recent developments in takeover law have eased the most extreme fears of incumbent managers, pressures from investors remain a central fact of life for senior executives.

There are important complications to this story. The rise of stockholder perspective also coincided with a new conceptualization of organizations that both rationalized the events and provided the foundation for their continued momentum. This "nexus of contracts" perspective on the corporation will be discussed later in the book. On the other hand, just because stockholders are dominant, it does not automatically follow that employees will be treated worse. If Human Relations–style practices truly improve productivity, then they will be in stockholders' interests. Again, this is a question I defer until later, but it is worth noting that to the extent that relatively generous compensation policies toward employees and reasonable employment security policies were adopted because of managerial values or because they made managers' lives more comfortable, these policies are in fact at great risk in the new environment. At the minimum this shift in corporate governance changed the priorities of management. As one generally sympathetic observer of the buyout firm KKR noted in the *Harvard Business Review,* "A ... potential weak spot for KKR has been its human-relations policy, or lack of one. Major owner-directors like KKR are driven by rigorous financial discipline, which sits at the opposite end of the spectrum from hard to quantify 'soft' issues."[58]

SUMMARY

The old labor market was not all of one piece. Union and nonunion firms coexisted in manufacturing. In addition, a "secondary labor market" provided unstable and low-wage employment and abided by few of the rules I have laid out.[59] However, despite this diversity, there was a central set of norms, behaviors, and institutions that structured the core of the labor market. This was reflected in the academic constructs such as "threat effects" and "wage contours" that described how the different elements of the labor market were tied together despite their apparent diversity. It was also reflected in public policies such as unemployment insurance that were premised on a single dominant employment model that cut across the main parts of the labor market.

It is not easy to demonstrate just how thoroughly this system has been shattered, and to do so I have relied on a wide variety of scattered evidence. None of the indicators are perfect, and each seen on its own yields somewhat ambiguous findings. However, taken as a whole, the indicators add up to a consistent story and conclusion. Norms regarding layoffs and "family" or "community" have been undermined, and this is reflected in data comparing the nature of layoffs twenty-five years ago and today, in the rhetoric of the business press, and in the harder data of rising dislocation rates and falling employment tenure. The wage structure has been shattered, and market forces have much greater impact on compensation than they have had in the past. Some of the institutions that provided a framework for the old labor market, namely, unions and a corporate governance structure that implicitly recognized stakeholders, have changed dramatically.

Finally, it may help to conclude this chapter with a parable that points out how in an important sense detailed analysis of survey data misses the point. Imagine that one hundred people worked together steadily for a number of years with no untoward events. One day I walk in and summarily fire one person and then walk out. It is true, as the researcher would argue, that only 1 percent of the group have lost their jobs. However, the world has been turned upside down for everyone. Henceforth the remaining ninety-nine employees will come to work every day wondering when their turn will come, and this worry will inevitably alter a wide range of labor market behaviors. The actual changes described in this chapter are more extensive than one in one hundred, and their consequences have reverberated on a yet larger scale.

Appendix: The Surveys

The National Establishment Surveys

The 1992 and 1997 surveys were both telephone surveys of a representative sample of American establishments that were in the private for-profit sector and that had at least fifty employees. Other than these restrictions the surveys (appropriately weighted) are representative of the entire economy. The surveys were directed to establishments, that is, specific business addresses, rather than to headquarter locations. Hence the questions were about practices at the given establishment as opposed to questions directed to headquarters about practices elsewhere in the country. This leads to more accurate responses. In the 1992 survey the response rate was 65 percent, and in the 1997 survey the response rate was 57.8 percent. Both rates are very high for surveys of this kind, and no important biases exist in the pattern of nonresponse.[60] The 1997 survey consisted of a follow-up to the establishments that responded in 1992 plus an additional sample of new establishments. When the 1997 results are reported alone, both sets of respondents are included; and, obviously, when the longitudinal data are reported, only the 1992 sample is used. Two sets of weights are used to make both samples representative, although the 1992/97 sample obviously excludes businesses that were founded between the two years, as well as ones that closed.

The survey reports information on the actions of establishments, and the data collection was designed to create a representative national sample of these establishments. Hence one way of reporting the data is to say something like: "Twenty percent of establishments have such and such a practice," and this would be perfectly accurate. However, this describes the actions of a typical establishment and not the experience of a typical employee. The reason for this distinction is that most establishments in this country are relatively small, but since the fewer number of large establishments have more employees, the experience of the typical employee is more influenced by events in large establishments.

To see this point concretely, imagine that there are ten establishments in the country, nine of which have fifty employees and one of which has five hundred. If all nine of the smaller ones follow practice "X" and the one larger one follows practice "Y," then I could say that 90 percent of establishments do "X," and this would be accurate. However, it would also be correct, and maybe more useful, to say that the majority of employees in the country are exposed to practice "Y."

I deal with this complication by presenting the data in two ways. When I want to describe establishments, I refer to the "percentage of establishments" or "establishment practice." When I want to describe the experience of the typical employee, I use the term "percentage of employees," or I indicate that I am using employee weights. In some cases one or the other formulation will be clearly appropriate, while in other instances it makes sense to present the data both ways. Finally, in statistical analysis, which is more sophisticated than simple tabular presentations (i.e., in regressions), I always include a variable for size, and these regressions use the establishment weights unadjusted for the number of employees.

The Dislocated Worker Surveys and the Current Population Survey

The Current Population Survey (CPS) is administered every month to a large sample of the U.S. population and is the basic source of data for well-known statistics such as the unemployment rate, employment levels, earnings, full- and part-time employment, and the like. In 1994, because of a major revision of the survey and the sampling methods, a number of the series were interrupted, and it is difficult to construct consistent data over time for some variables. For our purposes this is particularly a problem for part-time work. In many months an additional supplemental survey is administered on a variety of topics. In this book I use two of these supplements, the supplement on dislocated workers and the supplement on contingent work. As noted in the text, the dislocated workers supplements were administered every two years beginning in 1986, and the contingent workers supplement was administered in 1995 and 1997.

The Panel Survey on Income Dynamics

The Panel Survey on Income Dynamics was begun in 1977 as a longitudinal of five thousand families. Over time data were collected on the family members, and, as children left to form new families or families changed in other ways such as through divorce, the new "family" members were also tracked. In this way the overall sample size grew to more than twelve thousand. An additional sample of low-income people was also followed over time, as, for a period, was another extra sample of Hispanics. In the data I report I use only the core representative sample. Attrition has been something of a problem, but several researchers have studied the issue and report that attrition does not affect the results. In each year a weight is provided that corrects both for sample design and attrition, and I use these weights. Over the years different questions were asked of family heads and other adults, and when there was a male present, he was designated the family head. Although this problem was eventually corrected, the early disparity makes it difficult to construct as long a time series on women as on men, and hence I report only results for men.

THREE

▬▬▬▬▬▬

Experiencing the New Economy

T̲HE PROOF OF THE PUDDING is in the eating. The destruction of the old labor market is only of academic interest unless it has real consequences for people. If all is well for labor force participants, then there is much less urgency in understanding the nature of the institutional changes over the past two decades and what might be done about them. If, on the other hand, individuals are indeed in distress, then these themes are much more salient.

There are obviously good reasons to be skeptical about any doomsaying. The unemployment rate has fallen to the lowest levels in a quarter century, and the success of the American economy is held up as a model in both the developed and the developing world. In the face of such good numbers and widespread acclaim, it seems churlish to complain.

There is considerable truth to this viewpoint, and a one-sided negative depiction of recent events would be misleading. Indeed, when we come to policy, it will be important to avoid initiatives that hamstring the economy's strong points. Nonetheless, there is cause for concern even in these apparently good times. In the course of this chapter we shall see that

- Over a long stretch of time wages have stagnated for more than a majority of the labor force, and earnings have also increasingly grown unequal.
- These dismal earnings patterns are not offset by mobility. People are not moving in large numbers from the bottom of the earnings distribution to the top over the course of their careers.

- Job insecurity has increased along a number of dimensions. For example, the rate of dislocation has grown despite a seemingly strong economy. The consequences of dislocation are very severe for many people.
- People in certain categories of contingent work, particularly those who work for temporary help agencies or for internal temp pools organized by their employer, overwhelmingly would prefer a regular job. Employees in these kinds of employment settings pay a steep price in terms of low wages and low benefits.

These are some of the characteristics of a "successful" economy. One can easily imagine that the inevitable downturn will yield even more troubling outcomes.

A Portrait of the Labor Market Today

A useful way to begin is with a brief description of what the labor market looks like today and how it compares with the peak years of 1979 and 1989. Table 3.1 presents the basic facts with respect to employment, and table 3.2 does the same for earnings. Looking first at table 3.1, it is apparent that the two years were very similar in terms of the unemployment rate, but the structure of the labor market changed. First, it is much bigger, with more than thirty million jobs created in less than twenty years. This is the reason that the American labor market deservedly receives so much admiration.

Although the overall record looks strong, it is also apparent that the employment status of men has slipped, whereas the situation of women has

---

The Business Cycle

When making comparisons of economic data over time, it is very important to compare comparable points in the business cycle. This is because I am interested in seeing whether the underlying long-term structure of the labor market has changed and hence I want to avoid, to the extent possible, confusing possible long-run shifts with short-run developments due to the business cycle. Throughout this chapter I therefore use data from two business cycle peaks, 1979 and 1989, as well as data from the most recent year available.

TABLE 3.1
Employment Patterns, 1979 and 1998

	1979	1998
Civilian employment	96,945,000	132,424,000
Unemployment rate	5.8%	4.2%
Civilian employment to population ratios		
White men, 25–54	0.92	0.90
Black men, 25–54	0.83	0.80
Black/white ratio	0.90	0.89
White women, 25–54	0.58	0.74
Black women, 25–54	0.60	0.72
Black/white ratio	1.03	0.97
Percentage jobs blue-collar	0.33	0.24
Percentage jobs professional and technical	0.15	0.18
Percentage jobs service	0.13	0.13
Percentage jobs managerial	0.10	0.14

Source: *Employment and Earnings*, January 1980 and November 1998.
Note: The 1998 data refer to October of that year.

improved. For both blacks and whites the fraction of men who were employed (the "employment to population ratio") actually has fallen since 1979, while the surge in female labor force participation has driven up the ratio for women of both races. It is important to note that this decline in male employment occurs for men in their preretirement years and hence cannot be explained by a falling retirement age. Evidently men are simply having more trouble finding jobs despite the seemingly strong labor market. These divergent fates of men and women will also be apparent in the wage data.

It is also more than a little discouraging to note that over this period the relative employment situation of blacks has worsened relative to whites.

We can also see in table 3.1 that the employment distribution dramatically switched from blue-collar in the direction of white-collar work. The growth in managerial jobs is striking, especially given the popular view that firms have become "leaner" by eliminating managers. The growth in managerial and professional and technical jobs seemingly runs counter to the view that the quality of jobs has deteriorated over time.

The earnings data in table 3.2 show much less good news than do the employment figures. In this table I focus on full-year/full-time workers. The

TABLE 3.2

Earnings, 1989 and 1997

	1989		1997	
	Men	Women	Men	Women
Median earnings (1997 dollars) for all persons 15 years and older who worked full-time/full year	35,179	24,237	33,674	24,973

Source: Bureau of the Census, Current Population Reports, Money Income in the United States, P60-200, September 1998.

reason is that I want to understand how wage rates have changed over time and hence need to factor out the impact of changing labor supply on annual income (i.e., if I looked at shifts in annual income for all people or all families, the data would reflect both wages and the amount of time people work). I look at the last decade, a period that includes the strong recent job growth.

What is striking in these data is that, despite the very strong economy, the wages of men fell over this period and the wages of women barely rose. Clearly, the strong gains are not being shared with the average, or median, worker. Additional evidence is available from the Employment Cost Index. These data are drawn from surveys of firms, not people, and in other ways are also conceptually different from the census-based information provided in the table. They probably overstate wage growth.[1] They do, however, have the advantage of including benefits as well as wages and salaries. The trends in the index are quite revealing. From 1989 through (and including) 1998 the annual increase in the index after inflation was greater than 1 percent in only two years and was never greater than 2 percent. Clearly these data support the conclusion that earnings and compensation have been flat over a long period of time.

These discouraging earnings trends have fallen especially hard on young people beginning their careers. Among 25- to 30-year-olds, median weekly earnings between 1979 and 1996 fell by 23 percent for men and 4 percent for women. For both men and women in this age range, the ratio of their weekly earnings to the earnings of middle-age workers fell over these years.[2] These declining earnings across two cohorts apply to all occupations and not just, for example, to blue-collar work.

It is also important to note that on dimensions other than simply earnings the strong economy of recent years has failed to bring benefits to many employees. For example, in 1997 the number of people who lack health insurance rose to the highest level in a decade, 16.1 percent of the population. Much of the increase occurred in households with incomes of seventy-five thousand dollars or more, indicating that more than changes in the welfare laws lie behind these trends.[3]

The second striking fact about earning trends is the substantial growth in inequality. For example, the ratio of the hourly wages of the top 10 percent of the wage distribution to the wages of the bottom 10 percent was 3.6 for men and 2.7 for women in 1979. By 1996 these ratios had exploded to 4.4 for men and 4.0 for women. Increased inequality also occurred elsewhere in the wage distribution; for example, the so-called 90/50 ratio, that is, the ratio of the wages of the top 10 percent to the average wages, also widened for both men and women.[4] This increased inequality has been widely noted and the subject of a great deal of research and popular discussion. The previous chapter described how the wage-setting mechanisms of the postwar labor market served to stabilize the wage structure and to maintain relative differentials among occupations. With the erosion of these rules wages have been much freer to respond to market forces. In addition, the decline of unions and the erosion of the real value of the minimum wage have contributed to inequality.[5] Although economists do not agree in portioning out the explanation for this trend, it is quite apparent that the old wage system has radically weakened and as a consequence the division between economic winners and losers has grown.

CAREERS IN THE 1980S AND 1990S

The portrait sketched above reveals useful insights about the American labor market as experienced by its participants, but the picture is static. It is important to understand how people's careers unfold over time. It may be, for example, that someone who today is in an insecure job will, tomorrow, land lifetime employment with a good high-wage employer. The reverse may also be true: even people who seem in comfortable circumstances today may be at great risk of sharp setbacks in their economic fortunes. The way to get at these questions is to follow the unfolding of people's careers over time.

The most logical measuring rod is wages and wage growth. When all is said and done, the most important deliverable of a healthy labor market is decent and rising earnings. The data in table 3.2 show that earnings have stagnated. However, although useful and compelling, these facts miss an important part of the picture. They do not describe the evolution of people's working lives and careers because they do not follow the same group of people over time but rather are successive snapshots at different times. This is a problem because different people underlie the averages at different times. It is very possible, for example, that a typical worker might have actually experienced wage growth even though, as reported above, the average wage in the labor force fell. This is because the average wage in the final period includes different people—perhaps younger, perhaps less skilled—than those who made up the average in 1979. The solution to this problem is to follow the same group over time, and this is what I now do using the Panel Survey on Income Dynamics (PSID).

Figure 3.1 follows the average wage for each year between 1979 and 1995 of the group of men who were between 25 and 40 years old in 1979.

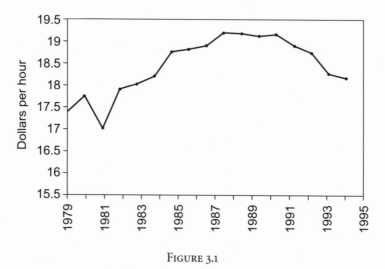

FIGURE 3.1

Male Hourly Earnings, 1979–1995

Source: Panel Survey on Income Dynamics. Data limited to males.

The same people are tracked over time. The average hourly wage increased only slightly over a sixteen-year period, from $17.40 to $18.17, a 6 percent increase. These are men who started out the period in the age group from which the greatest amount of wage growth would be expected, yet the average person experienced basically no increase.

Although the average outcome was virtually no improvement, some people were winners and some losers. Any specific standard for "winning" and "losing" is arbitrary, but I have adopted an approach that seems reasonable. Based on a conservative reading of the past, one might expect that someone doing well would experience a 2 percent real earnings gain per year. Over the 1979-95 period this translates into a total compounded gain of 34 percent, and so I designate as "winners" those people who had at least a 34 percent increase in their hourly earnings over this period. In a similar spirit I define "losers" as people whose earnings fell by 10 percent or more over those years. Figure 3.2 shows the distribution of these men into the two groups of "winners" and "losers." The winners only constitute 20 percent of the group, the losers nearly 40 percent. At least in terms of earnings this was not a happy time for the vast majority of male workers.

It would mitigate these grim results if there was economic mobility over this period. Perhaps the 20 percent who gained earnings were all people who

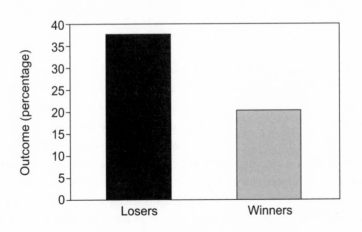

FIGURE 3.2

Earnings Outcomes, 1979–1995

Source: Panel Survey on Income Dynamics. Data limited to males.

TABLE 3.3
Earnings Mobility, 1979–1995

Quartile in 1979	Quartile in 1995	
	Top	Bottom
Top	54.3%	13.2%
Bottom	2.6%	49.2%

Source: Panel Survey of Income Dynamics.

started at the bottom of the earnings distribution in 1979 while the 37 percent who lost out over the period were people who began the period on the top. We might still regret the overall pattern, but we could be comforted by knowing that what might seem like an equitable reshuffling was occurring.

Unfortunately, the data do not support this optimistic interpretation. Table 3.3 shows the fraction of people who were in the bottom 25 percent of earnings who remained in that quartile in 1995 and the fraction who climbed to the top 25 percent in 1995. The table also shows the fraction who were in the top twenty-five percent in 1979 who maintained that status in 1995 and the fraction who fell to the bottom quartile. There is some mobility, but on balance it seems minimal. Not only did earnings stagnate for most people, but relative positions remained quite stable.

DISLOCATION

Perhaps the most central distinguishing characteristic of the new labor market is the high level of insecurity that many, if not most, employees feel. Chapter 2 showed that even in the face of an improving economy the rate and risk of dislocation have risen. I now examine the consequences of restructuring for the people who are affected. The unemployment rate is low, and the economy is generating jobs. It might be the case, therefore, that people who do lose their jobs land on their feet. If this was so, then, while we might be concerned about transitional problems associated with downsizing, on balance the problem would not be all that serious. On the other hand, if negative consequences were serious and long-lasting, we would have to take a very different view. Although some caution is necessary, we can get a good sense of the answers to these questions using the dislocated worker data

ANALYZING DISLOCATION

In examining the consequences of dislocation I combine two sets of surveys. To understand the consequences of dislocation in the 1990s, I combine the sample of people who reported being dislocated in the 1996 and 1994 surveys. To compare the consequences of dislocation in the 1990s with an earlier period, I combine the people who reported being dislocated in 1984 and 1986. In both sets of data their "current" situation is their employment status at the time of the survey itself.

In the section in chapter 2 on the rate of dislocation, I included all people who reported being dislocated except those who said that they had been dislocated from self-employment. In this section, however, the sample is somewhat more tightly defined. The survey only asked about the postdislocation experience of those who lost their jobs as a result of a plant closing, slack work, or large-scale layoff. No data were collected on the consequences of dislocation from the other three categories, end of a seasonal job, loss of self-employment, or "other." Given the absence of data, it is impossible to know how the inclusion of these people would change the results reported below, but this is a limitation with which we have to live. Finally, all wage data in this section are adjusted by the Consumer Price Index to 1996 dollars.

because the survey asked most people who had been dislocated about their current employment status.[6]

In studying the consequences of dislocation, I focus on people who were between the ages of 30 and 55 at the time they lost their job. These are people who are in the prime of their working career. Younger workers frequently change jobs, and hence dislocation may not have much meaning, and older employees have the option of retirement, which makes it difficult to assess the consequences of layoffs. Although I limit the analysis that follows to people between 30 and 55, I do not follow the convention in the literature by restricting the sample to employees with three or more years of tenure in the job they lost. In my view a 40-year-old worker with two years of tenure merits attention, whereas, by contrast, I would be less concerned about a 22-year-old who had worked at the same place for three years.[7]

It is most important to understand the situation of people who lost their jobs as a result of restructuring sometime during the years 1991 to 1995. However, to get a sense of whether the consequences of dislocation have wors-

ened, improved, or stayed roughly the same, I also report comparable data
for people who were dislocated in the three years prior to the 1984 and 1986
surveys.[8] In addition, to have a standard against which to judge whether people
who experienced dislocation are worse off than others, I look at the employment status of the age 30–55 population who had not been dislocated.
This comparison group enables us to judge the relative situation of people
who went through restructuring.[9]

Employment Status

The first question is whether people who lost their jobs managed to find new
ones. Table 3.4 shows the fraction of people who were employed at the time
of the survey for four groups: the 1994/96 dislocated workers, the 1984/86
dislocated workers, and the two relevant comparison groups.

There are two broad lessons. First, dislocated workers are worse off than
are people who did not go through this experience; for example, in 1994/96
the overall employment rate is nearly 10 percentage points higher for the
nondislocated than for the dislocated. This is a substantial difference.

The second important lesson, and a piece of good news, is that the disparity between the dislocated and the nondislocated is less in the 1990s than
in the 1980s. The gap between the comparison group and the dislocated
workers group fell from just under 16 percentage points in 1984/86 to just
under 10 percentage points in 1994/96. Although the employment disadvantage of people who are dislocated remains serious, the strong economy of the 1990s does help to an appreciable degree.

TABLE 3.4
Consequences of Dislocation, Percentage of People Employed

| | 1994/96 | | | 1984/86 | | |
	All	Men	Women	All	Men	Women
Dislocated	70.1	72.8	66.3	60.5	63.6	55.3
Not dislocated	79.9	87.6	73.1	76.3	89.9	64.3

Source: Dislocated Worker Surveys.
Note: Data are limited to people ages 30–55.

In table 3.4 I also ask whether the experience of men and women differs. In both 1994/96 and in 1984/86 women were reemployed after dislocation at a lesser rate than men. This is not altogether surprising because in general women are less likely to be employed than men. However, when we bring the comparison groups to bear, the gap between those who were dislocated and those who were not is larger for men than for women. In other words, it appears that relative to where they "should" be men are worse off after dislocation than are women. This continues to hold after more sophisticated analysis that tries to control for degree of labor market "commitment."[10]

Although the distinctions by gender and marital status are important, the central message is that all people, men and women, who experience dislocation find subsequent employment at a rate well below that of their comparison group.

There are two more useful ways to cut the data on reemployment. The first is by educational status. We have already seen that better-educated people who in earlier years were well protected from restructuring are now more vulnerable to job loss. What about their reemployment chances? Table 3.5 shows that the relative situation of the better educated has deteriorated. While it remains true that the employment and reemployment rate of people with a college degree is higher than those with less education, the gap between the groups has shrunk. Ten years ago people with a college education who were dislocated had outcomes much closer to their control group than did people without a college education. That is, for those with college the difference in employment between the control group and those dislocated was 10.4 percentage points, while for the noncollege group the gap

TABLE 3.5
Consequences of Dislocation by Education,
Percentage of People Employed

	1994/96		1984/86	
	College	Noncollege	College	Noncollege
Dislocated	79.6	67.4	77.7	58.0
Not dislocated	88.9	76.7	88.1	73.4

Source: Dislocated Worker Surveys.
Note: Data are limited to people ages 30–55.

TABLE 3.6
Reemployment Rates over Time,
Percentage of People Employed

	1994/96			1984/86		
	First year	Second year	Third year	First year	Second year	Third year
Percentage employed	60.4	76.2	79.7	47.2	68.9	73.0

Source: Dislocated Worker Surveys.
Note: Data are limited to people ages 30–55.

was 15.4 points. Today, however, the gap for the college group is 9.3 points, while for the noncollege group it is also 9.3 points. At least with respect to reemployment, the advantage of college has diminished.

Our final question regarding reemployment is for how long the disadvantage associated with being dislocated persists. One scenario is that after a short spell of difficulty victims of restructuring do eventually find new jobs and end up being indistinguishable from other labor market participants, whereas the other extreme is that their problems last indefinitely.

Table 3.6 shows the reemployment rates of dislocated workers arrayed by the number of years since they lost their job. The pattern is striking: employment rates increase sharply over time. If we compare the employment rate three years after the event with the employment rate for all people in 1994/96, the rates are essentially identical, and in 1984/86 the gap between the two rates was tiny. It would appear that after three years, at least as measured by employment rates, it is difficult to distinguish those who were laid off from others. It remains to be seen what the impact of the experience was on their long-term wages, and, of course, during the three years people who were dislocated experienced considerable income loss and personal difficulty. These qualifications notwithstanding, the long-term employment pattern is reasonably upbeat.

Earnings

The next question is the impact of dislocation on earnings. In assessing this it is important to keep in mind the obvious point that the earnings data refer

to those dislocated workers who did find new employment. The postdislocation earnings for the others are zero. In addition, unlike our analysis of
the employment rates, when we turn to earnings, the comparison group is
not some other set of workers but rather the dislocated employees themselves. How, I ask, do the earnings of the new job compare to what the laid-
off workers received at their old post?

To answer this question I transformed all earnings into 1996 dollars
and divided the dislocated workers into six groups based on how their old
and new earnings compared:

1. People whose postdislocation earnings were 20 percent or more below those
   of their old job.
2. People who lost between 10 and 20 percent.
3. People whose earnings were between 10 percent less than their old job and
   the same as their old job.
4. People who gained between 0 and 10 percent compared with their old job.
5. People who gained between 10 and 20 percent.
6. People who gained 20 percent or more compared with their old job.

Table 3.7 shows the distribution of these patterns for 1994/96 and
1984/86. One point that is immediately striking is the diversity of the experience. People fall into each of the categories, and, indeed, a considerable number of people gain earnings after being dislocated. It is difficult to make a
simple single generalization about the process.

TABLE 3.7
Earnings Consequences of Dislocation,
Percentage in Each Category

	1994/96	1984/86
20 percent or more loss	37.4	36.2
10–19 percent loss	9.6	9.8
0–9 percent loss	17.0	18.0
0–9 percent gain	10.8	10.3
10–19 percent gain	6.2	8.1
20 percent or more gain	18.7	17.3

Source: Dislocated Worker Surveys.
Note: Data are limited to people ages 30–55.

Having made this point, there are two other messages from this chart:

- A substantial number of people suffer very serious earnings losses as a result of dislocation.
- Unlike the reemployment rates, which improved between 1984/86 and 1994/96, the impact on earnings has not changed. This is consistent with what we know about the general stagnation of wages.

When I make the same calculations, this time differentiating by gender and by education, several strong lessons emerge. First, the experience of men and women is basically the same. Second, whereas in 1984/86 having a college degree provided some measure of protection against the earnings consequences of dislocation, this was no longer true in 1994/96. In 1984/86 the percentage of college graduates who suffered a loss of 20 percent or more was well below the percentage for the rest of the population, but by 1994/96 the two fractions were the same.[11] The college degree no longer provides protective coating with respect to earnings for people who are dislocated.

Finally, table 3.8 shows that, dramatically unlike the case of employment rates, the earnings data do not improve as time passes. Indeed, the data actually support the view that the longer it has been since time of dislocation, the worse off people are in terms of earnings.

Taken as a whole, then, the earnings data paint a basically grim picture. It is true that a substantial number of people do actually do better following dislocation. However, the bulk of people experience a decline in earnings, and for many of these the decline is quite sharp. Being well educated does not seem to protect against this decline, and as time goes by, the earnings picture does not improve.

TABLE 3.8
Earnings Loss with Years since Displacement, 1994/1996,
Percentage in Each Category

	Years since Displacement		
	1 year	2 years	3 years
20 percent or more loss	33.2	36.9	43.3
10–19 percent loss	9.1	9.3	10.3

Source: Dislocated Worker Surveys.
Note: Data are limited to people aged 30–55.

CONTINGENT WORKERS

The previous chapter described the extent of contingent work. Now I ask about the consequences of this type of employment. The data are taken from the February 1995 Current Population Survey. I will distinguish among four types of contingent work:[12]

- Temporary help firm employees.
- On-call workers: employees who work for a firm for a specific period of time but are not part of the regular workforce.
- Freelance workers/independent contractors: people who are self-employed and sell their services on a nonpermanent basis to others.
- Other people with jobs that are temporary for one of four reasons: they are temporarily replacing another worker, their job is seasonal, they are working only on a specific project and will lose their job what it ends, or they are working on a fixed-term contract.

Perhaps the most basic question is whether people want these kinds of jobs. There is considerable uncertainty and debate about this issue, with some arguing that these are "substandard" forms of work that no one wants and others pointing out that many people may enjoy the flexibility that this kind of work entails.

For people in each type of contingent work, the survey asked whether the person would rather have an alternative work form. The particular alternative cited depended on the kind of contingent employment involved. For example, if people were in a job of limited duration, they were asked if they wanted a job without such limits; if they were working for a temporary help firm, they were asked if they preferred a different type of employer. In each case the alternative cited was chosen as the appropriate choice representing what might be thought of as "standard" work.

Table 3.9 shows the distribution of views among the four types of contingent employment. Two points are apparent. First, there is a very sharp difference in the views of independent contractors and everyone else. Overwhelmingly, independent contractors want to be doing what they are doing. By contrast, a substantial fraction of other contingent employees would like a more standard job. Given this sharp gap, the remainder of this section focuses on the groups other than independent contractors. These people in total represent 7.2 per-

TABLE 3.9
Preferences Regarding Contingent Employment

	Want Other Kind of Work
Jobs of limited duration	40.7%
Temporary help firms	63.8%
On-call workers	61.0%
Independent contractors	8.2%

Source: Current Population Survey, February 1995.
Note: The data refer to people between the ages of 20 and 64 who are private-sector employees.

cent of the employed workforce who are between the ages of 20 and 64 and who work in private sector jobs. (A careful reader will note that 7.2 percent is higher than the total of contingent workers I presented in chapter 2; this is because the data employed here include the fourth category noted above: people who expect their jobs to terminate in a given period of time.)

Why are people doing contingent work? Table 3.10 tallies the answers people gave to this question, distinguishing between those who report that they want this kind of work and those who want something else.

TABLE 3.10
Reasons Why People Hold Contingent Jobs

	Want "Standard" Work	Want This Kind of Work
Only kind of work could find	43.0%	7.9%
Hope it leads to permanent employment	10.3%	2.8%
Obtain experience	1.6%	2.6%
Laid off and hired back	1.3%	0.9%
Other economic reason	10.7%	6.1%
Flexible schedule	8.2%	27.1%
Family/child care	3.6%	6.0%
In school	5.7%	21.2%
Other personal reason	11.4%	13.2%
Other	4.2%	12.2%
	100%	100%

Source: See Table 3.9.
Note: The data refer to people between the ages of 20 and 64 who are private-sector employees. Sample in this table excludes independent contractors.

It is quite apparent that the two groups are very different from each other. People who report that they are happy with contingent employment are by and large in these jobs for personal reasons. Personal reasons play some role for the involuntary contingent employees, but more important are explanations that center on economic constraints and failure to find something better. At the same time, of course, there is some overlap between the two groups, with some people who say they are happy with this type of work nonetheless giving responses that seem as if they lacked a broad range of choices while some people who say they want something better have personal reasons for wanting flexible jobs with fewer commitments. When all is said and done, however, the basic distinctions between voluntary and involuntary contingent employees seem to hold water.

What kinds of people find themselves in these jobs? The first column of table 3.11 shows the fraction of different subgroups who hold contingent jobs; the second shows the fraction who would prefer a standard job. To get a sense of whether any given personal characteristic makes a difference, each cell should be compared with the appropriate one in the final row that shows the pattern for the entire sample.

TABLE 3.11
Characteristics of People in Contingent Jobs

	Fraction Holding Contingent Work	Fraction Who Would Prefer "Standard" Employment
Ages 20–30	9.9%	54.9%
Ages 55–64	6.4%	29.2%
High school dropouts	9.1%	55.2%
High school graduates	6.8%	52.4%
Some college	7.5%	50.4%
College degree or more	6.7%	45.4%
African American	10.7%	57.5%
Married women	6.6%	40.9%
Unmarried women	9.4%	53.3%
Married men	5.6%	51.2%
Unmarried men	9.4%	50.5%
Entire sample	7.2%	50.5%

Source: See Table 3.9.
Note: The data refer to people between the ages of 20 and 64 who are private-sector employees. Sample in this table excludes independent contractors.

TABLE 3.12
Consequences of Contingent Work

	Have Contingent Jobs	Have "Standard" Jobs
Get health insurance from their employer	32.1%	52.5%
Have health insurance from any source	65.1%	80.4%
Hourly wage	$9.85	$14.67
Percentage who work less than 35 hours a week	30.3%	15.6%

Source: See Table 3.9.

Note: Wages are in 1995 dollars. The data refer to people between the ages of 20 and 64 who are private-sector employees. Sample in this table excludes independent contractors.

African Americans are more likely to be in contingent work than anyone else and are least satisfied with their circumstances. Older people are most content with this work form, and married men and people with college degrees are least likely to find themselves holding contingent jobs. By and large, however, the message of this table is the relatively even distribution of this type of work across different groups and the relatively similar attitudes people have toward it.

Finally, what is the impact of contingent employment on people's economic well-being? In table 3.12 I pull together several indicators.

It is quite apparent that contingent work is considerably less desirable than "standard" employment. This conclusion holds after more sophisticated controls, such as a regression equation estimating people's hourly wage as a function of a long list of personal characteristics and a variable that measures whether or not they are in a contingent job. For the roughly half of people who hold contingent jobs involuntarily, this kind of employment is very problematic.

SUMMARY

The new labor market is good news for some people. Roughly 20 percent of the labor force saw their wages rise since 1979. The majority of dislocated workers did find new work, and of these almost 20 percent actually improved their situation at least in terms of earnings. Independent contractors, who work in "nonstandard" jobs, overwhelmingly prefer their situation. All of this is good news and should not be overlooked.

Although the news is not universally bad, there is, unfortunately, plenty of room for concern. Aggregate employment is up, but for "prime age" males the ratio of employment to population has actually fallen. More people have experienced flat earnings than earnings growth, and a great many have lost ground. Poverty and near poverty rates have not fallen. For most people who are dislocated the consequences are quite negative. It can take three years to regain employment levels, and when jobs are found, the earnings stay on average much lower than in the lost job. The majority of people in agency temporary or on-call temporary jobs would prefer another arrangement, and these jobs pay less and are less likely to provide health insurance than does traditional work.

What all of this adds up to is the answer to the question of why we should care about the collapse of the old labor market structure. After all, the norms and institutions that constituted the old labor market had no value in their own right; they were only means to an end. That end was, of course, the welfare of people whose lives were shaped by the labor market. If these people are doing fine under the new system, then only nostalgic academics would care about the passing of the old regime. It turns out, however, that there is plenty of reason to worry and to think about what form the new labor market should take. Before turning to this question, however, the next chapter looks in much more detail at the behavior of employers in the new era.

F O U R

Restructuring within Firms:
The Shifting Employment Contract

AT THE HEART of the transformation of the American labor market is the firm. The pressures on employers and their response shape most of the outcomes that concern us. Wages are set by firms, hiring and layoff decisions are made by firms, and most training and career development is delivered by firms. When we turn to policy, a central theme is whether and how to influence the behavior of firms and the consequences of any specific policy for the ability of employers to compete and to generate jobs. In short, understanding the behavior of firms is at the core of both our positive analysis of what has happened and our normative analysis of what to do.

The remarkably strong economy and low unemployment rate make it easy to conclude that the widespread fear and attention generated by the highly visible layoffs and restructuring events in the early 1990s are behind us. This view is wrong. First, firms continue to engage in dramatic downsizing, and employees continue to believe that insecurity is a fact of life. The continuing layoffs can be seen almost every day in the newspaper.

However, despite the drama associated with large-scale layoffs, it would be a mistake to make these events central to our understanding of what is happening within firms. Layoffs, and the dissolution of the bonds between employees and employers that these imply, are important, but they are best seen as one element of a more general phenomenon: the rethinking and transformation of the employment relationship. In a variety of ways, and for a variety of reasons, the rules, procedures, expectations, and norms regarding work within organizations are changing. Not all these changes are for the worse. Under some circumstances employees come to enjoy increased opportunities to use their intelligence and skills. In other instances the changes clearly represent a deterioration of working conditions. Taken as a whole, the organization of work is being transformed.

Radical changes in the organization of work seem to be occurring in the midst of substantial internal dislocation and turmoil. That both are happening at the same time points to an apparent paradox: on the one hand some firms are broadening jobs and devolving higher levels of responsibility to their workforce, while on the other they are reducing their commitment to the same workforce and increasingly treating them as expendable. This is the opposite of what received wisdom would have led us to expect. The conventional view has always been that in order to obtain the high levels of employee commitment that decentralized and "empowered" work requires, the firm would also have to make a reciprocal commitment. Perhaps it is the case that employee expectations have changed, or perhaps the level of fear in the labor market has changed the terms of trade.

This chapter is organized around these issues and asks three questions:

- How has the organization of work been changing? Have firms continued to adopt so-called high-performance work organizations, such as teams and quality programs? Has the use of these innovations persisted even in the face of the turmoil caused by restructuring?
- How are changes in work organization linked to other organizational "innovations" that have characterized the recent period, namely, layoffs, the use of contingent work, and outsourcing? In short, how are the components of what is popularly considered restructuring linked together?
- Workplace innovations such as teams have commonly been seen as "win-win" in that they have the potential for improving the performance of the firm and generating gains that can be shared with the workforce. But has this really happened, or has the shifting balance of power in the labor market enabled firms to have their cake and eat it too, that is, to induce employees to generate new ideas and apply their creativity to the production of goods and services without sharing the benefits of these ideas in return?

In the end I reach a conclusion whose ambivalence mirrors the confusion many employees feel: innovative work arrangements have diffused with remarkable speed, and these systems entail higher levels of skill and responsibility. Furthermore, the evidence suggests that the labor force regards them as an improvement from the past. However, on average employers are not sharing the gains from these systems with their workforce, and, indeed, new work systems seem to bring with them higher rates of job loss and growing wage inequality. These last results speak dramatically to the growing power imbalance in the labor market.

Work Organization

The changes within American firms are not all of one piece. It is not accurate to speak of *a* single set of changes that are sweeping across the landscape. Consider the following vignettes:

- Digital Equipment Corporation was long known as one of the most employee-friendly firms in America.[1] It had a lifetime employment guarantee; it provided enormous amounts of training, both job related and "recreational," to its workers; it offered people numerous opportunities to shape their careers; and it did so in a setting that was more like a university campus than anything else. Yet by 1992 the firm had four billion dollars in losses, and by 1996 for twenty-two consecutive quarters the expense growth outpaced revenue growth. Revenue per employee at DEC lagged its competitors by a large margin as the "people-friendly" policies of the old regime proved far too costly in an environment in which DEC's proprietary computer systems no longer held sway. The result was a radical restructuring of the firm. The founder, Ken Olsen, was forced out; the power of the finance group within the firm increased; wages systems were changed to reflect individual performance better; job security was eliminated, with more than half the employees fired; and training budgets were sharply cut. Although the details are important, what fundamentally changed at DEC was the culture. The old "family" paternalistic model was replaced by a hard-edged market-driven approach to the world. This was symbolized by the opening screen that greeted employees when they logged on to their computers: the firm's stock price. The story of DEC comes to a close with its sale to Compaq.

- Diebold Corporation's CEO, Robert Mahoney, takes the following view toward his labor force: "Unionism is going down now because corporations have changed their views. We empower our people now. They work in teams with shared responsibilities. It's not management versus the workers in our plants now. We're all one for our shareholders." Be that as it may, employee earnings have been flat as CEO pay rose from $464,000 in 1990 to $2.37 million in 1995. Union jobs in Ohio were reduced from eight hundred to fifty, and the positions were transferred to Virginia and South Carolina, where annual pay was slightly more than half the Ohio rates.[2]
- In San Francisco twelve luxury hotels and the unions that represented hotel employees entered in 1994 into a lengthy problem-solving process resulting in a new contract that rewrote, to both parties' benefit, the rules governing work in the hotels.[3] The new contract provided substantial new flexibility in job design (for example, in the kitchen area twenty-seven job classifications were collapsed into three) and established joint employer/union problem-solving teams, a variety of incentive mechanisms to encourage employees to focus on customer satisfaction, and innovative benefits and training policies.

What is striking about these stories is both what is common and what is different across them. In each case the firm evidently "restructured" by trying to change its culture. The rules regarding careers and compensation seem to have changed in significant ways. However, in other important ways these cases seem very different. DEC was a classic example of a firm in a great deal of difficulty, indeed in danger of being swept away by shifting conditions in its industry. Part of the problem clearly lay in how the firm had organized itself, and it is difficult to conceive of plausible alternatives to a thoroughgoing transformation. By contrast Diebold looks like a different kind of classic example, in this instance a profitable firm that wanted to do even better for its senior management and stockholders and sought ways to accomplish this at the expense of the labor force. Finally, in the San Francisco hotel case, we find management and unions working cooperatively to restructure work organization in order to make the enterprises both more profitable and more rewarding for employees.

The diversity of these examples raises the obvious challenge of whether it is possible to move beyond anecdotes to understand the extent to which each example is representative of the transformations that are occurring in the labor market. By using the 1992 and 1997 National Survey of Establishments as well as other sources, I can paint a broad and representative portrait of the evolution of work inside American business.

Changes in How Work Is Done

One of the most important ways in which American firms responded in the 1980s and early 1990s to competitive challenges was by adopting a set of work practices that came to be termed "high-performance work organizations" (HPWOs). This vocabulary is most commonly applied to blue-collar work, but this is a mistake because many of the innovations are equally applicable in other settings.

In the traditional system the workplace was organized around tight divisions of labor and narrowly designed specialized jobs. Decision making was in the hands of supervisors, who decided how the jobs were to be performed, how work was scheduled, and how workers were judged. This traditional system has increasingly been seen as failing to meet the needs of firms and employees. The sources of failure are several. The efforts by firms to improve quality and to better meet customer needs require a reorganization of production that puts more power in the hands of employees further down the organizational hierarchy. This tendency is given additional impetus by efforts to cut costs, which also lead to elimination of bureaucratic layers and greater responsibility at lower levels. These shifts imply that job definitions need to be flexible and employees receive greater levels of discretion.

At the core of the new organizations are changes in how employees do their job. Perhaps the most typical innovation is the introduction of work teams. In many instances these teams are led by a management employee, but that person's role has changed to one of a "coach" or "facilitator." In other instances the teams are self-directed. In both instances the idea of teams is that the employees take responsibility for a group of tasks, that there is a sense of responsibility for the team's product, that the workers are broadly skilled, and that there is an element of job rotation.

In many "transformed" firms employees are involved in aspects other than direct work activities. The most common example is problem-solving groups, which often consist of a cross section of employees and hence to some extent obviate traditional managerial/nonmanagerial distinctions. These groups address problems such as production techniques, quality issues, and health and safety. In the most extreme form these groups can take up topics that in the past have been seen as clearly "managerial," for example, outsourcing and supplier policy.

Finally, it is important to recognize that these organizational principles are applicable outside manufacturing settings. Southwest Airlines has been phenomenally successful in part because it has organized itself along high-performance lines: employees do a wide variety of jobs (with pilots sometimes helping load baggage), are involved in hiring, and are compensated with various gain-sharing programs. In some telecommunications companies customer service representatives have been organized into self-managed work groups with considerable success,[4] and Eileen Applebaum and Rosemary Batt describe a life insurance company that "introduced self-directed work teams at some of its ... offices. Employees assumed responsibility for personnel as well as work-related issues and undertook cross-training in a pay for learning compensation system."[5]

The idea that these HPWOs could simultaneously meet the interests of employers and employees led to a great deal of interest in knowing just how widespread their adoption is. Indeed, one of the more important policy tracts of the early 1990s—*America's Choice: High Skills or Low Wages*—motivated its analysis and policy recommendations around the idea that the diffusion of these work systems was centrally important and, because of the low skill levels of workers, was being delayed. Other policy documents—for example, the Secretary's Commission on Achieving Necessary Skills (SCANS) report on changing skills—also used these work systems as the touchstone of their analysis.

Although the impression seemed to be that American firms were slow to adopt HPWOs, in fact research on the rate of adoption, including but not limited to the 1992 National Establishment Survey, found that somewhere between 20 percent and a third of establishments had adopted substantial elements of these systems.[6] This finding led to optimistic conclusions about the trajectory of firm strategy. The firms most likely to adopt these systems were those with relatively highly skilled technologies, firms that competed in international markets, firms that placed a high value on product quality, and those that were large and part of multilocation organizations.[7]

With these findings in hand, much of the public debate shifted to how to encourage even wider adoption via assistance to smaller firms, other kinds of information and incentive programs, and labor law reform.

The 1992 findings answered one question—the diffusion of these organizations was more substantial than had been realized—but left other questions unanswered. In particular, it remained to be seen whether new work systems would continue to spread. There were, in fact, good reasons to doubt that they would. Researchers identified a variety of barriers to diffusion. These included the availability to firms of what was termed the "low-road" option, that is, the opportunity to compete on the basis of cost cutting rather than quality and service. This cost-cutting strategy did not seem to require involving the labor force in the firm and, indeed, implied a hostility to the welfare of the employees. The argument was that in the United States, as opposed to Europe or Japan, limited labor market regulations and weak unions made this a viable option and that it would be difficult for a "high-road" firm to survive in an environment in which competitors followed the opposite strategy. Of course, this argument contained a paradox: if the "high road" was in fact more productive and profitable, it was not clear why the possibility and presence of the low-road option would deter firms that wanted to choose the other path. Additional obstacles included the weak institutional infrastructure in the American labor market, notably unions and employer associations, which in other nations seem to play an important role in spreading and providing support for new ideas. Finally, people concerned about poor performance of the American education system and the low levels of training in American firms, relative to comparable firms in Europe and Japan, argued that a skill gap would make it expensive for firms to adopt these new systems.

On top of these obstacles, a reasonable assumption was that the explosion of restructuring in the early 1990s would also undermine these new systems. There are basically two sets of reasons for predicting that in a period of extensive restructuring and layoffs the spread of HPWOs would stop and perhaps even go into retreat. The first is practical. Teams require a relatively stable membership so that members can learn their tasks and learn how to work together. This stability is at risk in restructuring, owing to turnover and job bumping, and this in turn makes it likely that the teams will not function well. Poor functioning means that the benefits of teams are unlikely to be achieved and that the organization's commitment to these innovations will weaken.

A case study that illustrates why teams are adopted and why they are so hard to maintain is the BellSouth Corporation.[8] Faced with increased competition in telecommunications, BellSouth responded in part by pursuing a cost-cutting strategy and reducing its workforce in its core local phone business (from about 83,000 in 1993 to about 60,000 in 1996), and by establishing an aggressively nonunion cellular business (despite the fact that the firm enjoyed a good working relationship with its union). The firm also sought productivity and quality gains in the regulated business by introducing self-managed work teams in a range of areas including outdoor equipment repair and customer service representative jobs. Evaluations showed that these self-managed teams were more productive and profitable than the old work systems they replaced. Surveys of managers and frontline employees demonstrated that they enjoyed their work under the new arrangements. Nonetheless, by 1997, of the 150 teams that had been established in the mid-1990s, only 10 were still functioning. The others were victims of layoffs of key personnel and qualms on the part of both management and union. Although the "high-performance work system" approach has not fared well, in most respects BellSouth is prospering in the new deregulated environment in which it finds itself.

The second reason for expecting retreat is that HPWOs work best with, in fact are predicated on, substantial employee commitment to the enterprise. Workers need to be willing to learn new skills, to offer ideas and suggestions based on their knowledge, and to care about quality and productivity. For example, Adler reports that in the General Motors–Toyota joint venture NUMMI (New United Motor Manufacturing, Inc.) employees offered ten thousand suggestions per year, of which 80 percent were adopted.[9] The conventional expectation in the industrial relations literature is that for employees to be willing to make these kinds of commitments the employer must offer a quid pro quo in the form of enhanced job security. Absent this offer employees will see any extra contributions they make as a threat to their job and those of their colleagues and will withhold effort. HPWOs are unlikely to do well in these circumstances. Yet as firms fire people, it is hard to see why the workforce would be willing to make these extra efforts.

As the foregoing suggests, there are good reasons to wonder whether HPWOs have continued to diffuse among employers and even whether firms that had these systems in place in the early 1990s have managed to maintain them. The 1997 survey can help answer these questions.

High-Performance Work Organizations in 1997

The 1997 survey enables us to pursue these questions by asking whether these new work systems have continued to diffuse and what, if any, has been the impact of the labor market turmoil of the 1990s on their adoption.

Table 4.1 shows the percentage of establishments that in 1997 engaged in each of the four practices with at least a 50 percent level of penetration (i.e., at least half of the "core" employees were involved). To provide a sense of how quickly these systems have spread, the table includes comparable data for 1992.

These data show a very extensive diffusion of these high-performance practices. Both the substantial rate of diffusion and the increase since 1992 point to the power of these ideas as well as their surprising ability to flour-

---

DEFINING HIGH-PERFORMANCE WORK ORGANIZATIONS IN THE SURVEYS

One obstacle to studying these questions systematically is that there is no unambiguous way of defining a high-performance work system and knowing whether or not the establishment is following this path. The approach I followed in 1992, and also in 1997, was to ask about a series of work practices, collecting data on whether or not the practice was in place and also on what percentage of "core" workers were involved.

I look at four work practices: self-managed work teams, job rotation, quality circles or off-line problem-solving groups, and total quality management. These are the practices that most of the literature sees as most central to the new forms of work organization.

The "core" workers were defined as the nonmanagerial employees most directly involved in the production of the goods or services sold by the enterprise. They could either have been blue- or white-collar workers. An establishment is given credit for a practice only if 50 percent or more of core employees are involved.

TABLE 4.1
Percentage of Establishments with High-Performance Work Practices
Involving at Least Half of "Core" Employees

	1992	1997
Quality circles/off-line problem-solving groups	27.4%	57.4%
Job rotation	26.6%	55.5%
Self-managed work teams	40.5%	38.4%
Total quality management	24.5%	57.2%
Two or more practices	26.0%	70.7%
Three or more practices	14.2%	39.5%

Source: 1992 and 1997 National Establishment Surveys.

ish even in an era of downsizing and employment insecurity. The only exception to the rapid diffusion is self-managed work teams. These are probably most affected by layoffs and other radical organizational changes, since they are hard to manage successfully if the personnel keep shifting. In addition, in some respects they represent the biggest threat to established power relationships in the organization. For these reasons their slower adoption should not be surprising. Furthermore, the growth of HPWOs remains even if the presence of teams is made a requirement. In 1992, 24.6 percent of establishments had two or more practices at the 50 percent level of penetration, one of which was teams, while in 1997 the figure was 38.3 percent.

The slow diffusion of teams notwithstanding, the central message of the survey is that the use of other components of HPWOs has surged. Even in the case of teams, it is striking that they have essentially held their own in the face of substantial organizational turbulence.

Another useful way of getting at these questions is to ask what fraction of establishments that in 1992 had HPWOs in place managed to maintain these practices in 1997. The answer to this question is in table 4.2, which assigns a "yes" to an establishment if it had at least two practices in place with at least a 50 percent rate of penetration. It is quite apparent that the capacity of employers to sustain these systems is quite high. More than 80 percent of the establishments that had a system in place in 1992 still did in 1997. Furthermore, this sustainability is not diminished if the firm had a layoff. Among those establishments that did not sustain the high-performance prac-

WHAT REALLY GOES ON IN
HIGH-PERFORMANCE SYSTEMS?

The nature of these surveys, and others like them, is that they ask relatively simple questions about broad categories of practices. It would not be possible to conduct a national survey in any other way, and without national data we have no way of knowing how generalizable are the more detailed cases that are often reported. However, national surveys, including the two reported here, vastly simplify the variety and complexity of actual practices. Indeed, in their extensive review of the literature, Eileen Applebaum and Rosemary Batt identify six different clusters of practices any one of which might be termed a high-performance work system.[10]

Paul Adler has shown that in NUMMI the work tasks themselves remain highly divided and the cycle times very short, both practices drawn from the older Tayloristic tradition.[11] The workforce has little say about technology choices or investment decisions. However, work teams are given considerable opportunity "off-line" to participate in job design. By contrast, Applebaum and Batt describe a Corning plant where employees "were actively involved in the design and layout of the plant and equipment. Teams work autonomously without shift supervisors, cross-train and rotate across semiskilled jobs, and communicate directly with engineers and other support staff."[12]

Given the range of actual models "on the ground," it is not possible, or desirable, to insist on one tight definition. The range of issues in which employees participate varies, the extent of their power varies, and the nature of supporting human resource practices (e.g., the characteristics of the compensation system) may also vary. It is also important to recognize that, from employees' viewpoint, not all designs are equally desirable. There are important differences in the intensity of work, in health and safety issues, and in the extent to which gains are shared. These concerns are discussed subsequently.

TABLE 4.2
Proportion of Practices Sustained

	Two or More Practices in 1997	
Two or More Practices in 1992	Yes	No
Yes	81.5%	18.4%
No	53.5%	46.5%

Source: 1992 and 1997 National Establishment Surveys.
Note: Establishment weights are used.

tices between 1992 and 1997, 28 percent had layoffs; among those who did sustain the practices, a nearly identical 27 percent experienced layoffs. This ability to sustain HPWO practices even in the face of layoffs is confirmed in more sophisticated statistical models that control for a variety of other factors.[13]

Overall these findings answer two questions quite clearly. First, American employers are indeed continuing to adopt new organizational forms. Second, and most surprising, both new adoptions and sustaining previous efforts seem quite possible even in the face of layoffs and organizational tumult. The traditional expectation, that employees will not cooperate unless they are protected, seems to be no longer valid.

ARE HIGH-PERFORMANCE WORK ORGANIZATIONS REALLY MORE PRODUCTIVE?

The widespread interest in innovative work systems stems in part from the perception that firms that adopt these techniques outperform others that do not.[14] There are several possible reasons why this might be true. First, HPWOs do a better job of tapping into the ideas and creativity of the workforce. Second, the participation they generate might increase the commitment of the workforce to the organization. Third, adoption might save costs as firms are able to eliminate some supervisors and other redundant employees (for example, extra quality control people). Finally, people might work harder because of increased peer pressure that emerges from being a member of a team. These are all reasons productivity might rise. Profits might also rise, although it is important to account for whatever costs are involved in adopting the new systems.

It is hard to research and prove these arguments. Classical random assignment or medical-type experiments (in which randomly selected firms adopt the systems and others do not) are obviously not possible. Absent this, the basic technique is to see if firms that use these systems do better either compared with other firms that do not use the systems or compared with their own performance in the past. Both strategies provide useful information, but both can be criticized. Statistically matching one firm with another is not a perfect process. Furthermore, it is possible that the direction of causality runs from doing well to adopting the systems rather than the reverse. Finally, per-

(continued)

haps the only firms that adopt the systems are the ones that know they will work, and hence there is no reason to suggest that results from one firm would be relevant to another.

With all these qualifications in mind, the research evidence does suggest that these new work systems outperform traditional models, at least with respect to productivity and quality. For example, this has been shown to be true in the automobile industry,[15] the steel industry,[16] telecommunications,[17] and apparel.[18] Although this research is more sophisticated than the following example, a sense of the dramatic impacts can be gleaned from the fact that two years after the Toyota version of high-performance work systems was introduced into the General Motors Fremont, California, assembly plant (with little new technology introduced and the old labor force rehired), labor hours per vehicle fell from 48.5 hours to 19.6 hours and quality dramatically improved.[19] In the telecommunications case self-managed customer service teams sold 20 percent more than did employees organized in a traditional fashion, and in a national sample of firms based on stock market data those with innovative work organizations had fifteen thousand dollars more in per employee profits than did other firms.[20]

Not all research shows impacts this large, and in particular it seems to be very important that the firm adopt the full range of innovations, not only in work organization but also in compensation and training. Nonetheless, the results are impressive. It remains to be seen, as I discuss subsequently, whether these gains are shared with the workforce.

WORK ORGANIZATION AND RESTRUCTURING

When people use the term "restructuring," more comes to mind than innovative work practices. The common understanding of the term also includes layoffs, contingent employment, and outsourcing.

There is a deeper reason, beyond the fact that they are linked together in common understanding, why these practices should be studied as a group. Each implies that the organization is changing the nature of its bonds or commitments to its labor force, that the character of the employment relationship is shifting. Layoffs are obviously the most severe, but outsourcing is in part a decision to move some tasks outside the firm's boundaries and thus to reduce the employer's reliance on its own labor force, while contingent work is a shift in the terms and conditions of employment.

I deal with the prevalence of layoffs and their relationship to HPWOs in the next section, when I take up the issue of whether these systems yield demonstrable gains for the workforce. For now I shall briefly examine contingent work and outsourcing as well as the loss of managerial jobs in firms that restructure.

I have already argued that the rise of contingent work represents a potential fundamental shift in how firms think about the employment relation. If there was ever a place where the fashionable idea of "core competence" gets applied to the labor force, then this is it. At the same time, the various forms of contingent employment represent more than simply techniques to ease the hiring and firing of labor. Anecdotes suggest that firms are increasingly using contingent employment as a screening device for hiring, and this "temp to perm" pattern suggests the emergence of a new labor market mediating institution, one that might have implications for a variety of public policies.

As I explained in chapter 2, the 1992 and 1997 surveys distinguished between two forms of contingent employment. The first is temporary staff who work on-site at the establishment but are on the payroll of another organization. These are the classic temporary help agency employees. The second group I asked about were on-payroll contingent employees, that is, workers who are on the payroll of the establishment but are regarded as contingent and lack whatever level of employment protections regular employees receive.

As chapter 2 described, the fraction of employers who use temporary or contingent workers is quite high. In the 1997 survey 50.1 percent of the establishments employed temporary labor, and 18.2 percent hired contingent employees. However, as we saw earlier, even though most establishments make some use of contingent work, the proportion of their labor force that is temporary or contingent is not very high. Among those establishments that do employ temporary and/or contingent employees, the temporary employees are equal to 5.7 percent of the regular employees, and the contingent workers are equal to 13.5 percent of regular workers. However, a substantial number of establishments make no use of one or both forms, and if these are included, then temporary employment accounts for 2.7 percent of total employment and contingent employment 2.4 percent.

The box entitled "How Contingent Employees Are Used" profiles the deployment of these temporary and contingent employees within the estab-

---

How Contingent Employees Are Used

In the 1997 survey temporary and contingent workers are found in a wide range of occupations: 36.7 percent of establishments said clerical work was the dominant occupation, 32.8 percent cited blue-collar work, and 15.5 percent cited service work.

The bulk of agency temporary employees are associated with the establishment for short durations: 62.9 percent of establishments said the typical length of employment was less than six months, while 24.6 percent said it was between six months and a year. By contrast, as would be expected, on-payroll contingent employees have a longer attachment: 28.7 percent of establishments said the typical duration was less than six months, 39.0 percent said it was between six months and a year, 25.3 percent said it was between a year and five years, while 6.8 percent said it was greater than five years

For both groups of contingent workers a nontrivial fraction eventually get hired by the establishment: 23.8 percent for agency temporaries and 44.4 percent for on-payroll contingent workers. Again, the disparity between the figures suggests—as did the figures on duration—that a somewhat different dynamic is at work in the two cases.

---

lishments. It is apparent that they work in a wide variety of occupations, and it is quite striking what a large proportion eventually get hired by the establishments. This suggests that temporary and contingent work, and the firms that provide these workers, are playing an important intermediary role in the labor market and are clearly part of the firm's employment strategy.

Outsourcing activities that in the past were done in-house are in many respects the equivalent of contingent work. They represent an effort to strip down the organization and to take advantage of what is available on the outside. Just what is available is a matter of some dispute. Every several months the United Auto Workers strike another General Motors plant in an effort to restrict outsourcing of parts to lower-cost producers, be they nonunion firms in the United States or yet cheaper plants in Mexico. This struggle captures one widely seen aspect of outsourcing: the effort to find lower-cost labor. On the other hand, researchers who have their roots in comparative economic development often take a different perspective. They point to the examples of Japanese supplier networks or northern Italian "industrial districts" and argue that innovative relations with suppliers are a source of positive economic advantages.[21] One line of thought is that because suppliers work with more than one customer they can often be more on the cutting edge of ideas and technology than can the customer firm. The other notion is that by establishing long-term stable relations with suppliers firms can gain the expertise of outsiders without the fixed costs of internalizing the production. These conceptions of outsourcing are tied to shifts in the definition and boundaries of the firm. In both instances, any increase in outsourcing clearly has implications for the careers of people within the customer organization.

The 1997 survey asked establishments whether, since 1992, they had outsourced activities or products that had previously been done in-house, and 38.5 percent of the establishments said they had. On a per-employee basis 48.2 percent of workers are in establishments that responded affirmatively. I asked those establishments that did outsource whether the labor costs at the new supplier were higher or lower than theirs. Lower costs are not the only story but are part of it: 30.6 percent said costs were lower at the new supplier firm.

Finally, another organizational change commonly associated with restructuring is the loss of managerial jobs.[22] The typical view is that organizations are flattening their hierarchies and hence reducing the number of managerial employees. Here the theoretical expectation regarding HPWOs is more clear: to the extent that HPWOs place decision-making power and skills in the hands of frontline workers, we would expect to see managerial employment decline. We shall see momentarily that the data are consistent with this expectation.

Links among the Practices

In what way are these various restructuring practices linked together? For example, as employers move in the direction of HPWOs, are they more or less likely to make greater use of contingent employees and to outsource more work? In principle it would be possible to argue the case in either direction. One view would be that it is very difficult to implement HPWOs employing contingent or temporary workers who are not fully committed to the firm and who may not be around for very long. Hence the relationship between these practices should be negative. A similar argument is that firms that increasingly outsource work, creating an insecure environment, will also experience difficulties convincing employees to participate in high-commitment systems. However, set against this view is what might be termed the "core-periphery" perspective. Employers may seek to implement HPWOs for some subset of their workforce, surrounding these workers with a more flexible buffer of less central employees via temporary/contingent work and via increased subcontracting.

Table 4.3 suggests that the former perspective is more accurate. Establishments that are further along in the HPWO direction make somewhat less use of contingent employees and are less likely to outsource (note, however, that they still engage in both practices). These differences are statistically significant (and remain after controlling for the size of the establishment and its industry). Although not overwhelming, these patterns clearly suggest that there is a logic to how the various restructuring processes fit together. However, while both of these findings imply that HPWO firms are relatively more friendly to their labor force (in the sense of not replacing them as much with contingent workers or reducing their ranks via outsourcing), it remains to be seen how these firms do when broader outcome measures—layoffs and wages—are considered. Examining this is the task of the next section.

TABLE 4.3
Link between HPWO Practices and Restructuring

	Two or More HPWO Practices	Less than Two HPWO Practices
Contingent employment, 1997	3.9%	6.2%
Percentage point change in contingent employment, 1992–97	–0.0002	3.6
Outsourcing work has increased in the past five years	37.5%	46.4%
Managerial employment 1997	10.6%	13.1%
Percentage point change in managerial employment, 1992–97	–0.01	2.2

Source: 1992 and 1997 National Establishment Surveys.
Note: All differences between columns are statistically significant.

Finally, as the theory suggests, these data show that managerial employment is less intensive and grew at a slower rate for the establishments that had HPWOs in place. This is quite striking and affirms the impact of HPWOs in diffusing greater decision-making power in the organization.[23]

ARE THERE MUTUAL GAINS?

Implicit in much of the discussion of high-performance work systems was the view that this approach to organizing work is "win-win," in the interest of both employees and firms. Indeed, an earlier book by Thomas Kochan and me, *The Mutual Gains Enterprise*, explicitly took this position.[24] The logic for this expectation is twofold. First, these systems sufficiently improve productivity so that there are gains to be shared. Second, there is a bias in these systems toward such sharing because they function best with high levels of employee commitment. Employees need to contribute their ideas and extra effort to the enterprise willingly, and they are unlikely to do so if the firm is not prepared to make a comparable commitment to them. This logic emerges both from observation of the Japanese system, in which employee commitment is exchanged for employment security, and from a long history of industrial relations in this country, in which firms found themselves trading various forms of job security for increased flexibility in work design.

There is, in fact, support for the first part of the proposition. We have seen that the evidence that there are important productivity gains inherent in these work systems is reasonably convincing and is drawn from studies of a variety of different industries. It is in the second half of the argument where things get shakier. There has not been any systematic research on whether the gains are shared, and there is a counterargument to suggest why they might not be. Perhaps HPWOs can coexist with downsizing and slow wage growth. This could happen either because employees so strongly prefer these systems that they continue to cooperate even in the face of restructuring or because the level of fear is so high and the power imbalances in the workplace are so sharp that the two quite different philosophies can coexist.

HIGH-PERFORMANCE WORK ORGANIZATIONS AND SKILL

As firms transform their work systems, it seems likely that the skills they need from their labor force will also change, in terms of both level and content. New and greater skill demands from employers are, in fact, often cited by education reformers as a major reason why it is important to transform the curriculum. For their part, economists trying to understand increased wage inequality also point to growing bias by employers in favor of more highly skilled employees.

There is, it should be recognized, a certain paradox in this discussion. Standard economic theory suggests that as employers reduce the length of time they expect to retain an employee the amount of training provided should likewise fall. This is because the firm will have less time over which to amortize its investment. This logic suggests that restructuring and downsizing should lower investments in training. The data, however, show the reverse: firms are spending more resources on training.[25] This reinforces the paradoxical nature of the current juncture: firms in some respects are clearly reducing their commitment to their employees but at the same time are investing more deeply in at least a subset of them.

In the 1992 establishment survey there was a very clear relationship between work organization and training: the level of training in those establishments that had two or more of the HPWO practices in place (with half or more of their core employees involved) was 35 percent higher than in establishments that were not on the HPWO road. This finding remains even after controlling for an extensive set of characteristics of the firm and the employees. Other research has also confirmed this pattern.[26]

These questions have been the subject of considerable speculation but very little systematic research. However, it is possible to make progress by taking advantage of the longitudinal nature of the two National Establishment Surveys. Specifically, I can ask what happened in 1997 in those establishments that had HPWOs in place in 1992. Do employees in 1997 seem better off than in establishments that had not adopted HPWOs in 1992? Using the 1992 data in this way is much more powerful and reliable than asking about the work practices and outcomes with the 1997 data only. If I were to compare work practices and employee outcomes just in 1997, it would be hard to be certain whether particular work practices explained the outcomes (e.g., HPWOs led to wage gains) or whether the causation

How Do Employees Feel about New Work Systems?

The text describes the economic consequences to employees as a result of working in firms that adopt high-performance work systems. Another important question is whether employees prefer these arrangements to more traditional ways of organizing work. There is some controversy about this because under some circumstances these systems can simply be an excuse to speed up and intensify work. Indeed, in the early days of the joint General Motors–Toyota NUMMI plant, a strong caucus emerged in the union that opposed the changes. From her participant/observer experience as an employee at a Subaru-Isuzu plant, Laurie Graham paints a complex picture: employees came to identify more with the firm than under traditional systems, and they also became committed to quality and productivity goals. They probably enjoyed the work more. Yet, under pressures of the intensification of work pace and health and safety concerns, they also came to be cynical and critical of just how "new" the system was and how committed the firm was to their welfare.[27]

There is little systematic information available on how employees feel about HPWOs, but what there is does suggest that they like the greater scope of teamwork and the opportunity to share their ideas while, at the same time, they remain wary of the firm's intentions. In a survey of private sector non-supervisory workers and low- and midlevel managers, a universe representing 70 percent of all private sector employees, Richard Freeman and Joel Rogers report, "Some 79% of non-managerial, nonunion participants in employee involvement programs report having 'personally benefited from [their] involvement in the program by getting more influence on how [their] job is done.' Among those without EI programs, 64% 'would like to have a program like this' at their company."[28]

In a difficult unionized environment the findings are similar. For example, in their survey of Chrysler employees working in plants organized by "modern operating agreements," John-Paul MacDuffie and Larry Hunter found that 76 percent preferred teams to the old system. In her survey of middle- and lower-level managers in a telecommunications firm that was introducing new work systems, Rosemary Batt found that 86 percent expressed satisfaction with their accomplishments, 68 percent with their participation in decisions, and 81 percent with their use of skills. Yet only 60 percent were proud to work for the company, 19 percent were satisfied with the firm's level of consideration of employees, and 29 percent had values similar to those of the firm.[29]

(continued)

> In a study that compared production workers in two very different indus-
> tries, telecommunications and apparel, Rosemary Batt and Eileen Applebaum
> surveyed workers and in a formal statistical model found that "job charac-
> teristics associated with teams . . . significantly improves job performance."[30]
> Open-ended interviews with network employees in telecommunications
> garnered comments that teams were better because "no supervisor is spying
> on you," or "now if a job goes well, we get the credit."[31]

ran in the other direction (firms doing well enough to pay good wages decided
to experiment with HPWOs). However, by looking at work practices in 1992
and outcomes in 1997, we have a much better chance at getting the direction of causation right, since it is obviously unlikely that some action in 1997
explains what the firm was doing in 1992.[32]

These ideas can be translated into the following statistical model, which
I employ:

$$\text{Outcome in 1997} = \text{Control variables} + \text{high-performance work system variable in 1992}$$

In asking about whether the gains for HPWOs are shared with the labor
force, I look at two outcomes:

- Whether or not the establishment reported in 1997 that it had laid off 5
percent or more of its employees between 1995 and 1997
- The average real wage increase (or decrease) experienced by the establishment's employees in 1996 (measured by compensation of core employees and also by compensation of all employees)[33]

As a first step it is helpful to start with a very simple version of the
model. Beginning this way will help us see what the broad patterns are in
the data. The initial control variables will be just measures of the establishment's industry and size. My measure of the presence or absence of a high-
performance work system variable will be the number of HPWO practices
in place with 50 percent or more core employees involved. Recall from
table 4.1 that the four practices are self-managed teams, quality circles, job
rotation, and total quality management.

The results are summarized in table 4.4, in which I put a "0" in those cells for which there is no significant relationship between the outcome variable and the HPWO variables, a "–" if the relationship is negative and significant, and a "+" if the relationship is positive and significant.[34]

An employer that had in place a high-performance work system in 1992 was more likely than others to have a layoff in 1995–97. Furthermore, as the utilization of HPWOs increased, the establishment was no more likely than any others to grant its employees (either core employees or all employees) a pay increase. These results certainly do not support the idea that the gains of HPWOs are shared with the labor force. It is also worth noting that the finding that employees do not obtain wage gains from HPWOs remains true even if the wage variable is restricted to wage gains for core employees (who are the ones whose participation in the HPWOs is measured by the survey).

There is some additional support in the survey for the finding that layoffs are associated with HPWOs. Establishments that had experienced layoffs were asked a "relative value" question that went as follows:

> We want to better understand how decisions to reduce employment levels are made. If we assign "poor current financial results" 100 points of explanatory power, how many points would you give to each of the other considerations I now mention as a reason you reduced staff? To get a score, if a factor is twice as important as poor current financial results for reducing staff give it 200, if it is half as important give it 50. There is no limit to the scale, so please tell me whatever number you think is appropriate.

The respondents were given several alternatives: organizational change (such as HPWOs), anticipation of future product market difficulties, outsourcing, technical change and capital investments, and a desire to rebalance the workforce. The results are shown in figure 4.1.

TABLE 4.4
"Mutual Gains" Outcomes

	Layoffs in 1995–97	Pay Raises in 1996–97
1992 HPWOs	+	0

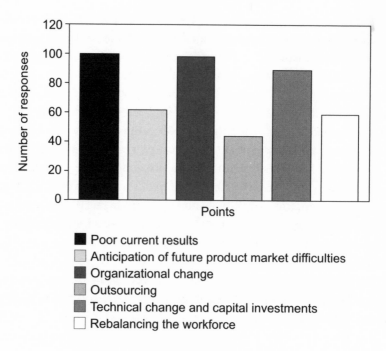

FIGURE 4.1
Explanation of Layoffs
Source: National Establishment Survey.

It is apparent that organizational change, such as HPWOs, ranks, along with poor current results, as the most important explanation of layoffs. Although subjective replies such as this should be interpreted carefully, the fact that these responses are consistent with the statistical analysis is certainly striking.

The overall results can be deepened by moving in two directions: first, by seeing if there are any differences in the impact of specific practices (e.g., teams), and, second, by looking more carefully at what characteristics of the employers help determine whether the potential "mutual gains" are realized.

With respect to specific workplace innovations, no practice stands out as an exception to the findings described above, or, to put it differently, no single practice can be said to produce mutual gains.

I searched for characteristics of the establishments that might influence the attainment of mutual gains. The factors I considered were the presence or absence of unions in general, the presence or absence of unions in those cases in which the firm implemented HPWOs, whether the establishment was a branch plant of a larger organization, the proportion of the labor force that was composed of women, the fraction of the labor force that works part-time, whether the establishment follows the "high-road" competitive strategy, whether the establishment had been subject to a hostile takeover attempt, and whether the establishment competed in markets against firms located in nations with low labor costs. All the explanatory variables except the low-wage-nation variable and the hostile takeover variable are taken from the 1992 survey.

The results are quite striking.[35] Even with the rich set of controls, HPWOs were still positively associated with layoffs, and the controls do not change the results for the compensation outcome. However, in the layoff model two of the additional variables make a difference. First, threats of hostile takeovers also induce layoffs. This is certainly consistent with the popular press accounts of how takeovers play out. Perhaps more strikingly, when unions are present and the establishment implements HPWOs, then, in a reversal, layoffs are less likely than otherwise. Put differently, with respect to employment security unions do seem to deliver the "mutual gains" that are possible from innovative work systems. Absent unions the impact of HPWOs is in the direction of a higher likelihood of layoffs.

Finally, recall from the earlier section that a reduction in managerial employment is associated with HPWOs. This might suggest that the finding that layoffs are linked to HPWOs could be largely driven by the efforts of employers to reduce their managerial ranks. In fact, among the establishments that reported layoffs, 75.8 percent indicated that some of the layoffs were among managers. However, among these employers (i.e., the ones that laid off some workers) only 22.2 percent of the total layoffs were managerial. While managers did indeed bear a disproportionate share of layoffs (since they accounted for only about 12 percent of employment), it is clear that the results in this section are not simply a function of the attempt to cut layers of managers.

SUMMARY

Events within firms are complicated and point in different directions. The spread of HPWOs has been dramatic and shows that managers have widely accepted the view that these innovations lead to higher productivity and quality. The widespread concern of a decade or so ago that barriers to diffusion would block these efforts seems not to have been justified.

At the same time that these new work systems have broadly diffused, companies have also been widely engaged in restructuring. Indeed, responses to the survey suggest that organizational innovation has been a prime driver of restructuring. This is an important point because it demonstrates that employment decisions and organizational change are driven as much by the "softer" innovations of recent years as by the spread of information technology and shifts in capital markets that have captured so much attention.

The spread of these HPWOs is, along some dimensions, good news for many employees. We saw that surveys show that workers, blue and white collar, prefer the higher level of responsibility and the greater opportunities for creativity that these work systems entail. These systems also require employees to increase their skills, and this is a good thing. The potential for mutual gains is clearly there. But now, the narrative turns darker because the data also show that mutual gains have not been realized. A central theme of earlier chapters was that the balance of power between managers and employees has shifted, and this shows up in the material in this chapter. The establishment of innovative work systems (in 1992) is associated with higher chances of layoffs in 1997 and bears no relationship to compensation gains. The only exceptions are the small number of establishments that are unionized.

It is more than a little surprising that employers have been so successful in spreading HPWOs even in the face of restructuring and layoffs. Recall that at the core of these new work systems is that employees are more forthcoming with their ideas about production and service and are more focused than before on the success of the firm and its relationship with its customers. That this higher level of employee commitment should exist, and even grow, in the face of reduced commitment on the part of the firm to its workforce is striking. On the one hand it reinforces the notion that employees find these new systems attractive. It also suggests that fear and insecurity have deep and broad consequences, influence a wide range of behavior, and have fundamentally shifted the terms of trade in the labor market.

Preliminaries to Policy

THE PREVIOUS CHAPTERS described where we have been and where we are now. This chapter and the next two are about where we should go. How best can we build labor market institutions that successfully deal with the problems laid out earlier and that are congruent with the new realities of the economy and the labor market? It is important that policies pass both these tests; it makes little sense to try to resurrect the old labor market structure. The trick is to preserve the strengths of the new labor market while tackling the outcomes that trouble us.

Rather than once again grind through each of the specific concerns, it is probably most helpful to begin by thinking at a more abstract level about the nature of the ills policy needs to address and the solutions that are feasible.

Many employees are doing quite well in today's labor market, and these people, maybe 20 percent of the labor market, succeed because they have market power that derives from scarce skills. This is one of the essential lessons of the Silicon Valley. However, it is simply not reasonable to expect that the bulk of the workforce can possess scarce high-level skills. In the past wages and working conditions for most employees were maintained in two ways. First, as I explained in chapter 1, widely held employer norms acted as at least a partial constraint and led firms to share productivity and profit gains with the workforce. Probably more important, employees had power that derived from unions and the threat of unionization as well as from government regulations such as minimum wages. Taken together these norms and power relations helped maintain the quality of many moderately skilled jobs.

The dramatic shift in these relationships is illustrated by the material in the last chapter, which demonstrated that even most "high-road" firms that have implemented high-performance work organizations do not share the gains from these systems with their workforce. In other ways, from general wage stagnation to the increased use of various forms of contingent employment, shifts in the balance of power in the workplace have led to a deterioration of employment conditions.

The second broad problem that policy needs to address is the issues raised by the increased rates of mobility in the labor market. Long-term careers with the same employer are less common, and even for those employees who do manage to hang on, the perceived risks are much higher than in the past. The adverse consequences of involuntary job changing are quite high, as chapter 3 demonstrated. High turnover and instability in low-wage labor markets are an additional concern. An important objective of policy should be to ease these transitions both by making employees more marketable, and hence more able to shift jobs, and by building effective institutions for facilitating mobility.

In short, the broad goals of public policy should be to redress an imbalance of power in the labor market and to improve the process of mobility and job transitions. No single tool can accomplish these objectives. Instead it will be necessary to build new labor market institutions that effectively perform a variety of functions. Taken as a whole, these institutions can provide a structure to the labor market and a framework within which work can be accomplished both efficiently and equitably.

In laying out these ideas it is important to realize that developments in the labor market have opened up new opportunities. Consider, for example, the role of labor market intermediaries. There were two main reasons why public intermediaries were not widely needed in the old labor market. First, most jobs were found by personal contacts. This is one of the long-standing findings of the older institutional labor economics literature, and it has been repeatedly rediscovered and elaborated on by more recent scholars. The second consideration suppressing intermediaries was that, after a period of initial search, rates of job changing and mobility were relatively modest. This follows from the characteristically long job ladders and lengthy employment tenures that we have already seen were an important part of the old order.

Several shifts in the labor market have made it more likely that intermediaries can be important. First, internal labor markets have weakened, and more people will need help throughout their careers in changing employers and finding new work. Another plausible story is that the nature of skill has changed. In the past, skills may have been quite firm-specific, and hence each firm did its own training. This explains why prior skill was not an important hiring criterion, and the role of the family/friend network was, in effect, to provide character references.[1] If skills have become more general (owing perhaps to the spread of microelectronics), then a hiring process that puts greater weight on skill may open the door to formal intermediaries. Although formal intermediaries are not the only way to accomplish this (witness the role of social networks in the Silicon Valley), the new hiring criteria may well create an opportunity for them to play a more significant role in the labor market. Certainly the growing importance of the temporary help industry suggests that new intermediaries have a future.

Some Preliminaries to Policy

The reader may well be wondering whether it even makes sense in today's environment to engage in a serious discussion of policy. This skepticism contrasts with the past, when identification of a problem led to a plethora of proposals for programs to solve it. Not every idea was a good one, but the shared assumption was optimistic: that good programs could solve problems. We obviously no longer live in that world, and both budget constraints and skepticism about government lead to a new shared assumption: that most policy ideas are suspect and most programs will fail. When it comes to thinking about new labor market institutions, these doubts about policy link naturally with the viewpoint that the market should be left unchecked. The rhetoric is indeed powerful, particularly when combined with the dominant negative attitude toward the possibilities of intervention. The burden on advocates of policy is made even heavier because there is much truth in the claims of their opponents. The competitive environment confronting employers is very tough and getting more difficult as the world economy opens up.

The size and diversity of the American economy are yet another challenge. It is not that difficult to design and implement what might be called "boutique programs," small interventions that do well and seem to hold promise. Be they training programs, modernization assistance to smaller firms, or labor market intermediaries, these programs look good but wilt when one asks how many people or firms they serve compared with the size of the universe of need. For an idea to be taken seriously, it must be plausible to envision how it can go to scale.

With these background worries in mind, it seems appropriate to begin by first considering the case against policy, that is, the argument that intervening in the labor market will just make things worse.

The Case against Policy

The theoretical argument against policy is that government interventions in the labor market have perverse effects. The intellectual basis of this view is the presumption that markets can solve problems better than can policy makers. Economic theory is deployed to argue that the uninhibited operation of the price system is the best solution. The penetration of this attitude into what had previously been more liberal enclaves is remarkable. For example, in a recent *Business Week* article, Massachusetts Institute of Technology economist Rudi Dornbush actually celebrated labor market insecurity. Even in recoveries ongoing international competition, he argued, means that employees are scared and that unions therefore cannot organize "cyclical raiding parties on corporate profits," which in turn means that wages will stagnate, which in turn means (he claimed) that the economy can continue on an unimpeded growth path. Mr. Dornbush applauded this turn of events.[2]

This intellectual perspective has been around for a long time, but its credibility and power are at their peak because of the conventional interpretations of what has happened in the world economy. There are two "facts" that undergird the argument. First, the failure of communist systems discredits national planning in its crudest form. Although no one seriously argues that old-style communist models are a solution to any of the themes in this book, the ambience of the policy debate cannot help but be influenced by such a spectacular failure of "antimarket" policies. The second, and more obviously relevant, "fact" is what is taken to be the superior economic performance of the United States, particularly in job creation, compared with Europe and the linkage that is made between this and labor market policy. The better economic performance is taken as evidence that efforts to regulate the labor market backfire. It is worth pausing to assess this claim because, if true, it would undermine a wide range of possible policy initiatives.

It is important to keep in mind that the goal is not to decide whether any particular European policy is a good thing that should be adopted but rather to ask the more general question of how strong the evidence is that labor market policy restricts employment growth.

Europeans regulate labor markets in a variety of ways. They make it more difficult than in this country to lay off workers (although there is considerable variation across Europe in the nature of these limitations, just as there is variation in other policies), they limit wage movements and hence create a more rigid wage structure than here, they have stronger unions, and so on. One theoretical expectation is that all of this stifles employment growth. For example, if firms are less able to fire people, then they will be more reluctant to hire them in the first place. If the wage structure is rigid and the wages of less-skilled employees are propped up, then these people will be less able to find work, since they cost too much relative to their productivity.

Why might these critiques not be true? One possible answer is that they may be accurate in principle but in practice of small importance relative to other factors that determine the employment level. This is much like the debate about the U.S. minimum wage. While most economists agree that the impact of the minimum wage on employment is in principle negative, much empirical work shows that the effect is very small and that hence other benefits of the minimum wage may outweigh its costs.

The other answer is that there may be offsetting advantages of labor market regulation that encourage employment growth. For example, if firms are unable to shed labor easily, then they may be more willing to invest in those employees, perhaps by providing more training, and this may in the long run raise productivity.

In recent years a number of scholars have assessed the impact of European labor regulation, and a fair reading of the evidence is that there is good reason to doubt that these policies are responsible for Europe's employment problems. As Rebecca Blank commented in her review of a wide range of studies: "The primary conclusion . . . is that while the design of social programs affects employer and worker behavior, these programs do not create major inflexibilities in the labor market."[3]

Some representative evidence includes the following:

■ Most European nations relaxed their labor market regulations in the 1980s, yet there was no change in employment growth after these modifications.

■ Although European wage structures are more rigid than in the United States and raise the wages of those on the bottom, the relative unemployment rates of the unskilled are no higher in Europe than in the United States, nor is there any relationship across European nations between the wage structure and the unemployment rates of different skill groups.[4] This means that decent wages for people at the bottom of the labor market are not a culprit for their employment problems.

■ A careful statistical examination of how German and U.S. firms adjust employment to changes in product market demand shows in both nations that firms are able to alter employment in response to shifts in their environment. The nature of the response differs in that German firms tend to adjust hours of work more than bodies and American firms do the reverse. Nonetheless, there is no evidence that German firms are handicapped relative to American ones.[5] In a similar vein, the Organization for Economic Cooperation and Development (OECD) reviewed the evidence and concluded that "there is little evidence that the responsiveness of job turnover to GDP growth varies significantly across countries grouped according to strictness of employment protection legislation."[6]

A final, and perhaps most striking, set of evidence is found in table 5.1, which shows the rates of gross job creation and destruction in a representative set of nations. The net changes in employment are consistent with the earlier evidence that the United States has created more jobs than other nations. However, underlying these small net shifts are very large flows of gross job creation and destruction. Critics argue that active labor market policy inhibits job creation, yet there is no evidence in this table that this is true. The United States does not stand out as creating more jobs than do other nations, and indeed the champion is Sweden, which is among the most heavily regulated of European labor markets.

The conclusion to take away from all of this is a relatively modest one. The European experience does not prove that labor market policy is a bad

TABLE 5.1
Annual Changes in Employment
(annual rates as a percentage of employment)

	Gross Job Gains	Gross Job Losses	Net Job Gain
Germany	9.0	7.5	1.5
France	12.7	11.8	0.9
Italy	11.0	10.0	1.0
Netherlands	8.2	7.2	1.0
Sweden	14.5	14.6	−0.1
United Kingdom	8.7	6.6	2.1
United States (a)	13.0	10.4	2.6
United States (b)	8.2	10.4	−2.2

Source: OECD, *Employment Outlook* (July 1996), 163.
Notes: Germany, 1983–90; France, 1984–91; Italy, 1987–92; Netherlands, 1984–91; Sweden, 1985–92; United Kingdom, 1985–91; United States (a), 1984–91; United States (b), 1984–88.

thing. There is no argument being made here that we should import European policies, only that the field of play remains open for considering the nature and scope of policy in this country.

A final point is just a general caution about the transitory character of arguments that are based on unfavorable comparisons of one nation's performance with another. It was not very long ago that American observers from a broad range of political and economic perspectives extolled the Japanese and German economic systems and compared them favorably with ours. At the time these comparisons were being made, our export performance and product quality seemed poor compared with these other economies. Yet, of course, at the time of these comparisons the German and Japanese labor markets were even more highly regulated than now, yet this was not seen as hurting performance. The worm has turned, and we now compare ourselves favorably with Germany and Japan and want to draw conclusions about the merits of the underlying structures. Given the evident transitory nature of economic advantage and of superior performance, it seems prudent to be restrained in any explanation that attributes the current difficulties of other nations to how they organize their labor markets.

It seems clear from the foregoing that the broad case against labor market policy is weak. With these considerations in hand, the next two chapters take up initiatives directed toward the main concerns that have emerged in the new American labor market. Chapter 6 examines how to deal with higher rates of voluntary and involuntary job changing, that is, mobility, and then I turn in chapter 7 to how to redress growing power imbalances in the American labor market.

Policies for a Mobile Workforce

THE NATURE OF THE NEW labor market is that people change jobs more often, sometimes of their own volition and other times because they are fired. In these circumstances there are two important elements of policy: as a first step we need to protect people during these transitions so that the consequences of job loss and job changing are less severe than they might otherwise be. Second, we need to build local labor market institutions that make movement through the labor market easier and more successful than it has been in the past.

I begin by discussing the safety net that is aimed at limiting the risks associated with job change, particularly involuntary shifts. The key pieces are improved unemployment insurance and making benefits more portable. I then turn to policies to rebuild pathways through local labor markets. This discussion includes ideas regarding the role of intermediaries as well as building networks that link together a variety of institutions.

THE SAFETY NET I: UNEMPLOYMENT INSURANCE

As turmoil in the labor market forces people to change jobs and induces higher levels of uncertainty and risk, one would expect that a central institution for alleviating some of this stress would be the unemployment insurance (UI) system.[1] This is a program that is literally intended to insure certain categories of employees against the risk of unemployment by paying them a benefit should they lose their job. Today only roughly a third of all unemployed people actually receive UI benefits,[2] and the fraction of the unemployed who are even eligible is well below half.[3] There is, therefore, good reason to be concerned that in recent years the capacity of the system to perform its function has weakened. Partly this is because the system has been cut back as it has been subject to the same kind of attack as other transfer programs, with questions raised about "perverse incentives" and "overly generous" benefits. The deeper problem, however, is that the system was designed around an image of the labor market—a single breadwinner in a family who was at risk of experiencing temporary, not permanent, layoffs—that is no longer descriptive of the labor market that confronts us today.

Unemployment insurance, like the U.S. Employment Service, was created during the New Deal and is a federal/state system. The system is funded by a payroll tax on employers that is experience-rated in that firms with higher levels of layoffs pay higher taxes. Washington establishes minimum national regulations concerning procedures and benefits, acts as a funding source of last resort if states exhaust their UI funds in a downturn, and during recessions provides various forms of extended benefit programs. Each state determines its own eligibility rules, benefit level, and duration of benefit. In addition, the states administer the program "on the ground."

There are four key parameters to the system: what kinds of jobs are covered, which individuals who held covered jobs are eligible to receive benefits, what the size of the benefit is, and for how long can one receive it.

Since its founding, the occupations covered by the UI system have been steadily broadened. Today 90 percent of all civilian jobs and nearly 100 percent of all wage and salary jobs are covered.[4] There is a case to be made for easing these restrictions, but the numbers of people involved (outside of the self-employed) are not great. The more complicated issue concerns which individuals among covered workers are actually eligible to receive benefits. At the core of this question are two central ideas that have been at the heart of the system since its founding. First, it is conceived of as an insurance system. Second, its major beneficiaries are intended to be employees who are in some sense "strongly attached" to the labor market.

Because UI is an insurance program (as opposed to a benefits program that pays support to any unemployed person), there is considerable concern about moral hazard problems, that is, how to avoid people deliberately taking actions to make themselves eligible for benefits. This is equivalent to wanting to make sure that no one crashes his or her car to collect insurance. For this reason self-employed workers are excluded, since it is very hard to know when they are truly "laid off." More broadly, this concern explains why eligibility is limited to job losers, that is, people who have been laid off. People who are entering or reentering the labor market are not eligible, nor, with a few exceptions, are people who quit their jobs.[5] We saw in chapter 2 that the pool of unemployed is increasingly made up of job losers and that among job losers a growing fraction have lost their job permanently. Concerns about moral hazard also explain the UI work test: people collecting benefits must be engaged in job search and available to take a job if one is offered. Exactly how this policy is implemented has been a central theme in debates about UI policy.

The issues of benefit generosity and duration of benefits are somewhat more straightforward. Standard measures of benefit levels suggest that UI payments replace about 36 percent of wages lost during the period the benefits are received. However, this measure is calculated by dividing the average UI payment by the average wage of all covered workers, and, as a matter of fact, UI recipients have lower wages than the average covered workers. Estimates that take this into account suggest that the actual replacement rate may be on the order of 60 percent for people who receive benefits.[6] Given the importance of this statistic, it is somewhat remarkable that generally accepted accurate data are not available. In all but two states people can receive benefits for a maximum of twenty-six weeks.[7] In times of recession the federal government has provided, under a shifting set of programmatic arrangements, extended benefits.

The most radical approach to UI reform would be to abandon its underlying premise and make UI benefits available to most unemployed people, not simply job losers. However, general policy abandonment of the insurance principle seems far-fetched in political and budgetary terms, to say the least. It is also probably bad policy in that it is hard to deny some basis for moral hazard concerns. Preserving the insurance principle does not, however, mean that the current benefit philosophy of the system is appropriate. Just as is the case with Social Security, a system that operates on insurancelike principles can still have room for policy and distributional concerns because there need not be a one-to-one relationship between taxes paid and benefits received. Furthermore, even the strict limitation of benefits to job losers might be reconsidered if done so in the context of the use of UI funds for more active training programs that require effort and sacrifice from participants. This possibility is taken up again below.

There are two broad issues regarding scope and coverage. The first is the duration of benefits, and the second concerns who is covered. At their root both of these questions go to the responsiveness of the UI system to the changing structure of the labor market. When the program was founded, the central image of the labor market was of a breadwinner (typically male) working full-time to support a family. The notion that the program is for "fully attached" workers has been built into eligibility requirements in the form of minimum earnings thresholds and minimum length of prior employment thresholds. These vary by state, but the tendency, driven both by budgetary issues and by political hostility to transfer programs, has been to make it more difficult to be eligible. This is, of course, somewhat ironic, as the labor force has increasingly looked less like the paradigmatic model that underlies the program.

When UI is thought of as a response to short-term temporary unemployment spells, the duration of benefits is unlikely to be a major issue, except in times of recession. However, as more and more people lose their jobs permanently, the situation of people who exhaust their benefits without finding new jobs becomes more worrisome. Since the labor market is indeed shifting in the direction of more permanent job loss, duration of benefits becomes a more pressing issue. There has, in fact, been a long-term rise in the exhaustion rate, and today roughly 35 percent of UI spells end in the exhaustion of benefits prior to acquisition of a new job.[8]

In response to this shift in the nature of job loss, it seems reasonable to lengthen the potential duration of insurance. There are at least two issues here. The first is that while virtually all states set twenty-six weeks as the maximum duration, only ten states make this duration available to all recipients. The remainder determine duration length on the basis of prior work history. A first step would be to establish a standard duration for all recipients. The second step would be to lengthen the maximum potential duration. Other than cost, the major concern is that this will simply encourage longer spells, that is, that here is a major moral hazard problem. There has been considerable research directed to this question, and Stephen Woodbury and Murray Rubin report that the best estimate is of a very small effect, that increasing potential benefits by one week increases the length of actual unemployment spells by one day or less.[9] Other worries regarding the consequences of increased benefit periods can be addressed by innovations such as "profiling," a technique for identifying and providing mandatory job search assistance for potential exhaustees that in fact does appear to speed job acquisition.

The second major concern is who is eligible to receive UI in the first place. Individual eligibility for receiving UI has been restricted since the early 1980s as a result of the general conservative reversal in social policy and the concern (parallel to the welfare discussion) that the program was being abused. According to the General Accounting Office, between 1981 and 1987 forty-four states increased individual eligibility thresholds and/or made it easier to disqualify a person in the middle of a spell of benefits.[10] Today, the UI system is biased against part-time workers, low-wage workers, and people who move in and out of the labor force. These biases result from the structure of the minimum hours and earnings requirements that most states impose for eligibility. To get a sense of the consequences, Lauri Bassi and Daniel McMurrer estimate that while 93 percent of full-time/full-year workers and 93 percent of workers who earn more than ten dollars per hour meet eligibility requirements, only 42 percent of part-time/part-year workers and 56 percent of people who earn less than around the minimum wage do so.[11] The recent report of the Advisory Council on Unemployment Compensation made a number of recommendations aimed at expanding eligibility, basing it on on hours worked over a base period (rather than earnings amount) and setting the hours threshold at eight hundred per year. Bassi and McMurrer estimate that these changes could establish eligibility for about an additional 15 percent of all unemployed workers.

The final area of reform is whether the UI system should be used in a more active way than simply check writing. Other than general aversion to active policy, the main obstacle to innovative programming is that employers who pay taxes and many unions see the system as "theirs" and intended to serve "their" workers and hence are more than a little reluctant to see funds used for broader objectives. There is also a concern that using UI funds that accumulate during good times might threaten the solvency of the program when recessions hit. Nonetheless, it is hard not to believe that more creative uses are possible for such huge pools of funds that are broadly aimed at alleviating labor market distress.

There have, in fact, been a few small initiatives—such as the profiling program and provisions that allow UI benefits to be used to capitalize self-employment—but in the aggregate these do not amount to much, and they are aimed as much at saving funds as at doing something more active with the system. Only two states—Massachusetts and Michigan—provide extra benefits to workers who enter training programs while they are unemployed. California diverted a small fraction of its UI tax to fund its Employment and Training Panel, a statewide program providing training assistance to firms that seemed in some kind of difficulty that threatened their employment base. This is a controversial program with many problems, but it does nonetheless represent an attempt to use the UI system to provide services that intervene prior to job loss.[12] It is absolutely worth thinking more broadly about how else to deploy the UI system's resources.

THE SAFETY NET II: PORTABLE BENEFITS

It is at least in part a historical accident that in the United States benefits, notably health insurance and pensions, are employer-based. In the 1920s leading nonunion firms seeking to defeat union-organizing drives created what came to be known as "welfare capitalism," a system of paternalistic firm-based benefits.[13] Many, though not all, of these plans died with the onset of the Great Depression,[14] but they did establish at least one image of corporate "best practice." Firm-based benefits received an even stronger impetus during World War II from the War Labor Board. The board was empaneled by the federal government to suppress wage inflation during a period of severe shortages. However, unions were able to argue successfully that even when wages were capped employers could improve benefit packages. As a result, there were strong incentives to move to an employer-based benefit system. Finally, the postwar tax system cemented this arrangement. Employers were allowed to pay their share of benefits in pretax dollars, as were employees. As a result, a dollar of compensation costs that took the form of benefits was worth more than a dollar paid in wages, and this tilted the compensation structure toward firm-based benefits.

Firm-based benefits pose two problems, one that has long been with us and one that is of growing importance. The long-standing problem is that nothing requires employers to offer benefits, and many workers (indeed, a growing number) find themselves in jobs that do not provide health insurance or pensions. Put differently, inequality is exacerbated in a firm-based benefits regime because the profile of benefits follows the profile of wages rather than being leveled by government provision. Second, and the issue that concerns us here, is that firm-based benefits are premised on a fairly low level of interfirm mobility. When people change jobs with greater frequency or increasingly work in nonstandard arrangements, firm-based benefits are a problem.

The issues involved in assessing the degree of loss due to increased mobility and the policies that seem most appropriate to remedy the situation are complicated, to say the least. With respect to pensions one issue is how to measure loss suffered by people who leave one employer and move to another. There are at least two possible sources of loss.

First, some people may move from a firm that provides a plan to one that does not. For example, in 1988, 18 percent of people who left an employer with a pension plan moved to another who lacked a plan.[15] Losses might occur because the person was not vested at the time of the move (and hence loses the contributions) or because had the person stayed he or she would have been on an earning trajectory that would have led to large benefits under a defined benefit plan. This latter point is particularly important because many defined benefit plans are back weighted, being generous for long-service employees but very skimpy for those who leave early.[16] Employees who leave, even though they are vested, cannot take their vested pension with them (investing it, for example, in an individual retirement account that would enable the value to grow) but rather are only entitled when they retire to the (likely small and not inflation-adjusted) defined benefit linked to their last pay rate.

The second kind of loss occurs even if a person moves to another firm that also provides a pension. Under most defined contribution schemes, the payout formula is based on years of continuous service. Hence a person who, for example, works for two employers and accumulates thirty years of work between them will receive a lower pension than another individual who receives the same pay each year of her or his career but stays at the same firm the entire time. The solution to this would be to enable the person to apply his or her years of service in the first firm to the pension calculation in the second firm, yet in 1992 only 13 percent of full-time workers covered by defined benefit plans had such a portability provision.[17]

An additional worry is that an increasing number of firms do not provide any pensions,[18] and many firms that do have plans exclude part-time and contingent workers from participation based on their failure to meet an annual hours threshold. Indeed, a person can be a full-time worker in the sense of working two thousand hours a year on a series of jobs but not be eligible for a pension at any of the jobs. This is analogous to the problem described above regarding unemployment insurance.

One solution to these difficulties would appear to be the growth of 401(k) plans, which are defined contribution plans tied to the person. These are indeed portable. However, these plans are useful only if the employee has resources to contribute, and employers need not contribute unless the employee does. Hence, in contrast to the older defined benefit plans in which all contributions were from the employer, the spread of 401(k) plans is only valuable to people at the upper end of the earnings distribution with available resources.

There are a number of ideas in circulation about how to deal with these concerns. In some sectors it may be possible to expand multiemployer plans that facilitate the transfer of years of credit from one firm to another. These are common in the construction industry and were also established among the firms that emerged from the breakup of the old Bell telephone monopoly.

Other ideas also hold promise. For example, Working Today is a New York–based organization that organizes contingent employees and independent contractors to solve collectively problems of health insurance, pensions, and other benefits. Its basic strategy is to build associational health and pension plans much like the TIAA/CREF plan, which enables university faculty to move easily from job to job while retaining their benefits. The Institute of Electrical and Electronics Engineers has been very active in this area, driven by higher rates of job changing among its members. Its proposals include reducing the time before vesting occurs and permitting employees who leave a job with a defined benefits pension to take the value of their current vested pension with them and transfer it into another pension plan. Yet another proposal, developed by the Pension Rights Center, is what might be termed a "reverse 401(k)," in which employers make an initial contribution that workers can then match on a two-for-one basis should they wish.

It is not clear what form a resolution of these issues will take (and health insurance is an even more difficult problem), and it would be foolhardy to try to sketch any specific proposal here. What does seem apparent, however, is that shifts in the labor market have given these issues new salience and that even if labor market policy is limited to the "pack your own parachute" approach policy makers will need to take up these benefit issues in a serious way.

BEYOND THE SAFETY NET: BUILDING INSTITUTIONS IN LOCAL LABOR MARKETS

Strengthening the safety net is an important first step in adapting the labor market to increased mobility. However, more active policy is also needed. We need to reduce the risks and enhance the benefits of mobility as people change jobs, involuntarily or not. This section discusses how to construct better pathways through the labor market.

When people think about active policy, they quickly turn to education and training as the most likely tools. Policy analysts and politicians across the political spectrum share a tendency to view job training as an attractive solution to a variety of social problems. Training has broad appeal because it relies on the notion that outcomes are determined by the attainments and skills of individuals and that labor markets will reward those who augment these capacities. The commonsensical quality of this idea explains the frequency with which policy makers return to this strategy. The Clinton administration invested heavily, both substantively and rhetorically, in proposing education and training as the appropriate response to economic dislocation, stagnating and increasingly unequal earnings, and youth unemployment. More than thirty years ago the War on Poverty was largely based on training programs delivered by numerous community-based organizations. Between these two endpoints Republicans as well as Democrats have seen training as the most appropriate tool to improve labor market outcomes for those who need assistance, be they welfare recipients or defense workers thrown out of work by shifting national priorities.

In fact, skills are important, but training alone is not enough. That this is true is demonstrated by the spotty record of the public employment and training system. Although these programs are typically defensible in a cost/benefit sense, the impact of most of them on the labor market and on the trajectory of people's lives has been limited (with the notable exception of community colleges). There are several reasons for this somewhat disappointing record, but the most important is that too often training programs are isolated from employers and are not linked to clear paths of job mobility. Making these connections is the job of labor market intermediaries, some of whom operate in tandem with training programs while others stand alone. Building up the importance of these intermediaries is the next important step we need to consider.

In its simplest form a labor market intermediary is an organization that makes a match between an employer with a job opening and a person who wants that job. The intermediary exists because it provides a service that is advantageous relative to people applying directly for jobs. There are several possible sources of this advantage. The most obvious is information. It is costly and difficult for the employer or the job seeker to learn as much as might be useful about the labor market: what (or who) is available, what going wages are, and so on. There are also economies of scale to information collection that an intermediary can capture. For many years employers have used search firms for higher-level jobs, and these search firms presumably exist for just this reason.

Given that the private market can produce and support intermediaries, why should public intermediaries exist? The most standard answer would be distributional: there may be people who would benefit from intermediary services, yet firms do not find it worthwhile to establish them for their stratum of the labor market. The fact of the matter is, however, that most public intermediaries have had a very sorry record of performance. Even though they are publicly supported and their services have been available to firms at no cost, they have not done well. In the old labor market the need for intermediaries was narrow and limited to the upper tiers of the labor market.

What is striking about the current period is that there appears to be an explosion of new intermediaries. Temporary help firms, with their "temp to perm" promises, are clearly one example. In the Silicon Valley the highly mobile upper-level workers rely on a web of interest groups, with names such as the Systems Administrators Guild or the Graphic Artists Guild or the Society for Technical Communication. These organizations may play a variety of roles, but helping their members find jobs is clearly one of the most important. Firms and other groups are increasingly using the World Wide Web to create job banks, and some employers, notably AT&T with its Talent Alliance, have created new formal intermediary organizations. The growth of these various intermediaries is supportive of the argument I made earlier: that increased rates of mobility and changes in the nature of skill have opened the door to new labor market institutions.

CLASSIFYING INTERMEDIARIES

In thinking about the role of public intermediaries, it is worthwhile to distinguish among three alternative models or types of intermediaries. These are:

- Traditional "one-on-one" intermediaries that passively accept job orders from firms and match these orders with people who have registered with the intermediary. The Employment Service is the classic example of such an intermediary.
- Intermediaries who are more active and aggressive in their relations to both sides of the labor market. These "customized" programs recruit employers to their service, design efforts—recruitment, training, and placement—to be responsive to the needs of those employers, and also reach out and recruit a labor force to match these job requirements.
- The third category of intermediaries share many of the operating characteristics of the second in that they are active on both sides of the labor market. However, they also bargain with firms or deploy power in order to alter firm behavior. These intermediaries see themselves as not only providing a service but also changing the terms of trade in the labor market. I defer discussion of this category until the next chapter.

ONE-ON-ONE INTERMEDIARIES

Any serious effort to explore the role of intermediaries must begin with the largest intermediary in the nation, the U.S. Employment Service. The track record of this agency is at best mixed, but it is important to keep in mind that, whatever its failures, the Employment Service represents a substantial investment of resources in intermediary activities. There are currently roughly 1,800 ES offices around the country that place about 1.5 million people in jobs.[19] The annual ES budget is more than $1.5 billion.[20]

The Employment Service was founded during the New Deal to facilitate the movement of unemployed workers into public employment programs, and two years later it was linked to the new unemployment insurance program because it was given the responsibility to administer the UI work test— the requirement that unemployment insurance recipients be available for employment. Like unemployment insurance, the ES operates under a mixture of federal and state control with the states retaining considerable authority over both administration and policy.

There have been ongoing struggles both over the control of the Employment Service and over its mission. The general theme is efforts by reformers to wrest policy control from what they perceive as rigid and unresponsive state bureaucracies and efforts by defenders of the system to explain away its failure by arguing that the ES has been given too many conflicting roles to play and too few resources. At the root of these conflicts is the widespread perception that the ES does not perform well.

Although there have been no random assignment evaluations of the ES, it appears acceptable on a cost/benefit basis because very little impact is necessary to offset its low expenditure per registrant (about eighty dollars).[21] Thus, for example, a recent study found that the ES reduced the duration of unemployment among those receiving UI payments by two weeks, a reduction adequate to justify the costs.[22] This type of finding is similar to those for job clubs that are fairly widely used in the employment and training system. They help people conduct their search more efficiently, cut a few weeks out of unemployment, and justify their costs. However, in the longer term it is impossible to distinguish between people who participated in job clubs from others with the same characteristics who did not.

The central fact is that the ES serves only the very bottom of the labor market and does not even do this very well. Only about 4 percent of all registrants who eventually find jobs do so via the ES.[23] Fully one-third of these jobs are temporary, lasting less than 150 days.[24] What success the ES has is in a very limited range of the labor market. In one data set from the mid-1980s the average male job placement was in a job that paid $10,700 per year, and the average female pay was $8,700.[25] As another researcher noted, "What is clear is that certain types of employers rely heavily on the ES. Those firms generally employ workers of few specialized skills, are willing to accept high turnover, and therefore pay low wages."[26]

It may be possible to improve on the ES in small ways via management reforms, and this is the line taken in a recent General Accounting Office study.[27] The fundamental issue, however, is why the system does not have more of an impact in the labor market. An important part of the answer is that, as noted above, until recently most good firms have not needed an intermediary except for a few specialized or very high level jobs. If there is a new opportunity for intermediary efforts, then the real question is whether the ES is appropriately structured to meet that need. Part of the answer is a bureaucratic one: the administration of the ES has traditionally been very conservative, very difficult to make responsive to national objectives and very reluctant to subject itself to any form of accountability. Part of the answer may also lie in the modernizing ideas currently afoot, for example, the Web-based version of the Employment Service called "America's Job Bank." However, it is also likely that passive one-on-one intermediary services are limited by their constricted ambitions. What, then, are the alternatives?

CUSTOMIZED INTERMEDIARIES

The Employment Service is passive. It takes job orders if firms call them in, and it works with the clients who walk in the door. Even if the ES takes the next step of contacting employers, the nature of the contact is inherently superficial. There is no sense in which the ES and the firm are partners, trying to accomplish something together. The next level of intermediary does, in fact, take this step and try to find ways to collaborate with employers. In doing so, these intermediaries stand a much better chance of accomplishing something on behalf of their clients. It is worth noting in passing that this kind of interaction is seen by the temporary help industry—the fastest growing intermediaries in the labor market—as its key marketing tool. When these temporary help agencies establish call centers for their clients or staff production lines, training their workers in firm-specific procedures, they are acting as customized intermediaries.

The public policy world offers a number of examples of intermediaries of this kind, and I shall briefly describe two. One of these, the Center for Employment and Training (CET), operates at the low end of the labor market. The other, community colleges, operates in higher reaches of the job queue. Together they illustrate both the possibilities and the limits of customized intermediaries.

CET is a job-training/intermediary program that was founded in California with close early links to the Farm Workers Movement.[28] Today there are more than twenty centers around the state, although the largest and best known is located in San Jose. The staff estimates that over the course of a year all the California centers serve around two thousand people. In recent years CET has been the subject of rigorous random assignment evaluations for its youth and welfare programs. It has done very well and hence has attracted considerable national attention as well as efforts to replicate it in other parts of the country.

CET, which costs roughly six thousand dollars per client, has several innovative program features. These include open entry/open exit training, a willingness to accept people with very weak backgrounds, remedial education that is done as part of job training and not as a separate feature, and a ten-day probationary period during which the staff and the clients get to know each other and learn if the program is appropriate. The program puts considerable public emphasis on the fact that it accepts people regardless of their educational background and hence does not cream, but this probationary period, which is not widely advertised, may help account for some of the strong results, since a nontrivial number of people leave before being officially enrolled.[29] The average enrollee is in the program for six months, and a list of placements suggested that the average wage upon graduation was in the $8.00–8.50/hour range.

A central aspect of the program, and why it is relevant to this discussion, is that the program staff work closely with firms not simply to develop job placements but also to determine which skills firms seek and where the industry is going. The job developers play a particularly active role in keeping the training program informed of what employers are looking for and how skills and technologies are changing. There are what appear to be active industry advisory boards for the different skill tracks, and industry staff visit the program with some regularity and sometimes help with the training. It is in this sense—that the program tries to understand what employers want and then designs a product that responds to these needs—that CET is more than just a passive intermediary between people seeking work and employers.

Although this is a strong program, there are limitations. When I conducted interviews with employers and wanted to discuss the CET program, I was invariably referred to the affirmative action or community affairs person in the organization. It was also made clear to me in interviews that the firms had strong alternative sources of labor recruitment for these jobs, notably temporary help firms, which could play a "temp to perm" role.

A second striking characteristic of the program, at least of the large operation in San Jose, is that despite its roots in the Farm Workers Movement it now lacks any community political base. The people who run the program do not think of themselves as a community organization in any sense but rather as a "stand alone" program. They are quite explicit in making this point when asked. The consequence of this, which I explore below, is that they lack any real power vis-à-vis employers.

Community colleges have emerged as the United States' premier training institution. In 1992, according to Norton Grubb, they accounted for 37.8 percent of all fall enrollments in postsecondary education and 45.2 percent of first-time freshmen enrollments. These are double the proportions of thirty years earlier.[30] These schools have become overwhelmingly vocational and frequently work with local employers. A description of the North Carolina system, written by Rosemary Batt and me, gives a good flavor:

> The North Carolina system . . . provides entry level training through associate degree and non-degree programs, further training for adults through continuing occupational education, and customized training to meet the needs of employers. The last category covers, among others, the New and Expand-

ing Industry Program for firms which are locating in the state and the Focused Industry Training Program that targets training to small, in-state firms to make them more competitive.[31]

In their most developed form community colleges respond to employer needs by designing degree and certificate programs that train for specific skills in demand. The evaluation evidence on community colleges is generally positive,[32] and it is clear that these institutions link employees with firms. It is true that there is considerable variation across community colleges in how broadly they see their mission and how aggressive and effective they are in making the match between firms and workers.[33] Indeed, many employment and training professionals are frequently frustrated by what they perceive as the rigidity of community colleges and their slowness to respond to labor market needs. Nonetheless, there are sufficient success stories to warrant highlighting these institutions as a generally successful approach to intermediary services.

Beyond Intermediaries: Building Networks

Creating effective intermediaries is an important first step. However, the ultimate objective of policy at the local level should be to create dense networks or pathways through the labor market so that there are multiple channels for mobility. The key to accomplishing this is to link training programs, intermediaries, employees, and firms together in a network that enables these actors to work together in an effective way. In the policy realm today there are basically two strategies toward building these networks.

One version is essentially an administrative reform strategy. Both the federal government, which finances many training programs, and state governments, which implement these programs and finance others, have come to believe that the key to better performance is to rationalize the employment and training system. This approach is fueled by reports that list the large number of government training programs, each with slightly different administrative rules.[34] In this view, both firms and individuals (both termed "customers" in the new restructuring-inspired jargon) are confused by the patchwork quilt of programs, and the solution is to bring everything together in a "one-stop shopping" career center. These one-stop centers would serve as a clearinghouse for both sides of the labor market and would be the gatekeepers for referrals to programs and to firms. Skill standards—which are government- and industry-developed blueprints for what incumbents in various occupations need to know and be able to do if they are to be designated a skilled such and such—play an important role in this vision because they provide a benchmark against which various training programs can be measured, and in principle they provide insurance to employers that if they hire someone with a given certification that person has achieved a designated level of competency. Related to this are performance benchmarks or "consumer reports" that enable both individuals and employers to judge the success of different training programs. Taken as a whole, then, this strategy seeks to rationalize the training and intermediary systems with various administrative reforms that are heavily driven by information (and information technology).

There is a fair amount of energy behind reforms along these lines. Legislation passed in 1998 consolidates a variety of federal training programs and provides incentives to create one-stop centers. The Clinton administration has established a national skills standards board that is attempting to induce industry groups to develop standards. A number of states have consolidated their employment and training system under one agency (or labor market board) and are trying to undertake the administrative steps necessary to build a more rational system.[35]

These efforts are certainly reasonable, and, in particular, attempts to build accountability into the employment and training system are to be applauded. At the same time, it should be recognized that most efforts along these lines are "content free" in the sense that they focus on improving the administrative structure of the system without paying very much attention to what the various components of the system actually do. The implicit assumption is that if the system is simplified, performance information generated, and a market for training programs created (with the invisible hand residing in the one-stop center) then the issue of content will work itself out. This may be true, but given the history of both training programs and most intermediaries, it is prudent to pay more attention to content.

The intuition behind this administrative reform strategy is that it is important to build networks that link the various actors in the local labor

market together. This intuition is shared by a different approach to local network building that is also attracting growing attention and that does have
a vision of content at its core. In this view the next step is to use training and
intermediary programs as the basis for building networks of firms, public
programs, and sometimes unions that work together to upgrade employers'
productive capacities and to provide mobility channels for the labor force.
This mixture of labor market policy, technical assistance, and cooperation
among firms in solving common problems goes under a number of different titles, the most current of which is sectoral employment programs.

The intellectual history of this idea, at least in the American context, can
best be traced to the idea of industrial districts popularized by Michael Piore
and Charles Sable in their book *The Second Industrial Divide*.[36] In these industrial districts, firms in a related industry function together in a mixture of
cooperation and competition that seems to produce innovation and growth
as well as a form of employment security if channels are created that enable
employees to move among firms as demand in any given employer ebbs and
flows. The challenge, then, is to create these districts and their associated labor
market institutions in this country. The building blocks are basically three
ideas: training programs, labor market intermediaries, and manufacturing
extension services. The last are a set of programs, modeled on the old idea
of the agricultural extension service, some of which are funded by the federal government under the auspices of the National Institutes of Standards
and Technology (NIST) and some of which are funded by states. Experts,
often industrial engineers or retired executives, help firms—usually small
and medium-sized ones—solve technical problems such as those involved
in plant layout, inventory systems, implementation of quality programs, or
installation of new technology. In the course of this the best of the extension services also help the employers upgrade their human resource systems.

A fully developed effort would bring together employers to discuss common technical, marketing, and employment problems and to find resources
to solve them, would engage these employers in designing common training programs for their labor force, and would create a mechanism to enable
people to move easily from one firm to another. In this way a network of
institutions would be created to structure the local labor market.

The individual pieces of these programs are far more common throughout the country than might be realized and have been created under a vari-

ety of different auspices. In some instances these networks are business-driven, a good example of which is the efforts of the National Tooling and Machining Association. In western Massachusetts and in seven other communities around the country, the NTMA has organized small machine shops into a network that trains young entrants, provides further training for incumbent employees, shares information on technical issues, and acts as an informal clearinghouse for job seekers. The western Massachusetts model, called the Western Massachusetts Precision Institute, trains about one hundred new machinists and two hundred incumbent employees a year in addition to performing the other "networking" tasks listed above.

Similar networks have been created under union auspices. An example is the Garment Industry Development Corporation (GIDC) in New York, which is affiliated with the apparel union, the Union of Needletrade, Industrial, and Textile Employees (UNITE). The GIDC is a well-established operation that runs on-site training for operators throughout New York City's large garment industry, provides training for employees dislocated from the industry, runs a marketing and technical assistance service for managers, and has established a job referral system called JOBNET.

Finally, networks can be created directly by public authorities. In 1994, according to one estimate, twenty-seven states supported 140 networks.[37] In addition, through the federal NIST program, an agency of the Department of Commerce, roughly one hundred manufacturing extension service centers have been created. These efforts are heterogeneous, and a good many are purely engineering-driven with few labor market components. Others, however, are broad ranging and share, for example, many of the characteristics of GIDC described previously. These programs are also politically popular, as witnessed by the ability of NIST to maintain the program in the face of congressional attacks after the 1994 midterm elections, and this suggests that they are serving their constituency.

One well-developed example of how networks can operate is the Wisconsin Regional Training Partnership. Annette Bernhardt and Thomas Bailey have provided a succinct description of this effort, which is reproduced in the accompanying box and which is based on material provided by the Center on Wisconsin Strategy, the organization behind the program.

This effort clearly aims to build a set of linked institutions that structure the local labor market and is striking for its scope and apparent success. There

THE WISCONSIN REGIONAL TRAINING PARTNERSHIP

The partnership consists of a consortium formed by manufacturers, unions, and public sector partners in the Milwaukee metropolitan area.[38] The goal of the partnership is to support the creation of high-performance workplaces and quality jobs in the region. About forty employers from the metalworking, electronics, plastics, and related industries currently participate, a significant share of the regional market. They employ roughly forty thousand workers, who are represented by industrial and craft unions. At the core of the partnership are a series of channels for active communication and planning between employers and unions, for example, working groups focused on plant modernization, and peer adviser networks to share best practices. Most of the employers either have or will have an on-site training center that provides continuous training and skill upgrading. A key component is the development of industry-specific skill standards, by employers, unions, and technical colleges in the region. Such standards have been successfully implemented at the entry level, and certificates to improve skill portability across firms are planned. In addition, the partnership has embarked on two major initiatives to systematize access to entry-level jobs (a youth apprenticeship program and a training program for inner-city residents).

is, however, some reason to be cautious. First, and most prosaically, most of what we know about this network, and others like it, is based on accounts provided by the people responsible for creating the program. Until outsiders have had a chance to assess the programs and their impact, and to do so over a period of time that includes downturns as well as the current very strong labor market in which it functions, we will not really know enough.

Second, as is true in many innovative labor market programs, scale and coverage are serious concerns. Even the most successful networks enroll only a small fraction of the firms in their area and reach only a very modest fraction of workers. In addition, although there are exceptions, network building seems most successful and prevalent in the metalworking, and even more specifically the machine shop, industry. This is an industry that seems to suffer from recurrent booms and busts and that, perhaps because of these, is frequently in crisis regarding its labor supply and hence is often involved in an ongoing cycle of programs that never seem to solve the problem. In 1975, when I was researching youth employment in Massachusetts, I frequently heard these complaints, and in that year the industry started a program called "More Machinists for Massachusetts." It would be helpful to have more examples of success in other industries, particularly outside manufacturing.

These red flags aside, these networks represent a design that brings together many of the significant players in the labor market to improve the competitiveness of firms and to upgrade the skills and create channels of mobility for the employees. There is ample opportunity for public policy to encourage and underwrite these models via planning grants, participation by industrial extension services, active involvement by economic development authorities and community colleges, and program funds to support intermediaries and training.

SUMMARY

Helping people deal with the challenges of reduced job security and higher rates of job turnover is one of the central challenges of labor market policy. In some respects the solution is straightforward, albeit politically difficult to implement: improving the safety net of unemployment insurance and moving toward a system of portable benefits. However, more serious institution building is also needed. We need to create mechanisms that facilitate the movement of people through the labor market. This is why the chapter focused so heavily on intermediaries and on networks.

While institution building is important, nothing in the history of American labor market policy suggests that it will be easy. The public record in this area is spotty, to say the least. The Employment Service has performed poorly over the years, and the federally supported job-training system, aimed at low-income groups, has a distinctly mixed record. Added to the poor track record are the challenges of going to scale, that is, serving a labor market as large and as diverse as ours.

Why should we expect anything better from another round of efforts? One reason is that economic conditions have changed so that these efforts are actually necessary for a broad swath of the labor market. In the past, most employees spent their work lives in sheltered internal labor markets, and only people at the bottom of the job queue were in need of these institutions. It is sadly the case that programs directed at poor people receive less support than those aimed at people in better circumstances, and hence as the universe of need broadens, we might well expect more credible efforts.

The second reason why we may do better this time is that some lessons have been learned about program design. The most important is that interaction between employers and programs is crucial. This does not necessarily mean governance: there is no reason to think that employers are better at planning or running programs than are professionals in this area. Indeed, there may be conflicts between the narrow interests of employers and the broader public interest. These might arise with respect to training content (employers may push for overly firm-specific training) or wages. However, successful efforts around the country have tied the content of what they do to the actual needs of firms and have involved employers fully in the design of programs. By making these links it is possible to build institutions that, because they are useful to the private economy, have a good chance of being sustained and growing.

Redressing the Balance of Power

T HE PREVIOUS CHAPTER described how to build institutions to address the heightened mobility characteristic of the new labor market. This is important but is not enough. The second leg of policy should be to redress the substantial shift in power from employees to firms. Many of the symptoms that worry us, ranging from stagnating wages to the spread of nonstandard work, can be traced to this changing balance of power. Most Americans do not believe that the current situation is fair—witness the broad support for the United Parcel Service strike as well as polling evidence I shall provide shortly. Certainly the postwar system was premised on a much more balanced distribution of power, and while changing economic conditions make the specific arrangements less tenable, there is no reason to believe that we as a society should be willing to accept that the end result must be such a dramatic shift as we have witnessed.

The implications of discussions about the balance of power point toward ideas aimed at altering the behavior of the firm at the top level, that is, influencing the objectives of the corporation in ways that rebound to the benefit of employees. Such a set of policies would not transform the labor market per se but might well have powerful impacts on employee welfare. What might be the directions such a policy might take? I want to distinguish between two alternatives. The discussion of governance often seems to confuse the distinction between *altering the goals of the firm* and the creation of *countervailing power*. When the goals of the firm have shifted, one might imagine the board of directors debating a policy and considering some trade-off between profits and employee welfare. In the case of countervailing power, the outcome is more like a bargaining process: the board and its managers push for one solution, the employees or their representatives push for another, and the outcome is some compromise determined by power relationships. In this latter scenario countervailing power can be created at many levels and in many locations: at the board level but also at the workplace level, in the political process, and in communities.

In short then, this chapter takes up two alternatives, corporate governance and employee representation, which might in principle address power on a broader scale:

- Rethinking corporate governance implies changing the objectives of the firm beyond single-mindedly maximizing the wealth to stock owners.
- Building up countervailing power means accepting that the firm will seek to act only in the interest of stock owners but actual outcomes can be altered by deploying economic and political power in other directions.

Whether either approach can be effective is very much an open question, but any broad effort at labor market policy must seriously consider both alternatives.

Corporate Governance

Just as the farmers and small-town businesspeople during the Progressive Era felt themselves buffeted by forces far away and outside their control, many of the events that today most distress us seem to originate from considerations unrelated to work organization or labor markets. The merger between two banks leads to the closing of numerous branches and consequent layoffs. A chief executive under pressure from investors to improve stock market returns announces a reorganization that includes substantial downsizing. Other actions are more immediately rooted in the labor market but may reflect ranking of competing values with which many disagree. Outsourcing production to low-wage countries might be an example.

Each of these examples has its defenders, and those defenders may very well be right. Bank customers may be better off if their bank can capture economies of scale and hence operate more cheaply, passing on some of the savings as lower prices for bank services. Low stock prices may reflect wasteful managerial practices, and the managers, frightened of takeovers invited by lagging stock prices, are prodded into action. Consumers are better off when their jeans are cheaper, and the economy is better off in the long run when resources are reallocated to their best use. However, there may also be instances in which the critics are right: the bank merger might reflect empire building and the egoism of a chief executive out of control; what the stock market perceives as inefficient management might be a long-term strategy aimed at building up the firm's human resources; the cost savings from moving production abroad might be outweighed by the social cost (not considered by the firm) to the communities that are disrupted.

It is possible to remain agnostic about the merits of particular actions, including some actions that adversely affect employees, but still believe that those actions should be debated and defended in a broader framework than that which is currently applied. To raise these questions is to raise the issue of governance.

The central issue posed by governance discussions is "In whose interest does the firm act?" Sorting through the answer to this is in part normative: Should the firm act only in the interest of stockholders, or should it act on behalf of a coalition of interests that also include employees and perhaps suppliers and local communities? There is also an important positive dimension: whatever goal is set needs to be carried out, and some worry that under current arrangements managers are free to ignore the wishes of their principals because there is little effective oversight or constraints on their actions.

The last several years have witnessed growing academic and political interest in these questions. What might be termed the "pro-employee voice" perspective on governance is motivated by takeovers and downsizing that seem driven by quick stock market gains regardless of the cost to employees or communities. Actions of this sort are contrasted with what would presumably result if the firm has broader objectives than only enriching those who own its stock.

Before taking up these issues, it is important to understand that most current interest in governance proceeds from a quite different angle. The debate is being driven by those who believe that stockholder interests are *insufficiently* valued by firms. The concern is that managers have not been restrained by effective oversight and hence have followed poor policies for too long (with General Motors serving as the cautionary example) or engaged in self-serving empire-building and perk-expanding activities. A variety of solutions have been offered, but they all start from the proposition that the ultimate goal of the firm is and should be to maximize the wealth of people who own its stock. Employee interests are considered only to the extent that they benefit when stockholders do well.

It seems clear that the pro-stockholder perspective is currently triumphant. In the academic literature the implicit assumption, deriving from microeconomics, has always been that economic efficiency is maximized when firms maximize profits and that, since the owners of these profits are the owners of shares, firms should in this view maximize the wealth of their stockholders. This view has been given greater credibility and a more sophisticated defense by the emergence of the so-called finance view of the firm. From this perspective the firm is nothing more than a "nexus of contracts" or a collection of financial assets. The problem is how to maximize the return on these assets, and this requires a market for corporate control that permits the buying and selling of these assets and hence applies the discipline of market forces to those who manage them. This discipline is effective because if the assets are mismanaged the stock price will fall, inviting takeover by those who will do a better management job and hence raise the stock price.

In the 1980s this finance view rationalized the surge in takeovers supported in part by financial innovations such as junk bonds. In his presidential address to the American Finance Association, Michael Jensen argued that we are living through a new industrial revolution caused by vast technological and organizational changes. These, along with globalization, have created excess capacity in many mature industries, and this in turn requires cutbacks in many firms in order to free up capital for more productive uses. He goes on to comment, "While the corporate control activity of the 1980s has been widely criticized as counterproductive to American industry, few have recognized that many of these transactions were necessary to accomplish exit over the objections of current managers and other constituencies of the firm such as employees and communities."[1]

Incumbent managers may have erected some defenses, but the trend remains in the direction of greater attention to the financial health of stock owners. Although hostile takeovers may be more difficult, mergers and acquisitions have increased to record levels after a period of decline in the late 1980s and early 1990s. Institutional investors, such as pension funds and mutual funds, have become increasingly active in prodding firms to take actions to raise the stock price.[2] Boards of directors are under pressure to become more assertive in monitoring the actions of managers. The dominant rhetoric of executives is shareholder value. When Kodak recently announced that it was increasing its planned layoffs from ten thousand to sixteen thousand people, a spokesperson explained the change by referring to Wall Street dissatisfaction with the previously announced lower number and commenting, "You cannot ignore important constituencies like shareholders."[3]

The finance view stands in contrast with the traditional conception of the American firm in which the wide dispersion of ownership gave professional managers a great deal of leeway in how they ran their business. Although these managers, and their defenders, never overtly questioned the assumption that ultimately they were managing in the interest of stockholders, in fact there is some reason to doubt that this was the case. While from the perspective of finance theorists the managers may have engaged in empire-building or even more wasteful activities (and they probably did buy too many corporate jets and hire too many friends), these managers also had an implicit stakeholder view of the firm and hence made decisions (increasing wages when profits were high, being reluctant to lay off except under duress) that were sometimes shaded toward the interests of employees and away from the immediate interests of stockholders (recall the language about "family" found in *In Search of Excellence*). The managerial firm may not be dead, but it is under intense pressure, and hence the debate over the legitimate objectives of the firm has been more directly engaged.

The "Employee-Friendly" View of Governance

Scholars and activists who view shifts in governance arrangements as a central strategy for improving outcomes experienced by employees make several different points, some of which are more threatening to the traditional conception of the role of the firm than others. The least threatening arguments focus on the particular institutional framework within which governance is conducted. One version accepts the centrality of stockholders but argues that the institutional setup of financial markets leads to an excessive focus on short-term stock gains rather than maximizing value in the long run. The emphasis on the short term makes it difficult for the firm to undertake investments, such as those in people, that have long time horizons. A second line of thought is that owners, or their agents, are too distant from the operations of the firm to value hard-to-observe investments, such as those in people, appropriately. As a result, investments of this sort tend to be undervalued by the stock market and hence by managers. Neither of these points fundamentally challenges the primacy of the stockholder, but rather both claim that their interests are being poorly served by the current system and that improvements would also make employees better off. A deeper challenge takes on the core belief that the only legitimate objective of the firm is to maximize stakeholder value.

The critique of short-term behavior begins with the observation that the fraction of stock held by institutions (notably pension funds and mutual funds) grew from 16 percent in 1965 to 46 percent in 1990. Among the one thousand publicly traded companies with the largest market value, institutions held 57 percent of the shares in 1994.[4] The managers of these institutional portfolios hold any given stock for a much shorter period than before (the average holding period of a stock has declined from seven years in 1960 to under two years),[5] and these managers are evaluated on the basis of the quarterly performance of their portfolios. As a result firms find themselves under pressure to boost short-term earnings (in order to maintain high stock prices), and this in turn leads to actions that undermine the long-run health of the firm and the well-being of employees. Surveys of chief executive officers and of portfolio managers show that both sides of the equation share the view that short-term performance is overvalued by the institutional setup of the market.[6]

These arguments are politically attractive because they provide the rationale for blaming Wall Street for irrational and destructive decisions by managers. The difficulty, however, is that neither logic nor evidence seems to support the argument. Logic fails because stock prices, even quarterly stock prices, reflect the best evidence available on the long- as well as the short-term prospects of a firm. If there were some publicly available piece of evidence about long-run prospects that remain unexploited, a knowledgeable investor could profit handsomely by buying that stock and holding it. No such opportunity is likely to remain unexploited in modern financial markets. Hence this information will be reflected in current stock prices, and as long as this is true, the fact that a portfolio manager aims to maximize returns every three months should not lead to any undervaluing of long-run investments. Some evidence on this point is provided by several studies showing that announcements that a given firm will increase its spending on research and development (hence depressing current earnings but increasing future ones) do not lower stock prices.[7]

A related, but more promising, critique is that the finance system in the United States is biased against certain kinds of long-term investments, in particular ones that are hard to measure and "touch." The argument here is that American investors have historically been distant from managers, buying and holding stock but having little direct contact or involvement in the managing of the firm. This arrangement follows from the small fraction of any given firm's stock held by even the largest institutional investor (for example, in 1990 the California Pension System owned stock in two thousand different firms, and its largest holding in any one firm was 0.71 percent)[8] and from laws and regulations that discourage investor cooperation. These patterns in turn emerged, as Mark Roe has documented, from a long-standing American distrust of concentrated financial power.[9] The consequence is that investors only have access to publicly available information and that their natural mistrust of management will lead them to trust only actions by the firms that they can observe and measure. These points are illustrated by a CEO who commented: "When I brief Wall Street analysts on our current earnings, sales projections, downsizing program, and capital spending plans they busily punch all these numbers right into their laptops as I speak. When I start telling them about our plans to invest in training and reform the workplace, they sit back in their chairs and their eyes glaze over."[10] These analysts may even be sympathetic to investments in human resources, but the problem they have is that these investments are hard to measure. Hence there is a bias in the system and a natural tendency to regard such activities with suspicion.

These arguments imply a positive assessment of the growing activism of institutional investors, who are paying more attention to the management of the companies in which they invest. This might herald the kind of "relationship investing" that could strengthen the hand of firms that want to invest in people. However, even here the evidence is weak. Michael Useem documents that a growing number of institutional investors are active in a range of activities, including proxy fights, resolutions proposed to boards of directors, and attempts to establish the kind of ongoing interactive relationship with managers that advocates of relationship investing support.[11] Nonetheless, most observers agree that real involvement by investors in day-to-day decisions or even large strategic ones remains uncommon. There are a variety of reasons for the reluctance of institutional investors to be involved, including their lack of expertise, their fear of becoming entangled in political struggles, and the fact that their small stake in any given firm limits their incentives to be engaged and raises fears that others will free ride on whatever contributions they make.

The bulk of investor activism seems focused on tracking stock prices and pressuring boards of directors via resolutions and efforts to assure that antitakeover tactics are kept to the minimum. Investors do not seem to develop the kind of in-depth knowledge that might lead them to support human resource investments that are shunned by more conventional analysts. Furthermore, employees benefit only if current efforts to maximize returns to stockholders are somehow less favorable to workers than the strategies supported by "more involved" investors, and there is no reason in theory or actual experience to believe that investors with a "relationship" would adhere to any goals other than maximizing long-run returns to stockholders. There is, for example, no evidence that Warren Buffett—the quintessential relationship investor—has any interest in or sympathy for actions that benefit employees at the expense of stockowners. Only if there were large unexploited profits to be had by adopting a different tack toward workers would this argument make sense, and while the literature does point to productivity gains from high-performance work organizations, it is very possible, as chapter 4 demonstrated, to obtain these gains without sharing them with the workforce.

What the foregoing suggests is that from the viewpoint of employees the core governance issue is efforts to rethink the fundamental assumption that the only legitimate objective of the firm is to maximize the wealth of those who own the stock. To raise this issue is to raise the governance issue most directly: In whose interests should the firm operate? Are the stockholders dominant, or does a stakeholder perspective make more sense?

Both Japan and Germany, whose economies have been successful over the course of the postwar period, take a broader view of the purposes of the firm than does the United States. In these countries the firm is seen as a public institution operating to maximize the combined welfare of stockholders and employees. Other constituents, notably suppliers, are also given weight, particularly in Japan. The consequence is that firms are willing to trade off some level of economic gain for stockholders in return for benefits to employees. This process was well described by Ronald Dore in his analysis of how Japanese firms seek to avoid layoffs, even in times of severe down-turns.[12] Despite the current economic crisis in Japan, the vast majority of firms continue to adhere to this policy.

To American eyes, or at least to the eyes of most American economists, the stakeholder view is an invitation to economic inefficiency. Profits, distributed to stockholders, are essential signals to achieve efficient allocation of capital. A stakeholder firm will be of the wrong size: if conditions indicate that it should grow (owing to increasing demand or technological dynamism), it will not attract enough capital because some of the returns are diverted to others. If the firm should shrink because it is in a declining sector or because of excess capacity for its product, internal capital will be retained for too long in order to appease the various constituencies. More generally, by contaminating relative price signals, in this case the returns to capital, the economy as a whole will be less productive than it otherwise could be. It would be better, in this view, to follow the rules of economic efficiency and then use the gains to remedy whatever negative outcomes the political process identifies.

One reply to this argument is to point to the past economic success of Germany and Japan. If the stakeholder system was so poor, how is it that these nations' economies did so well? As a matter of pure logic this point is not definitive, since it is always possible that Germany's and Japan's economies would have performed even more impressively under the U.S. system of governance. Nor has weak recent economic performance in both nations helped the shareholder case, particularly since one area in which the U.S. economy seems clearly superior is the allocation of capital to start-up ventures. The greater innovative capacity of the U.S. economy can be interpreted as evidence that our capital allocation process and therefore our system for assigning property (ownership) rights are superior. For example, it is possible that the venture capital business, which has been so central to the development of the information technology industry, would have been less vigorous in an environment in which returns to investment could not be fully captured.

An additional embarrassment is that firms in those nations, particularly in Germany, seem to be taking a quite different tack as they lay off large numbers of workers and move production offshore. Indeed, the business press is full of praise for German executives who have adopted the "American" model. As the *Wall Street Journal* pointed out in commenting on large layoffs at Daimler-Benz, "The emphasis is now on shareholder value, a concept only now being introduced into Germany by a new generation of young executives."[13] What this suggests is that in the past German firms were constrained by public policy and union power to behave in a more employee-friendly way and that as soon as the constraints were lifted they have begun to adopt a quite different approach.

In an effort to ground the stakeholder view more firmly, Margaret Blair and Mark Roe have made related arguments.[14] Blair points out that modern economic theory assigns ownership rights to shareholders on the grounds that they bear the residual risk of the enterprise. That is, employees and suppliers are paid according to a contract, whereas the owners receive a return on their investment only if something is left over. Because they bear this residual risk, they should have control, says the shareholder model. However, Blair and Roe both argue that in reality employees bear a residual risk because they have made specific investments in the firm, largely through learning skills that only pay off over time and to a large extent at a particular employer. For that matter, some suppliers have made similar firm-specific investments with a long payoff horizon. Hence in an important sense employees (and suppliers) are also bearers of residual risk. Furthermore, economic efficiency clearly requires that investments of this sort be encouraged. The conclusion of this line of thinking is that even if we ignore distributional concerns there remain efficiency reasons why employees (and suppliers) are legitimate stakeholders who should have a voice in governance decisions.

In the normal course of events one would expect that shareholders would be sensitive to these considerations because they, too, want to encourage employee and supplier investments in their firm. With this in mind, the firm would enter into explicit or implicit contracts to protect the investments of workers and suppliers, and reputational considerations (if these contracts are broken, the firm will not be able to attract workers or suppliers in the future) would be an effective enforcement mechanism. The problem, however, is that in an epoch of economic turbulence there may come a point when a firm finds it worthwhile to break these commitments whereas the stakeholders would oppose such an action. In fact, one interpretation of takeovers is that they provide rationale for such a "breech of trust" via the actions of new owners who bear none of the prior commitments of the old regime.[15]

Neither Blair nor Roe addresses the impact of stockholder governance on capital allocation. In a world of rapid, and international, capital flows, one might fear that investments would be distorted by the introduction of new claimants. However, it is not clear how seriously to take this concern. First, similar arguments can be made against any form of labor market intervention, for example, health and safety standards, yet not many people would be moved by such an argument. In addition, the capital allocation argument can be read as pointing to the conclusion that *all* firms should adopt stakeholder governance so that relative rates of return across firms are unchanged and hence capital flows unaffected.

As a preliminary to the discussion of the policy implications of these arguments, I want to take a slight detour and consider "corporate responsibility," a phrase that had considerable currency during the wave of layoffs in the mid-1990s. Imagine a firm whose leadership had "good values" with respect to its workforce. How would such a firm behave when faced with substantial economic pressure? Answering this question enables us to place some bounds on what we might expect from different approaches to the governance problem.

"Responsible" Corporations in Today's Labor Market

The rhetoric of corporate responsibility, as well as the strand of the governance literature that focuses on ownership structure and the values of the firm, both imply that many of the problems addressed in this book could be resolved were firms to behave differently, more "responsibly." It is hard to know with any certainty how true this is because there is no obvious way of testing the argument. The experience of the recent past does not lead to any special optimism that professions of values and commitment, no matter how sincere, can have any long-lasting impact when confronted with the stresses of the market. The behavior of a firm such as Malden Mills— whose CEO, Aaron Feuerstein, chose to maintain employment in the face of substantial financial costs—is exceptional. For example, both IBM and Digital Equipment Corporation shared long-standing explicit commitments to employment security, had very progressive (nonunion) human resource policies, and consciously positioned their wage structure above market levels. Yet, when faced with a crisis, both firms laid off tens of thousands of employees and radically transformed their internal management of people. I make no judgment here about whether these actions were necessary or unnecessary, and it is also worth noting that these changes did not happen quickly or easily and required a changing of the guard among top personnel. However, the central point is the impermanence of corporate values in the face of economic pressure.

It is, however, worth exploring a little more deeply just how much might be expected from firms that appear to be committed to the "high road." Were corporate America more thickly populated with such enterprises, would we still be worried about the themes developed in the earlier chapters? Three American firms that are widely regarded as exemplars of good corporate citizenship are Levi Strauss, Xerox, and Corning. Xerox has long been regarded as a leader among American firms in its commitment to diversity and equal employment opportunity. Furthermore, Xerox negotiated a widely admired contract with its union at its Webster, New York, plant, which established far-reaching employee involvement. Corning has been a family-controlled firm that also pioneered in implementation of high-performance work organizations negotiated in a very cooperative way with its union (it has both union and nonunion plants). Both Xerox and Corning have over the years shown considerable concern for the economic welfare of the communities in which they are located. Finally, Levi Strauss, controlled by the Haas family, has been a pioneer in a variety of employee benefits and health and safety issues in what is traditionally a low-wage and very exploitative industry. In addition, the firm has also been a leader in operating according to its values (e.g., avoiding child labor) in the overseas locations where it produces. It also signed an innovative contract with its union (about half of its American plants are unionized) and has worked hard to keep production in the United States despite considerable pressures to move totally overseas.

It would be hard to identify other large American firms that have a better long-term track record than these three of integrating positive values toward their employees into their production processes and investment decisions. It is therefore very interesting to know what happens when these firms find themselves under strong economic pressure.

Xerox. In December 1993, Xerox was profitable and had just rebounded strongly from a loss the previous year. Nonetheless, the firm announced layoffs of ten thousand employees, the first layoffs ever to occur during a profitable period at the corporation. These layoffs represented the third restructuring in three years. An earlier reorganization cut twenty-five hundred jobs. The layoffs combined white-collar involuntary departures, blue-collar "voluntary reductions in force," and incentive packages for service technicians to leave and become independent contractors.

When asked about the layoffs' impact on employees, Xerox president Paul Allaire conceded that they would disturb employee morale, but he predicted it would be a short-term disruption. "Clearly when you go through downsizing it has an impact on people's attitude toward the company. Nobody likes doing this. But the end result will be a stronger Xerox and a better place for people to work."[16]

These developments included the showplace high-performance/mutual gains program in Webster, New York. In June 1994, union workers at the Webster plant accepted base wage cuts from fifteen to ten dollars an hour, a two-tier wage structure for newly hired workers, and changes in work rules in exchange for job security through 2001. The company representatives had communicated that Xerox would take a strike, close the plant, and move jobs to Mexico if concessions were not made.[17] This plant is the home of the Wiring Harness Department and the widely reported work reorganization that has long served as a business school case of "mutual gains" bargaining.

Xerox also announced to the union that it was immediately laying off the four hundred workers not covered by the existing contract's "core" workforce's job security provisions. New hires in the better-paying job classes would start at 50 percent of the top pay rate and work their way up to wage parity over a five-year period. Xerox also won the right to hire part-time workers for periods up to a year as long as they make up no more than 15 percent of the total workforce.

One reason why the issues addressed in this book are so serious is that there is little reason to be reassured that restructuring is a one-shot event after which more secure times will return. Xerox illustrates this point. In April 1998 the company announced yet another round of layoffs (nine thousand jobs), again in the midst of a strong year. A financial analyst characterized the layoffs as "an heroic thing," while another noted, "There's a real paradigm shift here, from an engineering-driven company to one that really knows how to rip out infrastructure to get costs down."[18] In contrast one Rochester, New York, resident commented, "There is a kind of bewilderment around here; everyone is asking, 'If things are going well, why do they need to do this?'"[19] Another analyst, noting that Xerox already dominates its field and has no weaknesses, commented, "It's a watershed announcement for American industry. This is one of the first companies to embrace what I think is a new trend, of the best-in-class companies taking restructuring to distance themselves from any competitor."[20]

Corning. Like Xerox, Corning, after a long period of cooperation and high-road practices, has made what appears to be a radical shift in strategy. It sold its kitchenware products and plants, the very plants that much of the reengineering efforts and cooperative quality programs were designed to save. To its credit, the terms of sale included continued recognition of the union and no layoffs, but the sale nonetheless signaled a failure of and a retreat from efforts to save these jobs within Corning. Even more strikingly, Corning announced recently that it would open a new fiber optics plant in North Carolina and that when the plant was opened it would not recognize the union. In other words, despite Corning's rhetoric about the benefits of labor-management cooperation, it is not willing to "walk the talk" in its new plant.

Levi Strauss. In the past several years Levis has engaged in a series of quite radical restructuring actions, plant closings, and layoffs. In 1996–97 all managerial employees were required to reapply for their jobs, and in February 1997 Levis announced a 20 percent reduction in its white-collar labor force. However, the most dramatic action was a November 1997 announcement that Levis would close eleven factories with a loss of one-third of its domestic manufacturing jobs. Although the firm continued to be highly profitable, it has been losing market share to private label brands that produced jeans of comparable quality more cheaply than does Levis. These layoffs were explained as production cutbacks, not as an effort to ship production offshore.[21]

This radical downsizing plan contained a series of elements aimed at ameliorating some of the losses experienced by employees and their communities. The firm announced that it will spend $31,000 each on severance for lowest-paid workers and $25,000 on highest paid. The benefits include eighteen months of health insurance, eight months' pay without obligation to show up at work, three weeks of pay for each year worked, and $6,000 education/moving/job-training credit. The plan also included an $8 million grant to the communities affected. The union was remarkably restrained in its comments with Bruce Raynor, executive vice president of UNITE, saying that it was "by far the best severance settlement apparel workers have ever gotten, which will enable the affected workers to move forward with their lives."[22]

In February 1999 the other shoe dropped at Levis. The firm announced an additional layoff of 5,900 employees (again with generous benefits) and this time was explicit that it was planning to ship production overseas. The firm said that in the future it would largely be a marketing company.

What does all of this mean? These stories are not intended to denigrate the very real and distinctive value-driven actions by these firms. It is simply a fact that Xerox has been far better than most employers regarding equal employment opportunity and did enter into a pathbreaking agreement with employees at its Webster plant. It is a fact that when Corning sells a plant it requires the purchaser to protect the employees in ways that very few other sellers do. It is a fact that Levis offers a better benefits package than the rest of the industry, has better ethics regarding working conditions than do other employers in the industry, and, when it did shut down large numbers of plants, provided a level of assistance that most firms offer only to their senior executives. Nonetheless, it is also apparent that "good values" or "corporate responsibility" is not enough.

Despite the "corporate responsibility" of these firms, large numbers of employees face difficult labor market transitions. In this sense, the case for public policy is strengthened by these examples. And, of course, it goes without saying that most American firms do not share the values of these three.

It is also important to note two other distinctive aspects of these cases. At both Corning and Levis the "good values" of the firm were doubtlessly underwritten by the fact that these companies have a history of family ownership that helps shield them from stock market pressure. Perhaps more significantly, at all three firms there was a union in place that was able to bargain on behalf of the employees and reinforce the idea of "corporate responsibility." Hence, from these three cases one can reach two possible broad conclusions. The first is that even in the best of circumstances the need for public policy remains strong. Second, countervailing power remains an important consideration, again even in the best of circumstances.

Policy Regarding Governance

With the possibilities and limitations of "corporate responsibility" more clearly in mind, where do governance considerations leave us with respect to policy? To begin with, reforms directed at the stock market seem unlikely to be important in the labor market. First, as we have seen, critiques of short-term behavior have a weak theoretical and empirical foundation. Second, the problems confronting the labor market are far more extensive than disruptions caused by hostile takeovers. Consider that hostile takeovers declined sharply at the end of the 1980s because of the widespread adoption of poison pills and other defenses (including the passage by twenty-five states of laws permitting boards of directors to consider the needs of multiple constituencies). Despite this, rates of dislocation rose throughout the 1990s.

When it comes to changing the fundamental purpose of the firm, the implication of the shareholder argument is to initiate reforms that ensure that representatives of interests other than stockholders sit on the board of directors and have a voice in decisions. It is not clear, however, whether this approach will lead to any significant shifts in firm behavior. We have limited experience in this country with employee representatives on boards of directors, but what experience we do have is not particularly encouraging. A classic business school case is Eastern Airlines. As part of a deal regarding wage concessions, representatives of the airline's unions received four seats on the board of directors. Yet when it came to the decision to seek further concessions and to sell the airline to Frank Lorenzo, the employee board representatives were helpless.

Joseph Blasi and Douglas Kruse have moved beyond anecdotes and have carefully studied the diffusion and impact of employee ownership.[23] They find that employee stock ownership is considerably more widespread than might have been thought: 12.5 percent of the private sector workforce owns stock in firms in which employee ownership is at least 4 percent of the company's total market value.[24] Furthermore, the extent of employee ownership appears to have grown considerably in the past two decades. Blasi and Kruse focus much of their work on a group of one thousand publicly traded firms, representing 29 percent of the private sector market value in the economy, that have significant (4 percent or more) employee ownership. The median value of employee holdings in these firms was just over 10 percent. The employee ownership arises largely through pension plans and ESOPs.

Blase and Kruse carefully document the extent of employee ownership and the variety of ways it can arise, and they explore many of the economic and legal aspects of employee ownership. But for our purposes the important point is that there appears to be no evidence whatsoever that firms with substantial employee ownership behave any differently toward their employees than do other companies. According to Blasi and Kruse, only about 5 percent of their sample of one thousand firms treat employee ownership as anything other than a financial device. Blasi and Kruse note that "there is no evidence that employee ownership leads to participative management,"[25] nor is any evidence presented that firms with substantial employee ownership pay more equally distributed wages or provide higher levels of employment security.

COUNTERVAILING POWER

Neither trying to sell "corporate responsibility" nor taking the stronger remedy of reforming corporate governance seems a very promising path toward obtaining more satisfactory labor market outcomes. If we want to change how firms behave toward their employees, then it may be more promising to consider a strategy that builds countervailing power.

What does it mean to speak of countervailing power in the labor market? In a mechanical sense it means confronting decision makers in the firm with pressures that push them in a particular direction. Presumably they face other sets of pressures pointing toward a different outcome. The decisions that actually result represent some compromise between these competing pressures.

Implicit in this simple-minded, but still useful, rendering of decision making is the notion that many, if not all, economic decisions concerning the labor market can at least partially be viewed can resulting from the interaction of a complex set of considerations. Some of these are economic in the purely traditional sense. For example, if the wage rates of one category of labor rise relative to another, the firm will be inclined to substitute between the two groups. Other considerations, however, are more sociological or political. I have already discussed the role of norms in the old labor market, but these continue to be important today. In the 1980s there was considerable pressure on executives to imitate others in restructuring and downsizing. This came to be seen as the right thing to do, regardless of actual circumstances, and hence peer pressure arose in the management community pushing in this direction.[26] More broadly, in the organizational sociological literature there is a long tradition of seeing organizations as making decisions in response to a complex set of forces, internal and external, and not simply as a calculator responding unthinkingly to price signals from the market.[27]

The idea of countervailing power simply adds to the list of factors influencing decisions an organized group pushing in a particular direction. In some cases these pressures may seek to reduce the rate of profit in favor of a more equitable distribution of wages or more attention to employment security. However, the pressures need not always be oppositional or, in the language of negotiations, distributive. Pressure might be put on the firm to push it toward policies that enlarge the size of the pie available for sharing. In the narrow firm-as-calculator perspective, it is hard to understand why any pressure would be necessary to encourage an organization to be more efficient, since it should always be optimizing. However, once we adopt a more sophisticated view of organizational decision making, it is not hard to see that external pressures might, for example, enable decision makers to opt for actions that are in the long-run interest of both the firm and its employees in the face of internal organizational pressures for a less satisfactory outcome.

Implicit in this discussion is the assumption that organizations do indeed have some choices to make and that outcomes are not dictated by market forces. If any organization that deviated from some market-determined decision was always severely punished by capital markets competition, then there would be little scope for arguing for a broader view of decision making in labor markets. In fact, the capital market itself demonstrates that there is space for alternatives. First, most large firms draw a substantial amount of their investment capital from internally generated savings or profits, and most small firms have nothing at all to do with public capital markets. In both instances, even if public capital markets insisted on a single rate of return, the availability of alternative sources provides organizations with scope for choice. However, it is not even true that public capital markets push toward a single maximum rate of return. The evidence is that the typical premium in a takeover battle is about 40 percent over the current stock market value of the firm. Assuming, as do most financial economists, that current prices reflect the discounted future value of profits, this means that current management could in principle reduce the valuation of the firm by nearly 40 percent below current value before it would be a tempting target for the discipline imposed by raiders. Nothing proposed in this book implies anything near such a radical reduction in value.[28]

In thinking about the alternative that organizations have, it is important to understand that both sides of the argument can be true. On the one hand, firms are under more pressure than in the past, and this has to be recognized. There are legitimate limits to how far they can be pushed. On the other hand, in most circumstances there is still scope for choice. The market permits considerable long- and short-run variation across organizations in profit rates and in the share of the product that is divided between employees and stockholders. Just where in this permissible range the organization ends up remains at least in part a function of the political and social pressures it faces.

Once we accept the importance of countervailing power as a "policy response," it remains, of course, to ask what in practice this means and what forms it can take. I want to distinguish between countervailing power at the community level and countervailing power in the workplace.

Countervailing Power in the Community

Community organizations and community groups can organize in a variety of ways to shape the employment decisions of firms. One important trend in recent years has been the spread of Living Wage Campaigns. The typical form of such ordinances is to require firms that do business with the city to pay their employees a wage that is normally several dollars per hour in excess of the federal minimum. The idea is clearly to push up the wage structure, particularly for adults in steady jobs.

More than fifteen cities have enacted Living Wage laws, and it is on the agenda in many more. Evaluations of the impact of these efforts are scarce, but one of the first such ordinances, passed in Baltimore in 1994, has been the subject of two evaluations. Jared Bernstein recently summarized both studies and concluded that they showed that there was no evidence of job loss resulting from the ordinances, that prices did not rise because of the ordinances, and that the affected workers received a gain in wages.[29] On the more negative side, the number of employees who gained was small, on the order of two thousand or so.

It is, however, an error to think of these laws simply in terms of their direct impact on a small set of workers. Living Wage Campaigns have become an effective centerpiece of larger community organizing efforts around economic issues. Because of the commonsensical popularity of the idea of pushing up wages for the worst-paid workers (a popularity that is also reflected in the widespread support for the federal minimum wage), a Living Wage Campaign becomes an effective device for raising larger issues regarding economic structure and outcomes. It has helped build community organizations and in some cities has become linked to other campaigns, such as those aimed at linking tax breaks and abatements to job and wage commitments by employers.

Another example of efforts to build countervailing power at the community level is a training program in Texas, Project QUEST in San Antonio, which has ambitions and impacts far beyond those of typical training interventions. Project QUEST is a program that has enrolled roughly one thousand people since its inception in 1993.[30] Most accounts date the momentum for the development of Project QUEST from the January 1990 announcement of the closing of a Levi Strauss manufacturing plant. In response two community-based organizations began to organize around jobs and training. Both organizations are affiliates of Industrial Area Foundations (IAFs), a national network of community-based organizations. In the years prior to Project QUEST the Texas organizations had been quite successful in mobilizing their communities around issues ranging from local construction bonds to street safety to school reform. Thus the organizations had a strong and aggressive political base on which to draw.

An important part of the efforts of IAF leaders involved generating support for the training initiative from the San Antonio business community. They started by gaining the involvement of a few influential employers and then leveraged their commitment in larger meetings of business leaders. Ultimately a large number of employers expressed commitment, promising to provide information on their evolving staffing requirements, hire program graduates, cooperate in curriculum development, and offer financial or other support. Given the activist history of the IAF organizations in San Antonio, it is clear that the political and street-level power of these organizations played an important role in the willingness of the firms to play ball.

The design of the program itself was innovative,[31] but that is not the central point for the present purposes. It is important to note that, although the gains for individual clients are clearly significant,[32] Project QUEST thinks of itself in more ambitious terms than a traditional employment and training program. In a traditional program the nature of the external environment—the behavior of firms, the surrounding educational institutions, and the community itself—is taken as given, and the program simply seeks to place clients successfully in that environment. Project QUEST became an active actor in the San Antonio labor market and education system and effected institutional change. One example is that it bargained with employers to raise the wages of entry workers and to create job ladders attached to some entry jobs.[33] Its ability to do so was a reflection of its power in the market. Second, it pushed hard on the community colleges and led them to adopt innovative programmatic, curricular, and scheduling changes, all of which have subsequently been made available to all students, not just those from QUEST.[34] The fact that QUEST's effectiveness rests on community-based political power and that it seeks to interact with and alter its environment lies at the heart of what makes the lessons of this program important.

Countervailing Power in the Workplace

The construction of countervailing power in the community can accomplish a good deal, and there are other examples beyond those cited here. For example, some community groups have made good use of the leverage on firms gained by their efforts to obtain tax abatements and other forms of public subsidies. However, there are limits to what purely community-based power can achieve. First, although a variety of pressures can be placed on employers, it remains true that outsiders have a very imperfect knowledge of what goes on inside the organization with respect to production and careers. As a result, it is hard for any community-based organization to be effective in changing working conditions along a variety of dimensions. This is true with respect to purely distributive issues, such as raising wages or increasing security, but it is equally true for finding ways to improve the operation of the organization in a manner that rebounds to the benefit of both managers and employees. These outsiders simply lack the detailed knowledge needed to accomplish this.

The second limitation of community-based efforts is precisely that they are community-based. Many important decisions are made at high levels, for example, in the headquarters of a firm with locations throughout the country. It is difficult for community-based organizations to be effective in these circumstances, and, indeed, they may be weakened by the ability of firms to play one location off against another.

Finally, it is important to recognize that most community-based efforts are aimed at improving conditions in the lower range of the labor market. This is not a weakness; in fact, it is desperately needed given the widespread problems faced by employees in low-paying work. Nonetheless, the issues raised in this book also suggest that it is important to influence the behavior of firms throughout the entire labor market, and community groups have not historically been effective in this regard.

These considerations point to the importance of employer-based forms of countervailing power, and the obvious starting point is unions.

Thirty years ago any discussion about how to address the kinds of problems that concern us here would naturally have begun with unions. After all, the role of unions is to bargain with employers to protect job security, establish career lines, and ensure that employees shared in growing profits.

More generally, unions stand as a countervailing force to employer power. The surest way to modify the behavior of one party in the labor market (or any other market for that matter) is to confront it with another actor that has political and economic resources. In this sense strong unions are the alternative to the governance/corporate responsibility approach. Rather than trying to get firms to act differently by boring from within, unions try to alter behavior by bargaining from without.

In recent years unions have played this role with radically reduced effectiveness. The facts of union decline are well known, and the various explanations have been widely debated in both the academic and the popular literature and will not be rehearsed here. It must also be recognized that even in the best of circumstances unions are only a partial solution. Even the strongest of unions—consider the United Automobile Workers—have been unable to prevent radical downsizing and stagnating wages in their industries. Finally, the task facing unions is daunting. Despite the new energy unions devoted to organizing, the share of private-sector employees who were members of unions fell from 9.7 percent in 1997 to 9.5 percent in 1998. The net gain of members was a mere 57,000.[35]

So deep is the hole in which unions dwell that the first step in this discussion is to ask the simple question of whether unions, or at least unions in some shapes and forms, do indeed have a constructive role to play in addressing the problems that concern us here. In fact, it is not hard to show that the answer is yes.

To begin with, employees have a much broader interest in being represented than one might guess from current membership figures. Put differently, there exists what some researchers have termed a "representation gap." A survey conducted by Richard Freeman and Joel Rogers found a widespread interest among employees in having a greater say in how their work is organized. For example, 82 percent of nonunion workers thought employee involvement programs would be more effective "if employees, as a group, had more say in how these programs were run," and between 69 percent and 76 percent of nonunion workers would like to have committees that meet with management on a regular basis to discuss employment issues. Only 9 percent wanted management to select who served on such committees. In the survey there was also considerable concern that such efforts not lead to confrontations with management, and there was overwhelming support for a form of representation with which management cooperated. Finally, 32 percent of nonunion employees reported that they would vote today to establish a union (and 90 percent of currently organized employees would vote to keep their union).[36]

These results have been replicated in other research. For example, in 1996 Seymour Martin Lipset and Noah Meltz conducted a representative sample of American employees. Among nonunion workers they found that 47 percent said that they would vote tomorrow for a union were such an election held, 57 percent felt that unions on the whole were good, and only 37 percent felt that unions were not needed because workers were already being fairly treated.[37]

It is not surprising that many people want some form of representation because inherently unions can act in ways that are outside the scope of all other labor market institutions. Unions bargain with employers over wages, working conditions, and fairness issues, and in doing so they represent the views and choices of employees of a given enterprise or set of enterprises. Community organizations cannot typically play this role because their reach ends after their constituency is hired. Even very effective intermediaries, such as the IAF and Project QUEST, have difficulty maintaining contact with people after they are hired and have little role in subsequent working-life issues. Laws and regulations are an alternative approach to dealing with wages, working conditions, and fairness, but these are limited and blunt instruments. First, they typically set minimum standards, for example, the minimum wage, but are of much less use when it comes to dividing the economic pie above this minimum. In addition, in an imperfect world people have to make choices and trade-offs among objectives. Unions are a political institution within which employees can debate and make these choices. Laws and regulations provide no such options.

Although most of the material in this book has been aimed at understanding events in the core of the economy, it is nonetheless important to recognize that improving the quality of low-skilled service jobs is a key element in any attack on inequality. Unions can play a big role in this regard. A direct way to see this is to compare jobs before and after unionization. For example, in nonunion nursing homes nurses' aides deliver 90 percent of the hands-on care to frail, elderly, and disoriented residents.[38] These workers earn an average wage of only $6.06 an hour, although they are required to be certified and have seventy-five hours of training in most states.[39] House-keepers and dietary workers earn even less.

About 12 percent of all nursing homes are unionized, in both public and private sectors. In these facilities, conditions are quite different. Wages are higher, beginning at $8.00 an hour, and increase with experience. Most workers have health insurance and other benefits, such as paid holidays, vacation, and a reliable schedule with guaranteed hours. Some have tuition reimbursement, so they can continue their education in nursing and upgrade their skills to licensed practical nurse, a job that usually pays $12 to $14 an hour. Equally important, workers with a union have negotiated for such improvements as adequate supplies, more staff (and replacements when people are ill or absent), and even better food for residents. Injuries are fewer because unions negotiate for more training and for lifting equipment that is kept in working order.

Extending Employee Representation

Given the case for unions, why are they doing so poorly? One way of thinking about the problems unions face is to review the difficulties posed for them by the new labor market. The postwar success of unions was based on their ability to organize in the industrial core of the economy, yet conditions have changed in significant ways. A partial list would include:

- Employees outside the blue-collar/manufacturing world have a different view of what they want from work and what makes for success. They are individualistic, believing less in the importance of collective action and more in the value of their own skills and resources. From this perspective unions as traditionally understood (at least as understood by these employees) are less attractive.
- Higher rates of mobility between enterprises undermine the basic premise of most unions in America: that they can organize a stable set of employees whose careers are centered around one employer. Outside of the construction crafts, unions have few organizational forms designed to accommodate a mobile workforce.
- High-performance work organizations, and other workplace changes, build a sense of identity between employees and the firm. This poses a vari-

ety of problems for unions. First, it undermines the sense of "we and them" that lies at the heart of adversarial bargaining and the rationale for unions. Second, it blurs the distinction between employees and managers and in doing so creates problems for defining bargaining units and managing job ladders.

- The foregoing describes how shifts in the core of the economy have undermined unions. It is also the case that outside the core, in the low-wage service sector, unions face considerable difficulties. With a few exceptions, such as the Service Employees International Union, collective bargaining did not fare well in this sector even in the heyday of unions. Firms in this sector are small, and therefore to organize any substantial share of the market tremendous effort is required. The labor force has high turnover, and hence it is difficult to build commitments to an organization. The supply of workers willing to take positions for low wages is large and, given immigration trends, growing. All of this has made it hard for unions to make much progress in these jobs.

These shifting circumstances have led to an extensive discussion among those sympathetic to unions about what forms a revived union movement might take. More important, there are numerous experiments with new organizational models (and new organizing models), and these experiments both demonstrate the continued vitality of the union movement and provide a way of testing new ideas and learning. There is a growing academic literature that tries to learn from these efforts, and I shall not recapitulate that literature in any detail.[40] It is, however, worth highlighting some of the core ideas.

As a preliminary to this discussion, note that many observers now draw inspiration from a very old union idea, craft unions. In contrast to the larger industrial unions that dominated the postwar landscape, craft unions are based on occupational identity and do not rest on the tie between the worker and any particular employer. Hence the idea of mobility is presumed, and craft unions have historically also provided training and portable benefits to their members. This is what makes this model attractive in a newly mobile labor market. The drawbacks of the traditional craft union model are twofold: first, because of its occupational basis, it tended to put much effort into jurisdictional disputes about which craft/occupation was entitled to which work. The popular image of the carpenter refusing to plug in the power cord until the electrician arrives comes from this dynamic. Second, there has been a tradition of exclusivity: craft unions gained power by limiting membership and hence limiting the size of the labor force competing for jobs. The question is whether the fundamental craft ideas can be adapted without the these two less attractive characteristics.

When thinking about new strategies, it is important to remember that there is unlikely to be any single union model that makes sense in all circumstances. As the labor market has fragmented, the nature of organization in different sectors will have to vary. To help make sense of this, I distinguish among three types of employment: contingent workers, low-wage/low-skill service workers, and employees and firms within the older bastion of union power.

A variety of efforts are under way to organize contingent employees into craftlike organizations, for example, Working Today in New York City. The idea is provide a range of services in return for some degree of organizational commitment and the eventual capacity to negotiate with employers. As was described in the previous chapter, Working Today has based its strategy around providing benefits and other forms of assistance to contingent workers. Another example is the Bergen City Temporary Workers Campaign. This began with a guide identifying the temporary employers in the area who provided the best wages, benefits, and training to their workers. The guide was circulated among job developers, career counselors and social workers, and education and training systems. Some temp agencies realized that the guide was a tool for differentiating their firms in the marketplace for highly skilled temps as better employers. As a result the guide has increased the number of temporary firms willing to open up their practices to public scrutiny. The project is currently in the process of forming a Temporary Worker Association to organize temporary workers across firms. The hope is that the association would work with a Temporary Employer Association to provide legal aid and advocacy and direct representation, investigate complaints, hold public hearings on best practices, and establish minimum standards for multiemployer agreements. Another approach is to establish a temporary help agency that pays above-average wages and benefits, which competes by offering higher-quality service by more committed workers, and which therefore puts pressure on the rest of the industry. This is a strategy that is being followed with some success by the IAF organization, BUILD, in Baltimore.

With respect to the second group I distinguished above, low-wage workers, there have been a wide range of successful efforts to organize low-skill service employees. The problem is, once again, how to gain the allegiance of a geographically dispersed high-turnover group. The paradigmatic example of this style of organizing is the Justice for Janitors campaign.[41] In this effort organizers merged the organizational principles of craft unions—geographic coverage and portable benefits and rights—with the energy and commitment generated by viewing the effort as a social movement, akin to the civil rights movement, aimed at improving the lot of poor people. To this brew was added a set of innovative tactics such as effective approaches, often quite aggressive, to building owners who had hired the subcontractors who actually employed the janitors. Similar campaigns have been successful with other seemingly marginal groups, for example, home health care workers.[42]

Finally, we come to the fact that many workers will continue to be attached to a single enterprise for long stretches of their careers. Mainstream unions have been increasingly innovative and have contributed in many ways to the competitive advantage of firms. For example, in the steel industry the unions played a key role in helping to implement HPWO work systems and have taken responsibility for their firms by serving on boards of directors. Nonetheless, unions must find ways to expand their base. One approach is to find new issues and new organizing themes more attractive to today's employees. A prime example is the Harvard Union of Clerical and Technical Workers, which, by appealing to issues of training, day care, and sexual harassment, was able to fashion an appeal that connected with its largely female, well-educated constituency.[43]

The next question is how to get from here to there. This is a hard question not simply because of the complexities of the labor market but because of the difficult politics, internal and external to unions. Externally, efforts to enact labor law reform in the current environment seem problematic to say the least. Internally in a nontrivial way unions have brought many of their troubles onto themselves by failing to organize new groups of workers and by too often seeming to be the club of comfortable middle-aged white men defending their privileges. Under John Sweeney the AFL-CIO is trying to address these problems, and how successful the new regime is will be more important than any other consideration.

The last point merits repeating: it is worth discussing policies that can ease or facilitate the resurgence of unions. However, the more important determinant of success or failure will be whether the union movement itself can get its act together and effectively appeal to and organize new groups of employees. The limitations of public policy are shown by the fact that even in Canada—whose labor laws are typically held up by people sympathetic to unions as a structure worth imitating—the percentage of the labor force that unions represent is on the decline.

In any case, in the current U.S. political environment it seems quixotic to discuss labor law reform at any length, but setting these doubts aside briefly, there are three areas in which reform is warranted. These concern traditional organizing campaigns, facilitating the organizing of widely dispersed employees, and the role of unions in the workplace. With respect to traditional organizing, there is widespread agreement among lawyers and other researchers sympathetic to unions about some important steps.[44] These include shortening election campaigns, increasing substantially the penalties employers face for unfair labor practices during such campaigns, arbitration of first contracts, and restrictions on the use of permanent replacements for legal strikers.

With respect to the social movement–style organizing of low-income service employees, Howard Wial has emphasized the importance of overcoming the National Labor Relations Board's bias in favor of small, narrowly defined bargaining units.[45] Wial believes that areawide organization of low-wage workers in dispersed small employers could be facilitated by various administrative steps to encourage multiemployer bargaining.

It is obvious that labor law reforms of one stripe or another could strengthen unions' hands, although the sources of their difficulties are deeper than the law and it would be foolish to view labor law reform as a panacea. However, beyond the law there are other political steps that may also be helpful. In recent years, at both the national and local level, political leadership has seemed at best to be cool to unions and at worst to have run away from them. In order to legitimate the importance of employee voice, it seems important that national leadership visibly reincorporate unions in economic and social policy making. At the state and local level it would be helpful to find ways to make unions more central to state and local training and economic development policy. Whenever possible, local authorities should ensure that unions are "players," with respect to allocation of training funds, technical assistance to firms, local economic development, and the like.

New Forms of Representation

The foregoing discussion describes the problems and opportunities facing unions in different sectors of the labor market. However, the discussion takes for granted a fairly traditional form of representation, that is, unions as we have long known them, albeit drawing on more innovative organizing strategies. It is worth considering, however, more radically different ways of organizing for employee voice in the workplace. We do not, however, have good real-life models of these alternatives, and so the discussion has to be speculative.

Among academics who study this question, there is broad interest in the example of European Works Councils, which are enterprise-based employee groups that represent the entire range of the workforce, including midlevel managers, and that act as the employees' representative on a wide range of personnel and human resource decisions.[46] These organizations provide representation but generally do so in way that is supportive of the competitive success of the enterprise and cuts across the worker/manager divide.

One relatively modest first step along these lines is to provide incentives for the creation of employee committees to help administer such workplace regulations as health and safety laws, equal employment opportunity laws, or publicly supported job-training funds. A well-developed argument along these lines is made by David Levine, who adds the argument that employers might find this approach attractive if it is linked to deregulation.[47] For example, the Occupational Safety and Health Administration (OSHA) would offer to eliminate inspections and "bureaucratic" enforcement in return for the establishment of employee oversight committees responsible for health and safety. There has already been some experience along these lines, the most extensive of which is a comparable program in Ontario, Canada. In the United States, about ten states require employers to establish employee health and safety committees, and OSHA has launched an experimental program in Maine that provides a trade-off between inspections and the formation of committees. To concerns that this approach would diminish the quality of enforcement, Levine points out that this strategy has worked well when it has been tried and that, in any case, traditional enforcement mechanisms are already spotty, to say the least.

It is possible to think about expanding this approach beyond health and safety to other issues, such as the administration of public training funds and subsidies firms receive or some categories of dispute resolution. The hope would be that these relatively narrowly defined "single-issue" committees would expand over time to play a larger role in representing employee interests within the firm. Where a union was present, it could play this role, but employee involvement would have to be more inclusive than only the union members. In the absence of a union employee, representatives would be selected by a vote among all employees. Proposals along these lines do raise legitimate concerns about how to maintain minimum standards in the face of likely employer and employee tendencies to skimp on these standards in order to enhance the competitiveness of the enterprise. In addition, they likely would run into terrific opposition from employers who see these committees as nothing more than intrusions into managerial prerogatives. Unions also have reasonable concerns because they may view this approach as an invitation to establish company-dominated unions. All these difficulties make it likely that any movement along these lines will be slow and incremental, but nonetheless this may well be a promising avenue to enhance employee voice.

Turning to a different approach, earlier I listed three types of employees—contingent, low-skilled service, and traditional—for whom unions need to come up with distinctive strategies. There remains a question of whether some form of employee representation is feasible for more highly skilled professionals. The key characteristics are that people are more individualistic and more mobile. In this context Charles Heckscher has argued for what he terms "associational unions," which he defines as similar to professional associations but with a willingness to pressure employers.[48] Such an association would provide a range of services—educational, job matching, legal, portable benefits—but would also (in a largely undefined way) represent its members with employers. Worker organizations established along these lines would abandon the principle of exclusive jurisdiction (that only one organization can represent a similar group of workers within an enterprise). Much of the inspiration for these associational unions would come from the numerous self-help groups (e.g., the technical writers' guild in the Silicon Valley) and special interest organizations (e.g., women's groups, minority caucuses, and gay groups) that have sprung up in the workplace.

Another important idea is to find ways to combine the strengths of unions and community groups. Consider again Project QUEST in Texas. As things now stand, QUEST is a powerful presence in the local labor market but is only effective up until the point people get hired. It has little reach into employers beyond the initial bargains it strikes with them regarding entry wages and hiring plans. However, as the program grows, it will have alumni clustered in small groups in many San Antonio employers. A reasonable next step might be for QUEST to begin to offer these alumni further training and other services. If this effort is successful, QUEST can also offer these services to other employees who are not alumni. If QUEST can in this manner establish strong relationships with these people, it may eventually be able to represent them vis-à-vis employers on a range of issues. This representation may not be unionlike in the traditional sense, since QUEST will not represent a majority of employees or sign collective bargaining agreements. However, QUEST may be able to generate power and to improve working life in a variety of ways.

The foregoing examples are clearly speculative. Furthermore, even if they came to fruition, they would be weaker than traditional unions in important ways, notably the absence of a clear collective bargaining contract. In the best of all worlds traditional collective bargaining is preferable. On the other hand, in some ways the incomplete character of these alternatives is a virtue because they can be constructed in a step-by-step way without having to follow the rigid confines of labor law. They can take advantage of whatever openings appear, they can respond to changing circumstances and adjust their strategy and tactics accordingly, and they can undertake whatever mission circumstances permit. As such they have opportunities for success that are denied traditional collective bargaining arrangements.

Summary

A central characteristic of the current era is a striking shift in the balance of power between employers and employees. The consequences of this show up in a variety of ways, for example, in the finding of chapter 4 that employees have not reaped the gains inherent in workplace innovation. More generally, the stagnation of wages and the willingness of firms to treat workers as much more disposable than in the past surely both reflect the changing balance of power in the labor market.

This line of thought suggests that a key element in any effort to build new labor market institutions should be institutions that redress the power imbalance. The diagnosis, however, is easier than the cure. This chapter has reviewed the two most plausible strategies: altering the governance structure of firms and building effective countervailing power external to the firm. Both strategies seem logical, yet both face substantial challenges in the execution. Of the two it seems to me that the countervailing power approach is more plausible, but to accomplish it will require a great deal of imagination on the part of groups seeking to represent employees, as well as a more favorable political environment than we have experienced in recent years. The next chapter, in addition to pulling together the overall argument of the book, suggests why it is realistic to believe that these ideas have a chance of taking hold.

EIGHT

Conclusion

Wᴇ ʙᴇɢᴀɴ ᴛʜɪs ʙᴏᴏᴋ with a paradox: despite the good economic news on many dimensions, there remains a widespread sense that the labor market is a far riskier and dangerous place than in the past. In some measure this feeling is based what is in the air, as many firms continue to restructure and as rhetoric takes hold proclaiming that everyone is responsible for his or her own career and can expect little from his or her employer. However, there is also hard reality. On the one hand, it is true that many people find work to be more satisfying, that substantial numbers are benefiting economically from the new economy, and that in many firms workplace innovations promise better productivity and quality. However, for the majority of employees the benefits have been slow in arriving, and insecurity remains high.

Understanding these facts is hard both because of their paradoxical nature and because of the temptation to study specific symptoms rather than develop a broader understanding of what ties the various trends together. This book has tried to attend to the big picture: to describe how the labor market has changed, to provide a framework for understanding what has happened, and to think through policies that can respond to new realities.

The central story is that the postwar labor market was built around a set of institutions and practices that shaped behavior and that functioned reasonably effectively given the environment. Chapter 2 described these institutions in some detail. In the old labor market managers operated according to norms that placed substantial value on maintaining a long-term commitment to their labor force. Wage determination was strongly shaped by concerns regarding internal equity and fairness. Careers within organizations were governed by well-defined job ladders. All these patterns were supported by a corporate governance structure that was fairly lax in the pressures it put on management. The structure was also supported by unions that were strong and that could also pose a substantial threat in sectors where they were not present.

These institutions were put into place through a combination of economic and political pressures after World War II, and they shaped the labor market for nearly the next forty years. They have now collapsed with considerable resulting uncertainty about what comes next. This collapse is paralleled by the emergence of new ideas and practices within firms regarding how to organize work. Taken together, radical shifts in the structure of the external labor market and transformations within organizations have brought us to the current juncture of a labor market in flux.

What Comes Next?

Describing the end of an old system is one thing; understanding what will emerge is quite another. Important elements of the new system are in place, as the growing importance of temporary help firms and other mechanisms for contracting out work makes clear, as does the increased commitment of employers to innovative ideas about organizing work. However, the ultimate shape of the labor market is as of yet far from being determined.

In thinking about this it is centrally important to recognize that there is more scope for choice and alternative outcomes than might appear at first glance. The reality is that labor market behaviors are the result of a complex interaction of economic, institutional, and political considerations. It is important to see this because without this richer view any effort to think about policy will be truncated and incomplete. This point can be illustrated both at the level of the firm and at the level of the labor market as a whole.

Beginning with the firm, the nature of this brew is clear in our analysis of the transformation of work organization. The economic pressures on organizations are easy to see. In some markets foreign competition is fiercer, while in others domestic deregulation is driving competition. Whatever the case, firms across the board are feeling more heat. These market-driven pressures are intensified by changes in governance as newly energized investors demand higher levels of performance. When all this is added up, we have a powerful vector of economic forces pushing on organizations. The pressures are apparent, but how do firms respond?

One consideration influencing the response is the menu of technological and organizational options available. Some of these are technical in what I have termed the "hard" sense. Information technology provides numerous opportunities to rethink organizational structures, and this in turn can have substantial implications for both the numbers of people employed and the nature of their careers. Equally important are "soft" organizational technologies. New ideas about work organization have exerted wide-ranging influence on employment systems. The surveys I conducted, and which are reported on in chapter 4, document the striking explosion of innovative work systems.

The impact of economics and technology, hard and soft, is substantial. However, the story does not end here. These pressures are refracted through the political and social framework of labor markets to produce the actual outcomes we observe. One element of this framework is norms among employers about what degree of commitment they should make to their employees. In chapter 2 I developed in some detail evidence that these norms have shifted substantially in the direction of weaker commitments to incumbent workers. I also argued that these norms have some independent power, that they do not merely reflect other economic forces.

However, as important as norms may be, the most important lens through which organizational choices are refracted is the power balance between employers and employees. The potential repertoire of responses available to employers is shaped by this balance of power, and this can explain what are perhaps the most striking findings in chapter 4. First, despite the tremendous insecurity caused by downsizing and restructuring, employees have been willing to implement high-performance work systems that draw on their ideas and commitment to the enterprise. This willingness to cooperate despite the lack of any security is the opposite of what the traditional literature would have predicted. Second, the gains of these innovations have not been shared with the labor force. The "mutual gains" promise has not been realized.

It is important to understand the nature of this broad argument in its full complexity. It begins with the recognition that the pressures on organizations are real and not simply rhetorical efforts to squeeze out higher profits. The next step is to recognize that there are a range of possible responses to these pressures, some of which are relatively new responses that draw from innovative technology and ideas. However, which particular responses are chosen and the particular form they take are shaped by what can be broadly conceived of as the political framework within which these choices are made. Efficiency and technology have a role to play, but they are only part of the story. As the discussion in the last chapter on capital markets made clear, despite market pressure firms retain considerable leeway to pursue alternative policies.

The idea of choice applies to a broader canvas than a single firm or organization. In other key periods—the Progressive Era, the New Deal, and the years just after World War II—Americans engaged in a debate about what they wanted the labor market to look like, and they constructed institutions that endured for many years. In chapter 1, for example, I described how the postwar debate about the Full Employment Act and the so-called Treaty of Detroit between the United Automobile Workers and General Motors combined to shape many of the postwar labor market institutions. The Progressive Era was another time of strong debate and choice making about the role of markets in the economy and society. These periods were fundamentally a mixture of the political and the economic, and hence both were open to other outcomes and possibilities. The patterns that emerged were not inevitable.

We are again engaged in such a debate, and we have an opportunity to imagine and build institutions. The trick is both to develop a vision of what we want those institutions to look like and to be careful to ensure that that vision is responsive to the new realities of the labor market and the world economy.

BUILDING POLICY

One of the biggest obstacles to policy making in recent years has been the excessive respect given to the market. We have already seen that there is ample scope for choice. It is also worth noting that even from the more cramped perspective of economic theory an obsession with an unfettered market is a misreading. Welfare is maximized when actors pursue their individual (or firm) interest *subject to the constraints in their environment*. Some of these constraints are economic—scarce labor or land or capital—but other constraints are social and legal. There is nothing in economic theory that suggests that all constraints on firms should be eliminated. Economic production might be higher absent some constraint, but most economists recognize (via the idea of a social welfare function) that the greater good may involve some trade-off between the quantity of goods produced and other social goals. Not only does economic theory contain no prescription to eliminate constraints, nor does common sense. Very few people would argue that child labor restrictions in the United States should be eliminated even if a firm could make more money by getting 13-year-olds to assemble washing machines. The proper question is what restraints to impose and how to weigh the costs and benefits of any given restraint. Answering this question is what politics is about. The power of the market does not delegitimate policy; rather, it makes policy all the more important to a healthy economy and society.

Policy becomes particularly important because, as chapter 3 showed in great detail, there frequently are negative consequences for individuals of the current operation of the labor market. Much of this is because the structures that protected employees have been radically weakened or rendered irrelevant by the new environment. It makes sense, therefore, to think about how to rebuild the labor market in the face of modern realities. As chapter 1 pointed out, it is relatively straightforward to think about how to compensate people who made their careers under the old structure and are now victims of the new order of things. It is much harder to come to terms with what we want the labor market to look like in the future.

The institutional structure shaping the labor market is a mixture of norms, patterns of behavior within firms, and public policies. When we think about how to intervene, it is clear that while public policies are only one element of the larger picture nonetheless as a realistic matter this is where we have the most leverage.

It seems apparent that there is a mismatch between today's public labor market institutions and the new reality of the labor market. This mismatch can be seen in a variety of ways. For example, the public job-training system and labor market intermediaries are weak because it was assumed that most firms would hire people for long-term low-turnover jobs and provide training in-house. The unemployment insurance system is premised on support in the event that a long-term stable job is temporarily lost. Labor law as currently written and enforced assumes employer acceptance of the basic principle of employee representation. Social welfare is based on the idea of a single stable job being the basis for most benefits. In each instance shifts in the underlying economy and labor market have undercut the presumptions of the policies and institutions.

The response to this mismatch should be to build new labor market institutions that enhance the competitiveness and productivity of organizations but also assure better outcomes for more people. However, once we accept the idea of rebuilding labor market institutions, we are still left with the question of what kinds of institutions we want to build. In answering this question it is worth pausing to list again the goals I outlined in the first chapter. These were to build a labor market that embodied the following characteristics:

- *Efficiency:* The labor market should do a good job of allocating people to the firms and to the occupations in which they will be the most productive, and the market should provide the appropriate incentives and mechanisms to facilitate this movement as well as to encourage people to obtain the appropriate level of skills.
- *Equity:* Most Americans would agree that equity is an appropriate objective. In a rich nation it is hard to accept that there is no limit to the appropriate gap between the top and the bottom. There may be disagreement about how large that gap should be, but there is broad support for the idea that equity is a legitimate goal of policy and a labor market outcome that should be valued.
- *Opportunity:* The labor market should be structured in a way that permits people to make the most of their abilities and in which everyone has a chance to move ahead. This implies that there are opportunities for learning, and it also implies that the allocation of rewards is fair and not governed by inappropriate standards.
- *Voice:* People spend much of their lives at work, and most want to have some say in how their workplace is organized. Voice is not necessarily the same as

power or authority, and there is considerable variation in just where along the spectrum different people and different organizations want to be. However, a real opportunity to be heard and to participate seems fundamental.

- *Security:* No one can guarantee good outcomes for everyone. The economy is dynamic, and conditions change. However, we have long accepted the principle that through a combination of public and private policy some level of insurance should be available to ensure that there is a floor below which no one need fall.

In trying to achieve these goals, one way to think about the policy ideas developed in this book is to distinguish between two broad alternatives. In the first we take the generation of outcomes (e.g., wages, jobs, layoffs) as given and devise ways to enable individuals to cope better with the new environment. In the second, we try to influence more directly the actions of employers who, after all, drive labor market outcomes. Each approach can claim to be rooted in past approaches to social policy in the United States.

With a bow to the pop literature, we can call the first approach the "pack your own parachute" strategy. It is certainly congruent with current managerial rhetoric claiming that under the "new employment contract" people are responsible for their own careers and that the firm has some obligation to provide training to its employees but nothing further beyond that. More seriously, in what researchers have termed the "residual" approach to social policy, an important stream of American policy making has been to let the market generate whatever outcomes it will and then either compensate some people for the consequences, if these are seen as unfair, or simply enable people to do well in the market-driven environment. This philosophy has multiple roots: in a long-standing minimalist view of the role of government, in the political power of those who advocate leaving the market untouched, and in the intellectual ammunition provided by economic theories claiming that market outcomes are optimal.

The alternative is to try to influence the behavior of labor market actors, notably firms, so that the initial distribution of outcomes is more congruent with what we might desire. This more activist perspective also can claim historical roots. On a broad scale the Progressive movement, as we have seen, was a concerted effort to constrain and shape market forces. More modestly, labor market legislation ranging from minimum wage laws to health and safety rules to equal employment opportunity requirements all are aimed at changing the employment decisions of companies. Certainly efforts to build countervailing power fall into this category.

The importance of directly influencing the behavior of firms is apparent from the findings in chapter 4 about the absence of mutual gains, as well as from the limits, which I showed in chapter 6, to the corporate responsibility rhetoric. In recent years many observers have hoped that American firms would follow what they termed the "high road" of combining high-performance work systems with job security and good wages. A striking finding developed in the earlier chapters is that it is possible to follow the "high road" in organizing work while staying on the "low road" in terms of how employees are managed. This unexpected pattern means that outside pressure will be necessary to achieve fully the goals outlined above.

The analysis developed in the earlier chapters suggests two broad tasks for policy. First, it seems apparent that in the new labor market people will have to change jobs a great deal more often than in the past. We saw in chapter 3 that involuntary job changing involves considerable risk. This suggests that one objective of policy should be to enable people to do better in an economic environment of increased mobility. The second is more ambitious. The growing imbalance in the power of employees and employers has shaped how organizations have responded to new pressures and opportunities and is arguably responsible for much of what is bothersome about the current situation. The second broad objective of policy is therefore to ensure that employees have more voice and power than is true now.

I accept elements from both camps, and the proposals developed in chapters 5 and 6 fall all along the continuum from "pack your parachute" to changing outcomes more directly. The core of the proposals is to:

- Rebuild the safety net by fixing the unemployment insurance system and implementing portable benefits.
- Create local labor market institutions that can provide channels for successful mobility; these include strong intermediaries as well as networks of firms, training institutions, and schools.
- On a national scale rethink corporate governance (although my views are pessimistic about how much can be accomplished in this direction) and find new ways to enhance employee voice and build countervailing power.

Although the proposals developed here go beyond purely individualistic solutions, it is important to note that they are not intended to limit or restrict mobility or to create inefficient entitlements. Indeed, in many respects they are aimed at facilitating the movement of people from one job to another. In this sense they avoid the trap, or the perceived trap, of European labor markets. The main problem with European labor markets, I would argue, is not their institutions of employee representation or the social safety net that restricts the extremes of low income we see in this country. What is troublesome about European labor markets is the lack of mobility, the unwillingness of employees to change jobs and move geographically in search of better opportunities. This limits the reallocation of labor that an efficient labor market requires, and it keeps unemployment at higher rates than would otherwise be the case.

In contrast to a mobility-limiting approach, I want to make the job movement easier and more successful and to diminish the risks associated with it. This is why the combination of an improved safety net and local institutions that facilitate movement makes sense. The thrust of these policies is not to fight against the forces that have transformed the labor market but rather to make them operate in a more effective and fairer way.

Institution Building in the Labor Market

Just as the material in this book implies a theory of how organizations make employment decisions in response to a complex mix of economic, sociological, and political signals, it also implies a theory of labor market policy making. In particular, it points to the role of the overall structure of the labor market as distinct from specific policies or programs.

One step in this direction is to understand how institutions influence market outcomes. To begin, institutions can establish a minimum floor. In part this is via legislation, such as the minimum wage, but the influence is also more subtle. The norms of conduct I described in chapter 2 come to be seen as standard and best practice. Over time these norms take on a life of their own. They become broadly viewed as legitimate and proper and can influence the behavior of a wide range of organizations much the same way as does formal regulation. These twin pressures of minimum standards and norms can force laggards to upgrade their behavior.[1]

Institutions also provide mechanisms, such as intermediaries, that both directly influence outcomes and provide incentives for labor market actors to adapt their behavior and practices in particular ways. For example, an effective public training system and networks of intermediaries would influence hiring patterns, promotion paths, and even the choice of production techniques. Firms also have to adapt to the realities of the balance of power in the labor market. Many of the outcomes described in this book, ranging from wage stagnation and inequality to weakening employment security, would look different were the balance of power shifted.

In short, via standards, norms, mechanisms facilitating particular outcomes, and the power balance, the labor market comes to take on a particular shape. It is through this process that institution building can exert a powerful effect.

It remains, however, to ask whether it is possible to get from here to there. It is not hard to generate a wish list of programs that, if enacted, would respond to the issues raised in this book. Many policy documents have this quality. It would be nice to do better and be able to chart a plausible path leading to the steps that are advocated.

One pathway that seems closed is large-scale direct action at the national level. The constituency is simply not there to enact serious labor market policy. This, as Margaret Weir notes, can be seen in the failure of the Clinton administration to make progress on these issues.[2] An example is the so-called Dunlop Commission, which was established to broker a deal between business and labor. The implicit deal would have been modest improvements in the operation of labor law in return for greater flexibility on the part of organized labor toward high-performance work organizations. In the end the business community decided that they could have their cake and eat it too (as chapter 4 demonstrates they indeed could), and they walked away from any agreement. Weakness of national policy making is also illustrated by the failure of the mid-1990s political rhetoric about corporate responsibility to lead to any meaningful action.

Given this discouraging recent history, what reason is there to think that it is realistic to talk about policy? The basis for some hope is that most of the ideas developed here are about local institution building, and there is reason to expect—indeed, there are precedents in the history of American social policy for believing—that over time successful local initiatives will create a new politics.

The local institution building prescribed here can change politics in three ways. First, to the extent that programs are successful, they create a constituency for maintaining and expanding them. A good recent example is the ability of the NIST manufacturing extension services to prosper in the federal budget despite initial Republican antipathy to them. Second, the programs can serve as laboratories that illustrate the utility of new ideas and set the stage for national adoption. This is the classic role of state-level experimentation, and there are ample labor market precedents beginning with unemployment compensation in the 1930s.

Third, and perhaps most important, many of the ideas developed here can change politics by building power among local groups who, in turn, will favor active institution building at the national level. As community groups, unions, and policy activists become more successful at the local level and more integral to the operation of labor markets, they will both gain power and grow a constituency for their efforts. This will not be a quick process, but it is very plausible, as examples as disparate as the union movement during the depression and the environmental movement in the 1970s demonstrate.

Despite the grim politics at the national level, there is a tremendous amount of energy around the country in this arena. Community groups, local governments, unions, and policy activists have taken advantage of the vacuum in federal policy to experiment with new models for enabling people to navigate the labor market. Some of these efforts were highlighted in chapters 5 and 6, but there are numerous others in all parts of the nation. These efforts include a consortium of firms working together to solve common problems, community hiring halls, innovative job-training programs that are linked to employer needs, and associations of independently employed workers who pool resources around benefits and job. Not all these efforts will pan out, but the interest is widespread, and hence there is a substantial base for progress. Particularly hopeful in this regard is that many governors and local officials have begun to adopt these issues as their own, and hence resources and sustained political support may be forthcoming.

Constructing new labor market institutions is not a linear process. What actually emerges will be the result of a complex interplay of economics, politics, and experimentation. While the process is not easy or predictable, there is a history of success. The combination of a broadly recognized need and vigorous local experimentation may well once again yield a new crop of successful local labor market institutions and ultimately an effective national agenda.

Notes

ONE

INTRODUCTION

1. Neil Fligstein, "Markets as Politics: A Political-Cultural Approach to Market Institutions," *American Sociological Review* 61, no. 4 (August 1996): 658.

2. *Mackay Radio & Telegraph*, 304 U.S. 333 (1938).

3. Robert Kuttner, *Everything for Sale* (New York: Knopf, 1996).

4. *Business Week*, 26 February 1996, 47.

5. National Alliance of Business, *Thinking Anew about Worker Security* (Washington, D.C.: National Alliance of Business, 1996).

6. Wolfgang Streeck, *Industrial Relations in West Germany* (New York: St. Martin's Press, 1984); Gary Herrigel, *Industrial Constructions: The Source of Germany's Industrial Power* (Cambridge: Cambridge University Press, 1996).

7. BMW has opened a plant in South Carolina. As another example, the shoe maker Adidas moved all but 3 percent of its workforce to Asia. See the *Economist*, 30 September 1995, 79.

8. *Economist*, 16 March 1996, 72.

9. I owe this observation to Horst Kern.

10. I conducted interviews at Hewlett-Packard, and this was emerging as an important practice.

11. Manpower Inc. has formed an alliance with Drake Beam Morin Inc., the world's largest executive outplacement firm, to place into temporary jobs laid-off executives. *Business Week*, 10 June 1996, 81.

12. One of the key episodes in the creation of the postwar labor market was the struggle over the Full Employment Act, a story that has been told many times, including in Stephen Bailey's classic *Congress Makes a Law*. Had the Full Employment Act passed, it would have set the stage for national, centrally organized labor policies

that would in turn have created a different labor market than the one that actually emerged. The legislation did indeed have a reasonable chance of passage, but it was, as Margaret Weir explains, defeated by the mobilization of agricultural and business interests. Large-scale farmers were concerned that extensive federal spending, aimed at sustaining full employment, would undermine their control over low-wage farm labor. Business feared that the "social Keynesianism" inherent in the Full Employment Act would strengthen unions. The strong support of unions for the legislation was the opposite side of the same coin. The point to be emphasized is that at this juncture the nation indeed had choices regarding the institutional structure of the postwar labor market and that the resolution of these choices was the result of an explicitly political struggle. Invisible market forces and inevitable outcomes played very small roles.

A similar point can be made regarding other postwar labor market institutions. At the end of World War II, American labor felt both strong and frustrated. Unions emerged from the New Deal and their role in war production with a level of power and legitimacy unmatched in American history. At the same time grievances that had been repressed by the exigencies of war production and the power of the War Labor Board exploded. By the same token American corporations sought to push back on the boundaries of employee power and to reassert their unchallenged control of "management prerogatives." In 1945 and 1946 America experienced an unprecedented wave of strikes—more than two million employees on strike in the winter of 1945—which had the potential of reshaping the relationship between workers and employers. This is most clearly seen in the strike waged by the United Automobile Workers against General Motors. Walter Reuther sought to attack directly the prerogatives of American corporations by insisting that General Motors "open their books" and that the corporation allow unions to bargain over product prices as well as wage levels.

The struggle that ensued was not a garden variety labor conflict over pay increases but rather a battle to determine the shape of the postwar labor market. Had Reuther won the bitter 113-day strike against General Motors, there is every reason to believe that the pattern of realigned power relationships would have diffused and that the postwar labor market would have taken on a different shape than it did. With full knowledge of the stakes, both sides turned the strike into a national political issue. In the end, the UAW failed to achieve its objective. Reuther lost the support of both President Truman and other key unions such as the Steel Workers. With this defeat the strong unions settled into a bargaining relationship that led to the construction of the labor market.

In return for the freedom to manage, General Motors agreed to a wage-setting regime in which annual productivity gains (the so-called annual improvement factor) were automatically shared with the workforce. Put differently, "ability to pay" was institutionalized as a criterion for wage determination. This "Treaty of Detroit" also established the rigid internal labor markets—the job classifications, work rules, and wage relationships—that came to characterize the postwar labor market. This internal labor market structure was at least in part a political response to the inability of the union to influence employment levels and fluctuations directly. The fundamental pattern described above was spread, via imitation, throughout the unionized oligopolistic sectors of the economy. In the nonunion sector these patterns were also imitated, in large measure as an inoculation against the threat of organization.

Looking back, the pattern that emerged from these postwar struggles may not seem surprising. The emergence of the Cold War, the rehabilitation of the image of the business community that was achieved during World War II, and the continuing and indeed resurgent power of southern conservatives in Congress all combined to defeat the impulses toward more active labor market policy and stronger employee voice. Nonetheless, it is important to recognize that this outcome was a political outcome. The labor market that was created was one whose fundamental institutional structure was the product of a political struggle, a struggle whose outer limits may have been delimited by market forces and technology but one that admitted alternative outcomes with very different consequences.

See Nelson Lichtenstein, *The Most Dangerous Man in Detroit: Walter Reuther and the Fate of American Labor* (New York: Basic Books, 1995), and Margaret Weir, *Politics and Jobs: The Boundaries of Employment Policy in America* (Princeton, N.J.: Princeton University Press, 1992).

13. *New York Times,* 29 December 1997, D7.

14. Annalee Saxenian, *Regional Advantage* (Cambridge: Harvard University Press, 1994), 56.

15. Annalee Saxenian, "Beyond Boundaries: Open Labor Markets and Learning in Silicon Valley," in *The Boundaryless Career,* ed. Michael Arthur and Denise Rousseau (New York: Oxford University Press, 1966), 28.

16. *New York Times,* 23 November 1996.

17. See Michael Piore and Charles Sabel, *The Second Industrial Divide* (New York: Basic Books, 1994).

18. These networks go by names such as the Indian Professionals Association, the Korean-American Society of Entrepreneurs, and the Monte Jade Science and Technology Association. *Wall Street Journal,* 18 March 1998, B1.

19. *New York Times,* 29 December 1997, D7.

20. These wage data are taken from Working Partnerships, *Growing Together or Drifting Apart* (San Jose: Working Partnerships/Economic Policy Institute, 1998), 23.

21. Christian Zlolniski, "The Informal Economy in an Advanced Industrial Society: Mexican Immigrant Labor in the Silicon Valley," *Yale Law Journal* 103, no. 8 (1994): 2304–35.

22. Working Partnerships, *Growing Together or Drifting Apart*, 24.

23. Robert Weibe, *The Search for Order, 1877–1920* (New York: Hill and Wang, 1967), 12.

Two

THE CHANGING STRUCTURE OF THE AMERICAN LABOR MARKET

1. See, for example, William Landes and Lewis Soloman, "Compulsory Schooling Legislation: An Economic Analysis of Law and Social Change in the Nineteenth Century," *Journal of Economic History* 32, no. 1 (March 1972): 54–91.

2. For an interesting review of the field, see Bruce Kaufman, *The Origins and Evolution of Industrial Relations in the United States* (Ithaca, N.Y.: ILR Press, 1993).

3. See, for example, John Dunlop, "Job Vacancy Measures and Economic Analysis," in *The Measurement and Interpretation of Job Vacancies: A Conference Report*, National Bureau of Economic Research (New York: Columbia University Press, 1966); John Dunlop, "The Task of Contemporary Wage Theory," in *New Concepts in Wage Determination*, ed. G. Taylor and F. Pierson (New York: McGraw-Hill, 1957), 117–39; Clark Kerr, "The Balkanization of Labor Markets," in *Labor Mobility and Economic Opportunity*, ed. E. Wright Bakke (Cambridge: MIT Press, 1954), 92–110; Lloyd Reynolds, *The Structure of Labor Markets* (New York: Harper, 1951).

4. Paul DiMaggio and Walter Powell, "The Iron Cage Revisited: Institutional Isomorphism and Collective Rationality in Organizational Fields," *American Sociological Review* 48, no. 2 (April 1983): 147–60.

5. For an excellent description of the evolution of this employment system, see Harry Katz, *Shifting Gears* (Cambridge: MIT Press, 1985).

6. Reinhard Bendix, *Work and Authority in Industry: Ideologies of Management in the Course of Industrialization* (Berkeley: University of California Press, 1956); Stephen Barley and Gideon Kunda, "Design and Devotion; Surges of Rational and Normative Ideologies of Control in Management Discourse," *Administrative Science Quarterly* 37, no. 3 (September 1992): 363–99; Mauro Guillen, *Models of Management* (Chicago: University of Chicago Press, 1994).

7. Guillen, *Models of Management*, 58.

8. Thomas Peters and Robert Waterman, *In Search of Excellence* (New York: Harper, 1982), 5.

9. Ibid., 261, 239.

10. Robert Hall, "The Importance of Lifetime Jobs in the U.S. Economy," *American Economic Review* 72, no. 4 (September 1982): 716–24.

11. William H. Whyte, *The Organization Man* (New York: Simon and Schuster, 1956); Ann Howard and Douglas Bray, *Managerial Lives in Transition* (New York: Guilford Press, 1988).

12. See, for example, Oliver Williamson, Michael Wacter, and Jeffrey Harris, "Understanding the Employment Relation: The Analysis of Idiosyncratic Exchange," *Bell Journal of Economics* 6 (Spring 1975): 250–80.

13. Sanford Jacoby, *Employing Bureaucracy* (New York: Columbia University Press, 1985).

14. Donald Roy, "Quota Restriction and Goldbricking in a Machine Shop," *American Journal of Sociology* 60, no. 2 (April 1954): 255–66; Arthur Ross, *Trade Union Wage Policy* (Berkeley: University of California Press, 1948).

15. Arthur Ross, "The External Wage Structure," in *New Concepts in Wage Determination*, ed. George Taylor and Frank Pierson (New York: McGraw-Hill, 1957): 190.

16. Peter Doeringer and Michael Piore, *Internal Labor Markets and Manpower Analysis* (Lexington, Mass.: D. C. Heath, 1971), 72.

17. George Milkovich and Jerry Newman, *Compensation* (Plano, Tex.: Business Publications, 1984).

18. The most influential early formulations of these ideas are found in the chapters by John Dunlop and Arthur Ross in Taylor and Pierson, *New Concepts in Wage Determination*. Typical early empirical work includes John Maher, "The Wage Pattern in the United States," *Industrial and Labor Relations Review* 15, no. 1 (October 1961): 3–20, and Otto Eckstein and Thomas Wilson, "The Determination of Manufacturing Wages in American Industry," *Quarterly Journal of Economics* 76, no. 3 (August 1962): 379–414.

19. The role of "ability to pay" is discussed in Reynolds, Structure of Labor; see also the essays in Taylor and Pierson, *New Concepts in Wage Determination*.

20. Adolf Berle and Gardiner Means, *The Modern Corporation and Private Property*, rev. ed. (New York: Harcourt, Brace, and World, 1968).

21. Margaret Weir, *Politics and Jobs* (Princeton, N.J.: Princeton University Press, 1992).

22. *Wall Street Journal*, 10 May 1996, 1.

23. Eric Brynjolfsson, "The Productivity Paradox of Information Technology," *Communications of the ACM* 35 (December 1993): 66–77.

24. Although this does not necessarily imply an absolute loss of jobs. While computers substitute for labor when the amount of output is held constant, computers can also increase output by lowering the price of the product. See, for example, Earnst Berndt, Catherine Morrison, and L. Rosenblum, "High Tech Capital, Economic and Labor Composition in U.S. Manufacturing Industries," MIT-

EFA Working Paper 3414EFA, February 1992; Paul Osterman, "The Impact of Computers upon the Demand for Clerical and Managerial Labor," *Industrial and Labor Relations Review* 39, no. 2 (January 1986): 175–86.

25. *New York Times,* 11 August 1995, D1.

26. Robert J. Thomas, *What Machines Can't Do: Politics and Technology in the Industrial Enterprise* (Berkeley: University of California Press, 1994); Shosana Zuboff, *In the Age of the Smart Machine* (New York: Basic Books, 1988); Patricia Flynn, *Facilitating Technological Change: The Human Resource Challenge* (Cambridge, Mass.: Ballinger, 1988); Harland Prechel, "The Economic Crisis and the Centralization of Control," *American Sociological Review* 59, no. 5 (October 1994): 723–45.

27. Joseph Fucini and Suzy Fucini, *Working for the Japanese: Inside Mazda's American Auto Plant* (New York: Free Press, 1990).

28. Michael Jensen, "The Modern Industrial Revolution, Exit, and the Failure of Internal Control Systems," *Journal of Finance* 48, no. 3 (July 1993): 831–79.

29. Michael Useem, *Investor Capitalism* (New York: Basic Books, 1996), 138.

30. *New York Times,* 6 August 1995, F2.

31. *Wall Street Journal,* 4 May 1995, 1.

32. Ibid.

33. Susan Eaton did virtually all of this work.

34. *New York Times,* 7 January 1996, E19.

35. *Wall Street Journal,* 22 January 1996, A12.

36. *New York Times,* 19 March 1996, D4.

37. For example, for men quits as a proportion of the unemployed fell from 0.180 in 1979 to 0.165 in 1997 (the latest year for which data broken out by sex are available). For women the figures were 0.302 and 0.238, respectively.

38. Annette Bernhardt, Martina Morris, Mark Handcock, and Marc Scott, *Summary of Findings: Work and Opportunity in the Post Industrial Labor Market,* report to the Russell Sage and Rockefeller Foundations, February 1998, 1.

39. David Neumark, Daniel Polsky, and Daniel Hansen, "Has Job Stability Declined Yet? Evidence for the 1990s" (paper delivered at the Russell Sage Conference "Changes in Job Stability and Job Security," New York, February 1998).

40. For a description of this correction, see Henry Farber, "The Changing Face of Job Loss in the United States, 1981–1993," Working Paper 5596 (Cambridge, Mass.: National Bureau of Economic Research, 1996).

41. Between 1995 and 1997 the total number of dislocated workers was 8.0 million people. This is down from 9.4 million in the previous survey, but the decline is considerably less than the experience of past business cycles would have suggested. See the Bureau of Labor Statistics Newsletter, "Worker Displacement, 1995–1997," August 19, 1998.

42. Also included in this category are self-employed or independent contractors who have been in their job for less than a year and do not expect it to last for more than a year.

43. Thomas Nardone, Jonathan Veum, and Julie Yates, "Measuring Job Security," *Monthly Labor Review* 100, no. 6 (June 1977): 30.

44. Tracking over time the fraction of the labor force that works part-time is complicated by two significant technical issues. First, there is a major break in the time series after 1994 because of a change in design of the Current Population Survey. This increased the number of voluntary part-time workers but decreased the count of involuntary part-time workers. For this reason it makes the most sense to compare three years, the peak years of 1979 and 1989 and the final year, 1993, in which data were collected under the old system. Second, the census definition of *part-time* is based on the total number of hours per week an individual worked. This means that a person holding two part-time jobs of twenty hours each is counted as a full-time worker. This affects measurements of both the level and trend of part-time work. The impact on the level is obvious, and it would affect the trend if the rate of multiple job holding increased over time.

The data show the following: in 1979, 13.8 percent of men and 22.8 percent of women worked part-time voluntarily. In 1989 the figures were 13.8 percent and 21.4 percent, while in 1993 they were 13.3 percent and 20.0 percent. Thus there has clearly been no increase in voluntary part-time employment. There has, however, been some increase in involuntary part-time work. For men the 1979 rate was 3.7 percent, and for women it was 4.9 percent. In 1989 the figures were 4.3 percent and 4.2 percent, while in 1993 the rates stood at 5.5 percent and 6.4 percent.

Overall, these data therefore suggest that total part-time employment grew slightly for men and declined slightly for women, with a notable increase in involuntary part-time work. However, during the same period the rate of multiple job holding also increased, from 4.9 percent of the total labor force in 1979 to 6.2 percent in 1989. This implies that the number of part-time jobs in the economy probably grew more than the earlier figures indicate (since the combination of two actual part-time jobs would lead to a full-time job under the census definition and the rise of multiple job holding implies that more such combinations are taking place). It still remains the case that a balanced reading of the data would suggest that nothing dramatic has happened with respect to total part-time work but that more people involuntarily work part-time than in the past.

In 1997 the overall rate of part-time work was 17.4 percent, and the fraction of the labor force reporting themselves involuntary part-time workers was 3.4 percent.

See Thomas Nardone, "Part-Time Employment: Reasons, Demographics, and Trends," *Journal of Labor Research* 16, no. 3 (Summer 1995): 276–92; John Stinson,

"New Data on Multiple Jobholding Available from the CPS," *Monthly Labor Review* 120, no. 3 (March 1997): 3–8.

45. Judith Scott, Nina Frantzen, and Randall Mehl, *Temporary Staffing Industry Update* (Milwaukee: Robert W. Baird & Co., 1997), 5.

46. Ibid.

47. Angela Clinton, "Flexible Labor: Restructuring the American Labor Force," *Monthly Labor Review* 121, no. 8 (August 1997): 3.

48. *Staffing Industry Reports,* 12 January 1997, 8, 11.

49. The median duration of a temporary job (i.e., an assignment from a temporary help firm) was three months, and the median duration of an on-payroll contingent job was nine months. There are twice as many temporary as contingent jobs, hence the five-month figure.

50. Daniel Mitchell, "Shifting Norms in Wage Determination," *Brookings Papers on Economic Activity,* no. 2 (1985): 575–608.

51. Budd examined contracts reached by the United Automobile Workers with the Big Three auto firms and found that their impact in industries such as aerospace, auto parts, and implements had attenuated when he compared the period 1959–79 with 1987–89. Ericksen in his study of pattern bargaining in aerospace also found a diminished pattern in his comparison of 1959–78 with 1979–84. John Budd, "The Determinants and Extent of UAW Pattern Bargaining," *Industrial and Labor Relations Review* 45, no. 3 (April 1992): 523–39. Budd found that, while in 1955–79 average wages in auto parts, aerospace, and electrical equipment closely followed the average wage in the Big Three auto contracts, by 1987–90 the relationship was much weaker. Chris Ericksen, "Union Wage Determination in Manufacturing in the 1980s" (Ph.D. diss., MIT, Department of Economics, 1990).

52. Harry Katz and Owen Darbishire, *Converging Divergences: Worldwide Changes in Employment* (Ithaca, N.Y.: Cornell University Press, 1998).

53. Richard Freeman and James Medoff, *What Do Unions Do?* (New York: Basic Books, 1984), 153.

54. These figures are from Daniel Mitchell, "Wage Pressures and Labor Shortages: The 1960's and the 1980's," *Brookings Papers on Economic Activity,* no. 2 (1989): 191–232.

55. Thomas Kochan, Harry Katz, and Robert McKersie, *The Transformation of Industrial Relations* (New York: Basic Books, 1986).

56. *New York Times,* 5 December 1995, A18.

57. Useem, *Investor Capitalism,* 25.

58. George Anders, "The 'Barbarians' in the Boardroom," *Harvard Business Review* 10, no. 4 (July/August 1992): 87.

59. "Secondary labor market" is a term developed by Peter Doeringer and Michael Piore in their book *Internal Labor Markets and Manpower Analysis*. The term is linked to a large body of theory and research termed "dual labor market theory," which seeks to explain how this sector can emerge and coexists alongside the core labor market.

60. The 1992 and the 1997 surveys used as their sampling frame the Dun and Bradstreet database on all business establishments in the United States. For the 1992 survey in Paul Osterman, "How Common Is Workplace Transformation and How Can We Explain Who Does It?" (*Industrial and Labor Relations Review* 47, no. 2 [January 1994]: 175–88), I describe the nature of this sampling frame and show that it is the best available source. I also search for possible response bias in my survey and report finding none. For the 1997 survey, again using the Dun and Bradstreet data, which are available for all establishments in the sample regardless of whether they responded, I estimated a logit model with the dependent variable being whether or not the establishment responded and the independent variables being employment size of the establishment, whether or not the establishment was a part of a larger organization, and whether or not the establishment was in manufacturing. None of these variables were significant, indicating that no important biases exist in the response patterns. Also using the 1992 data I estimated a logit model in which the dependent variable was whether or not the establishment was reinterviewed in 1997 and the independent variables were size, whether the establishment was part of a larger organization, and whether or not it was in manufacturing. None of these variables were significant.

THREE

EXPERIENCING THE NEW ECONOMY

1. The index is based on a survey of employers and represents the compensation costs (wages plus benefits) for a fixed group of occupations. Hence, the data do not reflect the changing occupational mix of the labor force, as do the census data. This problem is analogous to the bias in the Consumer Price Index. For this reason actual wage growth is overstated. In other respects, however, the data are robust. See Michael K. Lettau, Mark Lowenstein, and Aaron Cushner, "Is the ECI Sensitive to Method of Aggregation," *Monthly Labor Review* 120, no. 6 (June 1997): 3–11.

2. Kurt Schrammel, "Labor Market Success of Young Adults from Two Generations," *Monthly Labor Review* 121, no. 2 (February 1998): 5.

3. *New York Times*, 26 September 1998, A1.

4. For both men and women the 90/50 ratio increased from 1.9 to 2.2. See Jared Bernstein and Lawrence Mishel, "Has Wage Inequality Stopped Growing?" *Monthly Labor Review* 120, no. 12 (December 1997): 9.

5. For a review of this debate, see Nicole Fortin and Thomas Lemieux, "Institutional Changes and Rising Wage Inequality: Is There a Linkage?" *Journal of Economic Perspectives* 11, no. 2 (Spring 1997): 75–96. See also Richard Freeman, "How Much Has Deunionization Contributed to the Rise in Male Earnings Inequality?" in *Uneven Tides: Rising Inequality In America,* ed. Sheldon Danziger and Peter Gottschalk (New York: Russell Sage, 1993), 133–63.

6. The caution arises because we do not really have a control group that would enable us to know what would have happened to people who lose their jobs had they not been laid off. Instead we have before/after, which may be subject to bias particularly if people who lose their jobs are worse workers than other folks. However, there is evidence that this is not a problem for workers who lose their jobs because of plant closings or large-scale layoffs. See Robert Gibbons and Lawrence Katz, "Layoffs and Lemons," *Journal of Labor Economics* 9 (1991): 351–80.

7. In fact, the patterns for everyone between the ages of 20 and 64 are not very different from what I present below.

8. These surveys asked about dislocation over the five years prior to the survey, but in order to keep the data comparable to those for 1994 and 1996, I only look at people who reported themselves dislocated in the three years before the surveys.

9. This, of course, runs the risk of selection bias, that is, the people who were not dislocated are in some way different (e.g., more productive) than those who were laid off. However, this concern is eased by the finding cited above in Gibbons and Katz, "Layoffs and Lemons."

10. Many women choose to spend some time out of the labor force raising a family, whereas the women who were dislocated were, by definition, working at the time and should be compared with a group of comparably committed women. A relatively straightforward way of getting at this is to look at married and single people separately with the expectation that single women aged 30–55 will all evince high labor force commitment. When I do this, it turns out that even after controlling for marital status it remains true that relative to their group dislocated women are better off than dislocated men. In fact, the group that takes the biggest hit is married men, whose employment rate in 1994/96 falls from more than 91 percent in the comparison group to 77 percent among those who were dislocated.

11. In the earlier period 37.7 percent of noncollege and 28.1 percent of college grads experienced a 20 percent or greater earnings loss. In the most recent period the figures were 38.7 and 33.9, respectively.

12. These definitions are created by me using the CPS data and do not fully correspond to the definitions used by the CPS in its own recodes. For example, I count as freelance workers/independent contractors only people who are also self-employed. In the residual temporary category I only count people who also give one

of the four reasons why their job is temporary. I do not include day laborers in the on-call group.

FOUR
RESTRUCTURING WITHIN FIRMS: THE SHIFTING EMPLOYMENT CONTRACT

1. The material in this description of Digital Equipment Corporation comes from a set of interviews Susan Eaton and I conducted with DEC employees over the past year, as well as a fairly extensive set of previous interviews I conducted at DEC about a decade ago.

2. The material in this paragraph was reported in the *New York Times*, 7 July 1996, 10.

3. This account is taken from Stuart Korshak, "Negotiating Trust in the San Francisco Hotel Industry," *California Management Review* 38, no. 1 (Fall 1995): 117–37; Annette Bernhardt and Thomas Bailey, "Making Careers out of Jobs: Policies for a New Employment Relationship," mimeo, Institute on Education and the Economy, Teachers College, October 1997.

4. Rosemary Batt, "Performance and Welfare Effects of Work Restructuring: Evidence from Telecommunications Services" (Ph.D. diss., MIT, Sloan School of Management, 1995).

5. Eileen Applebaum and Rosemary Batt, *The New American Workplace* (Ithaca, N.Y.: Cornell University Press, 1994), 110.

6. For a review of the various estimates, see Paul Osterman, "Work Organization in an Era of Restructuring: Trends in Diffusion and Impacts on Employee Welfare," Working Paper, MIT Industrial Performance Center, January 1999.

7. Paul Osterman, "How Common Is Workplace Transformation and How Can We Explain Who Does It?" *Industrial and Labor Relations Review* 47, no. 2 (January 1994): 175–88.

8. The material on BellSouth owes a great deal to the research of Rosemary Batt and is based in a lesser part on interviews I conducted.

9. Paul Adler, "The New Learning Bureaucracy," in *Research in Organizational Behavior*, ed. L. L. Cummings and Barry Straw (Greenwich, Conn.: JAI, 1993), 111–94.

10. Eileen Applebaum and Rosemary Batt, *The New American Workplace* (Ithaca, N.Y.: Cornell University Press, 1994). The six models are Swedish sociotechnical systems, Japanese lean production, Italian flexible specialization, German diversified quality production, American lean production, and American team production. The systems vary in the degree of autonomy they give the workforce, the nature of the supporting human resource practices, and the extent to which the gains from the systems are shared.

11. Adler, "The New Learning Bureaucracy," in *Research in Organizational Behavior*, ed. L. L. Cummings and Barry Straw (Greenwich, Conn.: JAI, 1993).

12. Applebaum and Batt, *New American Workplace*, 88.

13. Osterman, "Work Organization in an Era of Restructuring."

14. The issues raised in this box are discussed in more detail in Casey Ichniowski, Thomas Kochan, David Levine, Craig Olson, and George Strauss, "What Works at Work," *Industrial Relations* 35, no. 3 (July 1996): 299–333.

15. John Paul McDuffie, "Human Resource Bundling and Manufacturing Performance: Organizational Logic and Flexible Production Systems in the World Automobile Industry," *Industrial and Labor Relations Review* 48, no. 2 (January 1995): 197–221.

16. Casey Ichniowski, Katherine Shaw, and Giovanna Prennushi, "The Impact of Human Resource Practices on Productivity," *American Economic Review* 87, no. 3 (June 1997): 291–313.

17. Rosemary Batt, *Performance and Welfare Effects of Work Restructuring: Evidence from Telecommunications Services* (Ph.D. diss., MIT, Sloan School of Management, 1995).

18. Peter Berg, Eileen Applebaum, Thomas Bailey, and Arne Kalleberg, "The Performance Effects of Modular Production in the Apparel Industry," *Industrial Relations* 35, no. 3 (July 1995): 356–74.

19. James Womack, Daniel Jones, and Daniel Roos, *The Machine That Changed the World* (Cambridge: MIT Press, 1991).

20. Mark Huselid, "The Impact of Human Resource Management Practices on Turnover, Productivity, and Corporate Financial Performance," *Academy of Management Journal* 38, no. 3 (June 1995): 635–72.

21. Michael Piore and Charles Sabel, *The Second Industrial Divide: Possibilities of Prosperity* (New York: Basic Books, 1984); Michael Best, *The New Competition; Institutions of Industrial Restructuring* (Cambridge: Harvard University Press, 1990).

22. Charles Heckscher, *White Collar Blues* (New York: Basic Books, 1995); Peter Cappelli, "Examining Managerial Displacement," *Academy of Management Journal* 35, no. 1 (March 1992): 203–17; Paul Osterman, ed., *Broken Ladders* (New York: Oxford University Press, 1996).

23. As a check on these findings I regressed each of these outcome variables (contingent employment, outsourcing, and managerial cutbacks) upon the number of HPWO practices in place in 1992 at a 50 percent level of penetration, the change in the value of sales over the past year, and industry dummies. In each of the equations the HPWO variable was significantly negatively related to the outcome variable, thus confirming the findings in table 4.3.

24. Thomas Kochan and Paul Osterman, *The Mutual Gains Enterprise: Forging a Winning Partnership among Labor, Management, and Government* (Boston: Harvard Business School Press, 1994).

25. In a survey of employers conducted by the Bureau of the Census, 72 percent reported that their level of formal training had increased between 1991 and 1994 (these data were analyzed by the Institute for Research on Higher Education at the University of Pennsylvania). The 1992 National Establishment Survey showed a similar pattern.

26. See Paul Osterman, "Skill, Training, and Work Organization in American Establishments," *Industrial Relations* 34, no. 2 (April 1995): 125–46. See also Lisa Lynch and Sandra Black, "Beyond the Incidence of Employer Provided Training," *Industrial and Labor Relations Review* 52, no. 1 (October 1998): 64–81; and Harley Frazis, Maury Gittleman, Michael Horrigan, and Mary Joyce, "Results from the 1995 Survey of Employer Provided Training," *Monthly Labor Review* 121, no. 6 (June 1998): 3–13.

27. Laurie Graham, *On the Line at Subaru-Isuzu* (Ithaca, N.Y.: Cornell University Press, 1995).

28. Richard Freeman and Joel Rogers, "Worker Representation and Participation Survey; First Report of Findings," in *Proceedings of the Forty-Seventh Annual Meeting*, ed. Paula Voos (Madison, Wis.: Industrial Relations Research Association, 1995), 340.

29. John-Paul MacDuffie, Larry Hunter, and Lorna Doucet, "What Does Transformation Mean to Workers? The Effects of the New Industrial Relations on Union Employee Attitudes" (paper presented at the 48th Annual Meeting of the Industrial Relations Research Association, San Francisco, January 1996); Rosemary Batt, "From Bureaucracy to Enterprise?: The Changing Jobs and Careers of Managers in Telecommunications Service," in *Broken Ladders*, ed. Paul Osterman (New York: Oxford University Press, 1996), 55–80.

30. Rosemary Batt and Eileen Applebaum, "Worker Participation in Diverse Settings: Does the Form Affect the Outcome, and If So, Who Benefits?" *British Journal of Industrial Relations* 33, no. 3 (September 1995): 370.

31. Ibid., 358.

32. Although there still might be a permanent establishment fixed effect.

33. As a preliminary to this analysis, it is important to explain how the earnings data generated. A series of earnings questions were asked about three occupational groups within the establishment: core employees, managers, and everyone else. For each group we asked the following questions:

> Now I need to ask about . . . employee pay and benefit packages. We are asking about the paycheck before deductions, so please be sure to include these sources of compensation: wages and bonuses and profit sharing. Please omit employer contributions to benefits such as pensions and health, the value of

deferred compensation such as stock options, and overtime pay.

What is the typical compensation for . . . employees per year from these sources?

(Probe: By typical we mean about half the workers in this group will be paid more and half will be paid less.)

With compensation defined as above, the survey then asked about rates of change in pay for the previous calendar year for each of the three groups. Finally, with employment numbers for each group, I was able to calculate the rate of change in pay for the establishment as a whole.

34. The layoff equations are probit models. The independent variables include establishment size, whether or not the establishment participates in international markets, whether or not the establishment is part of a larger organization, whether or not the establishment has a human resources department, the age of the establishment, whether or not it is unionized, the degree of competition in the establishment's product market, a measure of the establishment's competitive strategy, and industry dummy variables. In order to control for the business success of the establishment, a factor that obviously will influence layoffs and may influence wages through the channel of recruitment and hiring, I include the percentage growth in the value of sales or product the establishment experienced in the three years prior to the survey. As controls for the composition of the labor force of the establishment, which might also affect layoffs and particularly wage patterns, I include the fraction of the labor force that is technical or professional, blue collar, and clerical. Finally, I include the fraction of the establishment's labor force that is female. All these variables, with the exception of the change in the value of sales, are taken from the 1992 survey. All the employment variables refer to regular, not contingent, workers. Finally, the variable I use to measure HPWO is the number of practices in 1992 that had 50 percent or more core employees involved. For a complete discussion of the model, see Osterman, "Work Organization in an Era of Restructuring."

35. These results are presented ibid.

FIVE

PRELIMINARIES TO POLICY

1. See, for example, Richard Lester, *Hiring Practices and Labor Competition* (Princeton, N.J.: Princeton University Industrial Relations Section, 1954). The basic findings in this book were replicated numerous times in a wide variety of studies.

2. *Business Week,* 11 August 1997, 20.

3. Rebecca Blank, "Does a Larger Social Safety Net Mean Less Economic Flexibility?" in *Working under Different Rules*, ed. Richard Freeman (New York: Sage, 1994), 158.

4. Stephen Nickell and Brian Bell, "Changes in the Distribution of Wages and Unemployment in OECD Countries" (paper presented at the American Economic Association annual meetings, San Francisco, January 1996); OECD, *Employment Outlook* (July 1996): 76.

5. Katherine Abraham and Susan Houseman, "Does Employment Protection Inhibit Labor Market Flexibility?: Lessons from Germany, France, and Belgium," in *Social Protection vs. Economic Flexibility*, ed. Rebecca Blank (Chicago: University of Chicago Press, 1994), 59–94.

6. OECD, *Employment Outlook* (July 1996), 171.

Six
Policies for a Mobile Workforce

1. In this section I shall, of course, provide citations as appropriate. However, I should also note that beyond any specific citation the material in this section draws heavily from the very useful book *Unemployment Insurance in the United States: An Analysis of the Policy Issues*, ed. Christopher J. O'Leary and Stephen A. Wadner (Kalamazoo, Mich.: Upjohn Institute, 1998).

2. In 1996, 36 percent of the unemployed received benefits. See Stephen A. Wadner and Thomas Stengle, "Unemployment Insurance: Measuring Who Receives It," *Monthly Labor Review* 120, no. 7 (July 1997): 16.

3. About 43 percent of the unemployed are eligible. See Daniel McMurrer and Amy Chasanow, "Trends in Unemployment Insurance Benefits," *Monthly Labor Review* 118, no. 9 (August 1995): 30–39.

4. Lauri Bassi and Daniel McMurrer, "Coverage and Recipiency," in O'Leary and Wadner, *Unemployment Insurance in the United States*, 57. The groups who are excluded are agricultural workers on "small farms" (although seven states including California, Florida, and Texas have included them), household workers who earn less than one thousand dollars a quarter, employees of religious organizations, and self-employed workers.

5. The exceptions have to do with what might be a "good cause," for example, sexual harassment.

6. The data in this paragraph are taken from Christopher O'Leary and Murray Rubin, "Adequacy of the Weekly Benefit Amount," in O'Leary and Wadner, *Unemployment Insurance in the United States*, 171–72.

7. Massachusetts and Washington permit a maximum of thirty weeks. An additional complication is that most states do not grant twenty-six possible weeks to all workers but rather vary the maximum with the person's work history.

8. Stephen Woodbury and Murray Rubin, "The Duration of Benefits," in O'Leary and Wadner, *Unemployment Insurance in the United States*, 232.

9. Ibid., 246.

10. General Accounting Office, "Unemployment Insurance Program's Ability to Meet Objectives Jeopardized," Report HRD-93-107, 1993.

11. Bassi and McMurrer, "Coverage and Recipiency," 77. These estimates are based on the Survey of Income and Program Participation and refer to the years 1989–91.

12. See Paul Osterman and Rosemary Batt, "Employer Centered Training Programs for International Competitiveness: Lessons from State Programs," *Journal of Policy Analysis and Management* 12, no. 3 (Summer 1993): 456–77.

13. Sanford Jacoby, *Employing Bureaucracy* (New York: Columbia University Press, 1985); Daniel Nelson, *Managers and Workers: The Rise of the Factory System in the United States* (Madison: University of Wisconsin Press, 1975).

14. Sanford Jacoby, *Modern Manors* (Princeton, N.J.: Princeton University Press, 1997).

15. John Turner, *Pension Policy for a Mobile World* (Kalamazoo, Mich.: Upjohn Institute, 1993), 37.

16. However, the actual economic loss depends on assumptions that are made about how to measure the value of the pension wealth the person takes with her or him from the first job and whether the wages on the second job are higher than they would be were there a pension (the economist's idea of so-called compensating differentials).

17. Ann Foster, "Portability of Pension Benefits among Jobs," *Monthly Labor Review* 117, no. 7 (July 1994): 49.

18. Karen Ferguson and Kate Blackwell, *The Pension Book* (New York: Arcade Publishing, 1995), 30.

19. See David Balducci, Terry Johnson, and R. Mark Gritz, "The Role of the Employment Service," in O'Leary and Wadner, *Unemployment Insurance in the United States*, 457–504; Louis Jacobson, *The Effectiveness of the Employment Service*, Advisory Commission on Unemployment Compensation (Washington, D.C.: U.S. Government Printing Office, 14 March 1995).

20. Jacobson, *Effectiveness of the Employment Service*.

21. Ibid.; Balducci, Johnson, and Gritz, "Role of the Employment Service."

22. Jacobson, *Effectiveness of the Employment Service*, 20.

23. Balducci, Johnson, and Gritz, "Role of the Employment Service," 485.

24. Jacobson, *Effectiveness of the Employment Service*.

25. Ibid., 20.

26. Ibid., 6.

27. See General Accounting Office, "Employment Service: Improved Leadership Needed for Better Performance," August 1991. The reforms it recommends are broader use of numerical performance standards and more active monitoring of local offices by the central state agencies.

28. The material that follows on CET was collected by me during site visits in February 1997. For another description of the program, see Bennett Harrison, *Building Bridges: Community Economic Development Corporations and the World of Employment Training* (New York: Ford Foundation, 1995).

29. I was told 20 percent.

30. Norton Grubb, *Working in the Middle* (San Francisco: Jossey-Bass, 1996), 53.

31. Rosemary Batt and Paul Osterman, "A National Policy for Workplace Training" (Washington, D.C.: Economic Policy Institute, 1993), 37.

32. Thomas Kane and Ceclia Rouse, "Labor Market Returns to Two and Four Year Colleges," *American Economic Review* 85, no. 3 (June 1995): 205–21; Grubb, *Working in the Middle.*

33. Grubb, *Working in the Middle,* chap. 6.

34. General Accounting Office, *Multiple Employment Training Programs: An Overhaul Is Needed* (Washington, D.C.: General Accounting Office, March 1994).

35. For a discussion of these efforts, see the National Center on Education and the Economy, *A Labor Market System for the 21st Century* (Washington, D.C.: National Center on Education and the Economy, 1997).

36. Michael Piore and Charles Sabel, *The Second Industrial Divide: Possibilities of Prosperity* (New York: Basic Books, 1984).

37. Erin Flynn and Robert Forrant, "Facilitating Firm Level Change: The Role of Intermediary Organizations in the Manufacturing Modernization Process" (Boston: Jobs for the Future, February 1995), 18.

38. The description in this box is quoted from Annette Bernhardt and Thomas Bailey, "Making Careers Out of Jobs: Policies for a New Employment Relationship," mimeo, Institute on Education and the Economy, Teachers College, October 1997.

SEVEN

REDRESSING THE BALANCE OF POWER

1. Michael Jensen, "The Modern Industrial Revolution, Exit, and the Failure of Internal Control Systems," *American Journal of Finance* 48, no. 3 (July 1993): 851.

2. Michael Useem, *Investor Capitalism* (New York: Basic Books, 1996).

3. *New York Times,* 19 December 1997, C4.

4. Useem, *Investor Capitalism*, 25.

5. Michael Porter, *Capital Choices: Changing the Way America Invests in Industry* (Washington, D.C.: Council on Competitiveness, 1992), 26.

6. Robert J. Schiller, "Background Paper," in *Report of the Task Force on Market Speculation and Corporate Governance*, ed. Twentieth Century Fund (New York: Twentieth Century Fund, 1992); James Poterba and Lawarence Summers, "Time Horizons of American Firms: New Evidence for a Survey of CEOs" (paper prepared for the Harvard Business School and Council on Corporate Competitiveness, 1992).

7. For evidence on this, see Schiller, "Background Paper," 64.

8. Porter, *Capital Choices*, 42.

9. Mark J. Roe, *Strong Managers, Weak Owners* (Princeton, N.J.: Princeton University Press, 1994).

10. Thomas Kochan and Paul Osterman, *The Mutual Gains Enterprise: Forging a Winning Partnership among Labor, Management, and Government* (Boston: Harvard Business School Press, 1994), 114.

11. Useem, *Investor Capitalism*.

12. Ronald Dore, *Flexible Rigidities: Industrial Policy and Structural Adjustment in the Japanese Economy, 1970–1980* (London: Athlone Press, 1986).

13. *Wall Street Journal*, 26 January 1996, A7.

14. Margaret M. Blair, *Ownership and Control* (Washington, D.C.: Brookings Institution, 1995), chap. 7; Roe, *Strong Managers, Weak Owners*, 261.

15. This argument is developed in Andrei Shleifer and Lawrence Summers, "Breach of Trust in Hostile Takeovers," in *Corporate Takeovers: Causes and Consequences*, ed. Alan Auerbach (Chicago: University of Chicago Press, 1988), 33–68. Some support for this argument with respect to the treatment of senior workers is found in Jagadeesh Gokhale, Erica Groshen, and David Neumark, "Do Hostile Takeovers Reduce Extra-Marginal Wage Payments?" *Review of Economics and Statistics* 77, no. 3 (August 1995), 470–85.

16. *New York Times*, 9 December 1993, D1.

17. "Xerox Workers Take a Wage Cut," *Washington Post*, 9 June 1994.

18. "Xerox to Cut 9,000 Jobs, Saving $1 Billion," *New York Times*, 8 April 1998, D1–D2.

19. Ibid.

20. "Xerox to Cut 9,000 Jobs, Close Plants," *Boston Globe*, 8 April 1998, C2.

21. *Wall Street Journal*, 4 November 1997.

22. *New York Times*, 4 November 1997, D1.

23. Joseph Blasi and Douglas Kruse, *The New Owners* (New York: Harper, 1991).

24. Ibid., 12.

25. Ibid., 228.

26. Gerald Davis, Kristina Diekmann, and Catherine Tinsley, "The Decline and Fall of the Conglomerate Firm in the 1980's: The Deinstitutionalization of an Organizational Form," *American Sociological Review* 59, no. 4 (August 1994): 547–70.

27. See, for example, Richard Cyert and James March, *A Behavioral Theory of the Firm* (Englewood Cliffs, N.J.: Prentice Hall, 1963).

28. I owe this point to conversations with Jeremy Stein.

29. The first evaluation was conducted by the Preamble Center for Public Policy and the second by the Economic Policy Institute and the Johns Hopkins University Department of Geography. See Jared Bernstein, "Living Wages: A Step in the Right Direction" (paper prepared for the Task Force on Reconstructing America's Labor Market Institutions, Institute on Work and Employment Research, MIT, Sloan School of Management, June 1998).

30. The account that follows is drawn from joint work with Brenda Lautsch. See Paul Osterman and Brenda Lautsch, *Project QUEST: A Report to the Ford Foundation* (New York: Project QUEST, 1996).

31. There are several important elements in the Project QUEST design. The first concerns the involvement of employers in the program. In addition to the employment commitments that the program had in hand when it began, QUEST worked with employers to design training curricula and to forecast future needs. This was accomplished (like CET) via occupational advisory committees that were established in the main training fields. Second, training took place almost exclusively in community colleges, and QUEST worked closely with the community colleges in designing appropriate and innovative training curriculum. QUEST has trained in a variety of fields, though there has been a notable focus on medical occupations. The high level of support provided to participants is a further distinguishing characteristics of Project QUEST. This help is financial but also includes assistance from counselors in navigating the community college system and a wide range of emotional, personal and family support.

32. The evaluation we conducted showed that Project QUEST participants earned more than seven thousand dollars per year more after participation than they had prior to the program. This estimate is based on a pre/post design, and there was no control group available. Hence there is a possibility of selection bias. However, we carefully studied the intake procedures and also read folders on a randomly selected sample of participants and concluded that people who had enrolled in the program did in fact suffer from serious barriers to employment that would have been difficult to overcome in the absence of the program. The pre/post design is also vulnerable to what is termed the "Ashenfelter dip," that is, the tendency of participants to experience a temporary decline in earnings just prior to enrolling in a program.

There was evidence of such a dip in the data, but it was not nearly large enough to explain away gains of the magnitude we found.

33. QUEST insisted that jobs pay at least $7.50 an hour. In several cases it succeeded in raising wages. In other cases it convinced employers to transform low-paying jobs into entry steps on a job ladder.

34. For example, it convinced the community colleges to establish a Remediation Academy for entering students to prepare them for Texas admissions tests. In other cases it modified curricula to allow for open-entry/open-exit designs.

35. Bureau of Labor Statistics, "Union Members in 1998," BLS Release, 25 January 1999.

36. Richard Freeman and Joel Rogers, "Worker Representation and Participation Survey; First Report of Findings," in *Proceedings of the Forty-Seventh Annual Meeting*, ed. Paula Voos (Madison, Wis.: Industrial Relations Research Association, 1995), 336–45.

37. Seymore Martin Lipset and Noah Meltz, "Work and Institutions," *Perspectives on Work* 1, no. 3 (December 1997), 18.

38. This example was developed for me by Susan Eaton, who has done considerable research as well as organizing in this industry.

39. Gooloo S. Wunderlich, Frank A. Sloan, and Carolyne K. Davis, eds., *Nursing Staff in Hospitals and Nursing Homes: Is It Adequate?*, Institute of Medicine, National Academy of Sciences (Washington, D.C.: National Academy Press 1996), 161, table 6.6.

40. See, for example, Janice Fine and Richard Locke, "Unions Get Smart," *Dollars and Sense* (September/October 1996): 16–19; Thomas Kochan, "Labor Policy for the Twenty-first Century," *Journal of Labor and Employment Law* 1, no. 1 (1998): 117–31.

41. See Stephen Lerner, "Strategic Labor Organizing," *Dollars and Sense* (May/June 1996): 32–37, and Fine and Locke, "Unions Get Smart."

42. Dorothy Sue Cobble reports that in California more than forty-five thousand home health care workers have been organized and that strong organizations also exist in New York City, Chicago, New Orleans, and other cities. See Dorothy Sue Cobble, "The Prospects for Unionism in a Service Society," in *Working in the Service Sector: Critical Paradigms and Problems*, ed. Carmen Sirianni and Cameron McDonald (Philadelphia: Temple University Press, 1995).

43. John Hoerr, *We Can't Eat Prestige: The Women Who Organized Harvard* (Phildelphia: Temple University Press, 1977).

44. This discussion is taken from Paul Weiler, "Governing the Workplace: Employee Representation in the Eyes of the Law," in *Employee Representation*, ed. Bruce Kaufman and Morris Kleiner (Madison, Wis.: Industrial Relations Research Association, 1983), 81–104.

45. Howard Wial, "The Emerging Organizational Structure of Unionism in Low-Wage Services," *Rutgers Law Review* 45 (Summer 1993): 671–738.

46. See, for example, Thomas Kochan, "Principles of a Post–New Deal Employment Policy," in *Labor Economics and Industrial Relations,* ed. Clark Kerr and Paul Staudohar (Cambridge: Harvard University Press, 1994), 646–72.

47. David Levine, "Reinventing Workplace Regulation," *California Management Review* 39, no. 3 (Spring 1997): 98–117.

48. Charles C. Heckscher, *The New Unionism* (1988; reprint, Ithaca, N.Y.: Cornell University Press, 1996).

Eight
Conclusion

1. There is a substantial sociological literature along these lines. See, for example, Lauren Edelman, "Legal Ambiguity and Symbolic Structures: The Organizational Mediation of Civil Rights Law," *American Journal of Sociology* 97, no. 6 (May 1992): 1531–76; Frank Dobbin, John Sutton, John Meyer, and W. Richard Scott, "Equal Employment Opportunity Law and the Construction of Internal Labor Markets," *American Journal of Sociology* 98, no. 2 (September 1993): 396–427.

2. Margaret Weir, "Wages and Jobs: What Is the Public Role?" in *The Social Divide,* ed. Margaret Weir (Washington: Brookings Institution, 1998), 268–311.

Index

Page numbers for entries occurring in boxes are suffixed by a b; those for entries in figures, by an f; those for entries in notes, by an n, with the number of the note following; and those for entries in tables, by a t.